PUNISHED

PUNISHED

Policing the Lives of

Black and Latino Boys

Victor M. Rios

NEW YORK UNIVERSITY PRESS
New York and London

NEW YORK UNIVERSITY PRESS
New York and London
www.nyupress.org

References to Internet websites (URLs) were accurate at the time of writing.
Neither the author nor New York University Press is responsible for URLs
that may have expired or changed since the manuscript was prepared.

Library of Congress Cataloging-in-Publication Data
Rios, Victor M.
Punished : policing the lives of Black and Latino boys / Victor M. Rios.
p. cm. — (New perspectives in crime, deviance, and law series)
Includes bibliographical references and index.
ISBN 978–0–8147–7637–7 (alk. paper) — ISBN 978–0–8147–7638–4
(pbk.   ) — ISBN 978–0–8147–7711–4 (e-book)
1. Punishment—California—Oakland. 2. African American
boys—California—Oakland—Social conditions. 3. Hispanic American
boys—California—Oakland—Social conditions. I. Title.
HV7254.A7O25   2011
364.60835'10979466—dc22   2010053655

New York University Press books

Manufactured in the United States of America

c 10 9 8 7 6 5 4 3 2 1
p 10 9 8 7 6 5 4 3 2 1

CONTENTS

Contents

PREFACE

A word of caution: our stories are not just for entertainment.
　　　　　—Leslie Marmon Silko, *Ceremony*, 1977

You know nothing, and worse than nothing, about the working class. Your sociology is as vicious and worthless as is your method of thinking.
　　　　　—Ernest Everhard in Jack London's *The Iron Heel*, 1907

An old, rusty refrigerator had been knocked over on the side of Pelon's garage. It was white and dented on the edges and looked like it had not been used in a decade. Its metal cooling rods faced the open sky. A twenty-four case of Corona beer filled with empty bottles sat on top of the rods. We had tagged the refrigerator at the height of our delinquent careers; finely scrawled on the side in black marker were nicknames for sixty-eight of our "homies."[1] I was with Pelon, a former fellow gang member. We turned the refrigerator over and read aloud to each other, "Dre, Moreno, Sleepy, Conejo," each homey coming to life as we said his name. Eventually we couldn't help but count. Out of sixty-eight members in the gang—we estimated, based on memory and after making a few phone calls—twelve were in prison serving three years to life, sixteen were in jail or prison serving sentences ranging from three months to three years, and the remaining forty had been incarcerated at one point in their lives. We knew this because we had spent years on the streets together, looking out for one another, protecting each other, and taking part of each other's lives, like family. At this moment, on a cool spring evening in 2002, in front of this old refrigerator, it dawned on us that by the time we reached our early twenties, none of the homies had avoided incarceration.

Most of us who were not currently locked up still fared miserably: seven murdered, six permanently injured from bullet wounds—one had been blinded, two paralyzed from the waist down, and three with permanent scars and debilitating injuries—and about a dozen were severe drug addicts, some of whom begged for money on the streets. From our estimate, out of sixty-eight homies, only two of us graduated from high school, and only I had made it to college. About a dozen had managed to evade major tragedies and, by the standards of the inner city, had become successful. Pelon had started a family and worked as a laborer for a moving company making twelve dollars an hour. He was the most stable homeboy I kept in touch with.

As we sat in front of Pelon's old garage with splintering green paint chips scattered on the ground, we reminisced about "back in the day" when we first met Smiley. We were about fourteen years old and had just recently joined the gang. Smiley was a naive kid our age who was physically abused by his parents. They often kicked him out of his house and onto the streets as a punishment for questioning them or telling them about his teachers' treating him negatively. We called him Smiley because no matter how bad his circumstances were—homeless, victimized, or hungry—he always kept a radiant grin on his face. But his smile got him in trouble. When we gave him the nickname, he told us he thought it was appropriate because he remembered always smiling in class, and the teacher always thought he was laughing at her. When he didn't understand what was going on in class, he would smile, and when the teacher yelled at him, he would smile. I remember one time when we were hanging out on one of our gang's street corners, on International Boulevard, rival gang members drove by shooting at us, and, as I turned to tell him to run, I could see he was looking at them with a big smile.

Smiley was an innocent kid who I felt was growing up in the wrong place at the wrong time. Smiley told us stories that from a young age his teachers treated him punitively. He was seen as a problem kid in school and spent many of his school days in the detention room. On the street, police often stopped him as he walked home from school, even before he joined the gang, because from their perspective the baggy clothes he wore marked him as a gang member. I was there many times when this happened. I had already joined the gang, but Smiley was not involved. Yet police treated him like the rest of us. He was followed around, constantly searched, handcuffed, and harassed. Over time, I noticed Smiley increasingly turn to the gang because he believed it was his only source of support.

I joined the gang seeking the protection that I thought police and other authority figures in my community had failed to provide. Smiley, like many other homies, wanted to join for similar reasons. When he was fourteen, we offered to jump him into the gang: a group beating that was the standard initiation ritual. He agreed, and that same night we took him to the side of Pelon's garage, where, next to the abandoned white refrigerator, a group of about eight of us punched him in the face, slammed him to the ground, and kicked him in the stomach. One of the homies grabbed a tall umbrella and hit him with it until the umbrella's aluminum structure collapsed and the fabric ripped off. After a few minutes we picked him up, gave him hugs, and handed him an "8 ball," a forty-ounce bottle of Old English Malt Liquor. He was officially one of us, part of our "familia," our "street family."

Eventually, Smiley and I became best friends. We took care of each other. One day, when his parents permanently kicked him out of the house, I told him not to worry. "I'm going to find you a house," I said. That night, I stole a 1980s Oldsmobile Cutlass Supreme, breaking the steering column with a large, heavy-duty flat-head screwdriver to gain access to the ignition rod. I drove it to our neighborhood, walked up to Smiley, handed him a screwdriver, and told him, "Here's your new two-bedroom apartment." Referring to the front and rear bench seats, I joked, "I'll sleep in the front room, and you sleep in the back room."

A few days later, I was pulled over by police for driving this stolen car. When I stopped in the parking lot of a large drug store on the intersection of Fruitvale Avenue and Foothill Boulevard in East Oakland, the cops dragged me out of the car, knocked me on my back, and repeatedly kicked me in the stomach and legs. I remember yelling like a little boy: "Awww! Help! Awww! Help!" The officer kicking me shouted back, "Shut the fuck up! You want to be a criminal, then you're going to get treated like one!" He stomped my face against the ground with his thick, black, military-grade rubber boots, his shoe's sole leaving scrapes and gashes on my upper lip and cheek bone. I was fourteen years old. After the beating, I was taken to "One-fitty," the name we had given the juvenile justice facility in our county because it was located on 150th Avenue (in the city of San Leandro). Neither the beating nor the few days I was held at One-fitty taught me a positive lesson. Instead, while I was doing time, a boy I met by the name of Tony taught me how to sand down a 1980s Honda car key to convert it into a master key for all early-1980s Honda cars. The day after my release, I got a hold of a 1980s Honda key, scraped it on the cement over the course of a few hours, went to a BART (subway) station parking lot, and stole another car to pick up Smiley and "go cruising."

A year later, after a few stints in juvenile hall and many experiences with violence, crime, drugs, and punishment, Smiley, Big Joe, and I visited some girls we had met. They lived in a neighborhood where many of our rival gang members lived. When we arrived, we spotted the girls sitting on their front porch. As we began talking with the girls, we noticed that a group of about eight rival gang members were walking down the street toward us. We were all about the same age, fourteen to seventeen years old, and all dressed the same: baggy, creased up, Ben Davis or Dickies brand work pants, with tucked in white T-shirts or baggy sports jerseys. The only difference is that we wore different colors to represent our affiliation.[2] Apparently word had gotten out that we were intruding in their neighborhood. They recognized us from previous fights we had with them over the past few months. Trying to prove our toughness, we threw up our gang signs and called them out for a one-on-one fight. Their plan was different. They wanted to gang up on us and beat us down. Once they reached us, they surrounded us, and we began to fight. I fell down a few times, and the last time I got up, one of them pulled out a gun. I ran. Hearing gunshots, I leaped between two cars for protection. I turned back: our enemies faded away as they scattered behind apartment buildings. I checked my body for blood to see if I had been shot. I was fine. I found Big Joe lying on the ground. He stood up and told me he was fine. We looked for Smiley. He was nowhere in sight. I turned the corner on the car I hid behind. There he was, face flat on the ground. I ran over to him, kneeling over his body and grabbing him, trying to get him to stand up. Smiley had been shot. The bullet hit him in the head.

Fresh human blood painted a picture of death on my brand-new pair of white Nike Cortez tennis shoes. I stood on that dark street knowing that my best friend was dying. I thought, as the movies had taught me, he should have been dead the instant the bullet hit his skull, but he continued to twitch and shake as we drove him to the hospital. We'd decided not to call an ambulance; we knew from previous experience that it wouldn't arrive in time. In the past we had been told by law enforcement that standard procedure dictated that the police had to clear a crime scene before EMTs could move in, and we had lost many friends and relatives to this policy. The ambulance often took over forty-five minutes to arrive when someone was shot in my neighborhood. A few hours later at the hospital, Smiley was declared dead.

The police told me that it was my fault that my homeboy had died and threatened to arrest me for being present at the shooting, with a charge of accessory to murder. I asked them if they were "going to catch the murderer." "What for?" one of the officers replied. "We want you to kill each other off." Smiley's death, and my negative interactions with police, forced me to reflect on the larger picture of youth violence and criminalization in Oakland. Without knowing it at the time, I began to develop a sociological imagination. I began to realize that in order to understand my personal predicament, I needed to find out how youth and police violence became so prevalent in my community. Although I could not articulate it at the time, it was at that moment when I recognized, "Neither the life of an individual nor the history of society can be understood without understanding both."[3] It was at this critical juncture that I began to seek answers.

I made it "out the game" only because of the various support programs that I was fortunate enough to find. Before Smiley died, I had dropped out of high school for two semesters. After Smiley's death, a teacher, Ms. Russ, found out about my troubles and reached out to me. She began to guide me. After ten years of schooling, I finally felt that a teacher cared about me. She contacted my probation officer, recruited university students to mentor me, and demonstrated a genuine commitment to my well-being.

One day, as I walked the line, deciding whether I would take my teacher's support seriously and engage in my education, I had an encounter with a police officer. His name was Officer Wilson. I had been drinking on a school day and provoked a fight with a rival gang member in front of Oakland High School. Officer Wilson arrived at the scene, breaking up the fight. He took me inside his patrol car and asked me if I was on probation; I told him that I was. Officer Wilson told my rival to go back to school. He put me in his patrol car, drove me to the police station, and dropped me off in an interrogation room. He told me, "You know I can arrest you and charge you with multiple infractions. . . . Tell me, man, what is going on in your mind?" I poured my heart out. I told the officer my story, my perspective. For about an hour, he listened. He then told me, "I'm going to give you a chance. . . . I'm going to let you go, but I want to see you make an effort to change your life around. Next time I catch you, I will make sure to lock you up." This last chance, combined with the multiple opportunities offered by my teachers and mentors, motivated me to begin the transformation process. I was ready to change, and, at that very moment, I found key individuals who were ready to help me along the way. I returned to my teacher and told her that I was ready. She began the process of advocating for me and convincing administrators to give me a second chance. Ms. Russ and Officer Wilson shared an insight in working with troubled young people: if they were to make a change in gangs, youth violence, and negative police-community interactions, a pipeline of opportunities had to be provided for street-oriented youths.

By the time I was ready to graduate, I had brought up my grade-point average from 0.9 to 1.9. I was encouraged by college-student mentors to apply to college, and I did. A few months later, I received a letter of conditional acceptance to California State University, East Bay. The letter informed me that I was accepted under "probationary status." I pictured myself being followed around campus by a probation officer. I told myself, "Probation? I'm already on probation, so it won't matter." I didn't realize that probation in college meant I would be expelled if I received below a C average, not that I would have someone constantly watching over me.

I completed my B.A. degree in four years while I worked full-time to help support my siblings. I chose not to live in the university dorms, instead moving in with my mother, Raquel; my sister, Rosa, aged twelve; and my brother, Miguel, aged fourteen, who was in a gang, addicted to crack cocaine, and in and out of juvenile hall. Throughout my childhood and adolescence, my family had lived on 88th Avenue and D Street in "Deep" East Oakland, 33rd Avenue and East 15th in East Oakland, and the "Lower Bottom" of West Oakland—wherever my mother could find an affordable apartment. During my first two years of college, we lived in a small, dilapidated shack in West Oakland. It had a cracked foundation that made the termite-infested house rock any time we walked up the stairs. Crack dealers usually sat on our steps in the middle of the night. They were often loud, yelling, and beating up on their girlfriends or crack-addict customers.

Despite my making it into college, conflict continued. Again, I asked the police for help, and again, they ignored me. We were forced to move after my mother's brother, my uncle Dario, was gunned down and killed while he stood between my mother and me on the corner of our street. It seemed that police were there selectively, to arrest my family and friends for petty acts but not to arrest the main drug dealers and victimizers who continued to prey on my community. As a researcher in the making, I wanted to understand why and how these officers would ignore certain major crimes and at the same time arrest so many residents for such minor infractions.

These experiences made me hanker for an understanding of urban violence and the government's treatment of the poor. In my college courses, I read books that discussed the government's neglect of the poor. While insightful, these books missed a key process that I had personally experienced: the state had not abandoned the poor; it had reorganized itself, placing priority on its punitive institutions, such as police, and embedding crime-control discourses and practices into welfare institutions, such as schools. In my perspective, the state, in my community, had punitively asserted itself into civil society. However, I could not be certain that the ideas I developed from my personal experience applied to anyone else. I needed to see if these experiences applied more broadly to the youth growing up in the flatlands of Oakland during a different time period. I applied to graduate school to pursue this study. In 2000, I was accepted as a Ph.D. student at the University of California, Berkeley. Given the opportunity to study race, inequality, and crime with some of the leading intellectuals in the country, I decided to try to understand the social forces that impacted the community where I was raised. To begin to understand this process, I befriended, mentored, observed, and interviewed Black and Latino boys in Oakland for over three years. As I spent more time in the field, I realized that while violence was very prevalent in the community, criminalization was also a "fabric of everyday life" for the youths I studied.[4] As my research unfolded, it became clear that in this community there existed a powerful culture of punishment, which shaped the ways in which young people organized themselves and created meanings of their social world.

The insights I gained by observing and interviewing these young men, as well as participating in the environment they navigated daily, helped me expose the role that criminalization played in their lives. I define *criminalization* as the process by which styles and behaviors are rendered deviant and are treated with shame, exclusion, punishment, and incarceration. In this study, criminalization occurred beyond the law; it crossed social contexts and followed young people across an array of social institutions, including school, the neighborhood, the community center, the media, and the family.[5] The young men in this study found themselves in situations in which their everyday behaviors and styles were constantly treated as deviant, threatening, risky, and criminal by adults in the various social contexts they navigated. I define this ubiquitous criminalization as the *youth control complex,* a system in which schools, police, probation officers, families, community centers, the media, businesses, and other institutions systematically treat young people's everyday behaviors as criminal activity. The youth control complex was fueled by the micropower of repeated negative judgments and interactions in which the boys were defined as criminal for almost any form of transgression or disrespect of authority. Young people, who become pinballs within this youth control complex, experience what I refer to as *hypercriminalization,* the process by which an individual's everyday behaviors and styles become ubiquitously treated as deviant, risky, threatening, or criminal, across social contexts. This hypercriminalization, in turn, has a profound impact on young people's perceptions, worldviews, and life outcomes. The youth control complex creates an overarching system of regulating the lives of marginalized young people, what I refer to as *punitive social control.* Hypercriminalization involves constant punishment. Punishment, in this study, is understood as the process by which individuals come to feel stigmatized, outcast, shamed, defeated, or hopeless as a result of negative interactions and sanctions imposed by individuals who represent institutions of social control.

Although I began this project from the perspective of my own life experience, I resumed with a systematic and empirical examination of the lives of the youths in this study. Life stories and voices of youths teach us about the mechanisms of criminalization that are a part of their daily lives. Observations allowed me to uncover the contradictions between what was being said and what actually occurred and to corroborate or confute what young people told me. From this point forward, the generalizations that I make come from the empirical data, unless otherwise noted.

My central argument is that criminalization was a central, pervasive, and ubiquitous phenomenon that impacted the everyday lives of the young people I studied in Oakland. By the time they formally entered the penal system, many of these young men were already caught in a spiral of hypercriminalization and punishment. This cycle began before their first arrest—it began as they were harassed, profiled, watched, and disciplined at young ages, before they had committed any crimes. Eventually, that kind of attention led many of them to fulfill the destiny expected of them. Criminalization left these marginalized young people very few choices, crime and violence being some of the few resources for feeling dignity and empowerment. Previous theorization has stopped here, describing this entrapment, blocked opportunity, and victimization. I move beyond these ideas and demonstrate that agency is very prevalent among these youths. A paradox existed among the youths in my study: criminalization became a vehicle by which they developed political consciousness and resistant identities. Unjust interactions with the youth control complex created blocked opportunities, but they also ignited the boys' social consciousness and developed worldviews and identities diametrically opposed to the youth control complex and mass incarceration. Some boys even developed a more formal political identity that called for a change in the system which so oppressed them.

My hope is that the first-person account and evidence I provide of the overarching reach of criminalization and punitive social control in the lives of young people will inspire policymakers to create alternative, more reintegrative approaches to law and order; that education, criminal justice, and community practitioners will change punitive practices and establish genuine caring relationships with these youngsters; that researchers will shift their levels of analysis so that we can account for other processes in the inner city beyond violence, pathology, or fixed typologies; and that by reading this book, young people will become further inspired to succeed despite the obstacles they might find in common with the boys in this book.

There is a way to transform punishment, to generate creative means of social control, which provides viable rehabilitation for delinquent youths and which does not spill over and affect young people who have yet to commit crime. It will take imagination and the courage to adopt successful models that attempt to transform the punitive way in which young people are treated in marginalized communities. There are a few individuals, such as my teacher, Ms. Russ, and Officer Wilson, who have broken away from punitive social control and aim to change the way young people are treated, and they can serve as examples. Maybe then a new generation of former gang members and delinquents will read names from an old refrigerator and celebrate multiple high school graduations and college degrees, instead of mourn the incarcerated and excluded lives of their friends and family.

ACKNOWLEDGMENTS

It takes a village to write a book. I am grateful to everyone that took part in the collective sowing to see this project flourish. The following colleagues and mentors read or discussed parts of my manuscript and provided me with crucial feedback: Elijah Anderson, Randol Contreras, Waverly Duck, Mitch Duneier, Robert Duran, Sarah Fenstermaker, Alice Goffman, Melissa Guzman, John Hagedorn, Paul Hirschfield, Gaye Johnson, Nikki Jones, Aaron Kupchik, Patrick Lopez-Aguado, Cid Martinez, Jody Miller, David Minkus, Pamela Oliver, Howard Pinderhughes, Carolyn Pinedo, Cesar Rodriguez, Ronald Takaki, Heather Tirado-Delgado, Diego Vigil, Howard Winant, and Clyde Woods. I also benefited tremendously from the mentoring and funding provided by UC Berkeley's Institute for the Study of Social Change, Center for the Study of Race and Gender, and Department of Ethnic Studies, the University of San Francisco's Irvine Dissertation Fellowship Program, the University of San Francisco's Sociology Department, the Ford Foundation's Predoctoral and Postdoctoral Fellowship programs, and the Racial Democracy Crime and Justice Network at Ohio State University. The colleagues at the Department of Sociology at the University of California, Santa Barbara, have been extremely supportive. My department chair, Verta Taylor, epitomizes the meaning of an outstanding mentor. She has been instrumental in my early professional career. Anonymous reviewers gave me the insight needed to complete this manuscript. Ilene Kalish, my editor at NYU Press, and John Hagan, the series editor, were always enthusiastic about this project, even when I felt otherwise. The young men in this study who shared their lives with me have granted all of us the gift of gaining deeper insight into the lives of young people who encounter injustice. My mother, Raquel; my brother J.T.; my brother Mike; and my sister,

Rosa, struggled and persisted with me growing up. My in-laws, Nadine, Enrique, Anita, Darrell, and Sarita, have taken me in as their own son and brother. I have made it this far thanks to the support and encouragement of my decade-long companion-partner-best-friend-wife, Rebeca Mireles. My twin daughters, Marina and Maya, and son, Marco, have taught me how to be a good father while striving to become a grounded professor and intellectual.

To the entire village I am deeply grateful.

Inevitably I have forgotten some names of people who helped me out along the way. I apologize and hope that you can remind me so that I can make it up to you.

PART I

Hypercriminalization

Dreams Deferred

The Patterns of Punishment in Oakland

What happens to a dream deferred? Does it dry up like a raisin
in the sun? . . . Maybe it just sags like a heavy load. Or does it
explode?
    —Langston Hughes, "Montage of a Dream Deferred," 1951

Just as children were tracked into futures as doctors, scientists,
engineers, word processors, and fast-food workers, there were
also tracks for some children, predominantly African American and male, that led to prison.
                —Ann Arnett Ferguson, *Bad Boys*, 2000

Fifteen-year-old Slick, a Latino kid born and raised in Oakland, showed
me the "hotspots": street intersections and sidewalks where life-altering
experiences linger, shaping young people's perspectives of the area. As
he walked me through the neighborhood, he pointed to the corner of
International Boulevard and 22nd Avenue, where a few months before
his best friend took a bullet in the lung during a drive-by shooting. He
watched his homey die slowly, gasping like a waterless fish, gushes of
blood inundating his respiratory system. We approached the corner of
23rd Avenue and International, and Slick warned me that "at any given

moment something could jump off, fools could roll up, and shit could go down." He did not have to tell me; I had been on these streets in the past as a resident and as a delinquent and later on in life as an ethnographer, observing the young people who spent so much of their lives on these streets. We stopped at a mobile "taco truck" to order a burrito. Standing on the corner watching cars and people pass by, Slick continued to "break it down" for me: "Just the other day, mothafuckas rolled up on me and pulled out a strap to my head. . . . Fuck it, today is my day, . . . so I threw up my [gang] sign and said, 'Fuck you.' . . . The thang [gun] got stuck or some shit, 'cause I saw him pulling but nothing came out." Slick seemed to pretend to show no trauma as he told me the story, but his lips quivered and his hands shook ever so slightly as he grabbed his soda from the taco vendor.

As we took our first bite and wiped our hands on our baggy jeans, an Oakland Police Department patrol car pulled into the taco-truck lot. Two officers emerged from the car and ordered us to sit on the curb: "Hands on your ass!" Slick looked down at his burrito, and I realized we were being asked to throw our meal away after only taking one bite. The officer yelled again. Our fresh burritos splattered on the chewing-gum-dotted concrete, and we sat on the curb with our hands under our thighs. An officer grabbed Slick's arms and handcuffed him. Another officer did the same to me. One of them lifted us up by the metal links holding the cuffs together, placing excruciating pressure on our shoulder joints.

As they searched us, I asked the officers, "What's going on?" They provided no response. They took out a camera and took pictures of Slick and me. "Who is this guy?" they asked Slick, pointing to me. Slick told them, "He's from UC Berkeley. He's cool, man!" The officers unlocked our handcuffs, told Slick to stay out of trouble, and got in their cars and drove off. The officers had noticed me in the neighborhood and had asked many of the boys about me. They knew I was some kind of college student trying to help the boys out. One of them later told me that I was doing the boys no good by studying them and advocating for them. The officer told me that I was enabling them by harboring their criminality and that I should be arrested for conspiracy.

I looked around and saw that a crowd of pedestrians and taco-truck patrons had gathered a few feet away from us. I made eye contact with a Mexican man in his fifties wearing a cowboy hat. He nodded his head with a disappointed look and said, "Pinches cholos" [fucking gangsters] and walked away. I turned to Slick and said, "You OK?" He replied, "That happens all the time. They got nothin' on me." "How often does it happen?" I asked. "Shit! Come on, Vic! You know wassup. It happens every day," Slick replied.

This kind of interaction with the police was common in my observations and in the accounts of Slick and the other boys I studied. All forty of the boys whom I studied in depth, and most of the other seventy-eight youths whom I informally interviewed and observed, reported negative interactions with police. Only eleven of the one hundred and eighteen youth reported any positive experiences with police. The majority of interactions between police and youth that I observed over the course of three years were negative.

A paradox of control took precedent: based on informal conversations with officers, I found that many of them seemed to sympathize with the poverty and trauma that many young people experienced; however, in an attempt to uphold the law and maintain order, officers often took extreme punitive measures with youths perceived as deviant or criminal. However, police officers were not the only adults in the community involved in criminalizing young men like Slick. As school personnel, community workers, and family members attempted to find solutions to rule breaking, defiance, crime, and violence, they seemed to rely on criminal justice discourses and metaphors to deal with these young "risks." In this social order where young people placed at risk were treated as potential criminals, social relations, worldviews, and creative responses were often influenced by this process of criminalization. In order to understand the process by which young people came to understand their environment as punitive and to observe, firsthand, how criminalization operated in their lives, I shadowed a group of young men for three years. This chapter describes this process and begins to show the way that ubiquitous criminalization operated in some of their lives.

Ubiquitous Criminalization

Leaving the corner where the police had stopped us, Slick and I continued to walk through his neighborhood. As we walked away from the avenue and through an alley to Slick's house, he told me he started evading school at age fourteen in fear for his own life, threatened by the same boys who killed his friend. Slick told me that teachers treated him differently after his friend's death, as if he were responsible for the shooting. When he arrived late to class a few weeks after the murder, his teacher picked up the phone and called the police officer stationed at the school. She told the police that Slick was a threat to her and to other students. The officer took Slick to his office and told him that he was on the verge of dying, just like his friend. Slick was sent to the vice principal. "The vice principal told me, 'I have to kick you out because you have missed too many school days,'" Slick explained.

I found that schools pushed out boys who had been victimized. Six of the boys in this study reported being victims of violence. All six of them returned to school after being victimized, and all six described a similar process. The boys believed that the school saw them as plotting to commit violence as a means to avenge their victimization. As such, the school commonly accused the boys of truancy for the days that they missed recovering from violent attacks and used this as justification to expel them from school. Four of the boys were expelled from school under truancy rules shortly after their attacks. After being expelled from school, feeling a sense of "no place to go," Slick spent most school hours hanging out with friends in front of the same intersection where his homeboy was gunned down, risking further victimization.

On our way to Slick's house, we took a break, sitting on his neighbor's squeaky wooden steps. As we began to talk, the resident opened the door and told us to leave "or else."

"Or else what?" asked Slick.

"Or else I will call the police!"

Slick cussed out the neighbor, murmuring out his frustration. The neighbor slammed his front door. Nervous about another encounter with police, we walked away. Defeated by the degrading events of the day, we continued walking toward his house, our heads bowed and mouths shut, both of us silenced. Slick and I sat on his steps until 7 p.m., when his mother arrived. She greeted me. She knew me as the *"estudiante"* [student] who was trying to help her child.[1]

I talked with Slick's mother, Juliana, for about an hour. She told me her frustrations with Slick. I listened attentively and told her that I would try to convince him to join Youth Leadership Project, a local grassroots youth activist organization that helped young people involved in gangs transform their lives by becoming community organizers.

I drove home, to 35th Avenue, in the same neighborhood, where I had taken residence to be closer to my research participants. I wrote some field notes and opened up *Policing the Crisis*, a book about how the media and politicians create scapegoats to deal with economic crises by sensationalizing crimes committed by black people.[2] I read about moral panics, those events or people—for example, black muggers, AIDS, pregnant teens, gang members—deemed a threat to mainstream society. According to the book, moral panics are often constructed as a result of economic and cultural crises. Often, it is the media and politicians who become central players in determining who or what becomes the moral panic of the time. They generate support for an increase in spending on crime or a decrease in spending on welfare for the "undeserving" poor.[3]

I asked myself whether Slick and his homies had become the moral panics in this community, and if it was this attention on their perceived criminal behavior which had led to the intense policing and surveillance that I observed and that the youth spoke about more broadly.[4] This is where my research questions for this project became clear: How do surveillance, punishment, and criminal justice practices affect the lives of marginalized boys? What patterns of punishment do young people such as Slick encounter in their neighborhoods in Oakland? What effects do these patterns of punishment have on the lives of the young men in this study? Specifically, how do punitive encounters with police, probation officers, teachers and administrators, and other authority figures shape the meanings that young people create about themselves and about their obstacles, opportunities, and future aspirations?

Shadowing Marginalized Youth

To answer my questions about criminalization, I observed and interviewed young males who lived in communities heavily affected by criminal justice policies and practices. Delinquent inner-city youths, those at the front line of the war on crime and mass incarceration, were the best source of data for this study. Their experiences spoke directly to the impact of punitive policies and practices prevalent in welfare and criminal justice institutions. I got to know forty Black and Latino boys who were between the ages of fourteen and seventeen when I began the study. I interviewed them, conducted focus groups with them, met with their friends and their families, advocated for them at school and in court, and hung out with them at parks, street corners, and community centers during the course of three years, from 2002 to 2005. Thirty of these young men had been arrested and were on probation. Ten of them had not been arrested but were related to or closely associated with boys who had been arrested.

I shadowed these young men as they conducted their everyday routine activities, such as walking the streets, "hanging out," and participating in community programs. I walked the streets and rode the bus with them from home to school and as they met with friends or went to the community center after school. There were days when I met them in front of their doorsteps at 8 a.m. and followed them throughout the day until they returned home late at night. I met their parents, probation officers, and friends. I attended court with their parents when the boys were arrested. Shadowing allowed me access to these young people's routine activities, exposing me to major patterns prevalent in their lives, including criminalization.

Shadowing enabled me to observe regular punitive encounters and the way these became manifest in the lives of these youth in a range of different social contexts, across institutional settings. Interviews with the boys supplemented my observations and allowed me to hear their perspectives on these patterns of punishment. By getting to hear these young people's definitions of criminalization, I was able to conceptualize aspects of their lived experiences that would be difficult to see otherwise. I decided to make young people's perspectives central to my understanding of crime, punishment, and justice in their community. Sociologist Dorothy Smith explains that "we may not rewrite the other's world or impose upon it a conceptual framework that extracts from it what fits with ours. . . . Their reality . . . is the place from which inquiry begins."[5] I took this goal to heart in conducting this study. The voices of these young men supplement the scholarship, much of it theoretical, that attempts to explain the expansion and social consequences of the punitive state.[6] These observations and voices would help me to test these theories on the ground and, if needed, to develop new ways to understand the consequences of the punitive state on marginalized populations.

Although a study of authority figures and social-control agents—school personnel, police, politicians, and other adults who hold a stake in overseeing the well-being of young people—could have provided a broader array of perspectives on punishment, I decided to focus on the voices of the youth. This is partly because I found that the perspectives of social-control agents were commonly represented in the media and institutional discourses and practices. For example, in the news media, when youth crime becomes an issue, police are often the "experts" who are interviewed to discuss their perspectives on why young people commit crime. However, the perspectives and experiences of the youths experiencing this violence, criminalization, and punishment are rarely taken into account in public discourse.

Readers may consider the accounts of the youth in this study to be one-sided. I urge readers to eradicate a dichotomous, either/or, perspective and instead focus on how young people come to understand their social world as a place that sees them and treats them as criminal risks. Even if adults make individual attempts to treat young people with empathy and respect, some youngsters have come to believe that their environment is systematically punitive. How do young people come to believe that "the system" is against them? I could provide interviews with police officers that discuss their desires to help these young men. However, the point of this project is to show the consequences of social control on the lives of young people regardless of good or bad intentions. A sociological cliché clarifies my point: "If men [and women] define situations as real, they are real in their consequences."[7] If young people believe that the social ecology in which they grow up is punitive and debilitating, then they will experience the world as such. If institutions of social control believe that all young people follow the "code of the street"[8] or that defiant or delinquent poor, urban youth of color are "superpredators"—heartless, senseless criminals with no morals—then policies, programs, and interactions with marginalized youths will be based on this false information.[9]

In order to create a study that would uncover the process of criminalization that young people experienced, I combined the methods of critical criminology with urban ethnography to develop an understanding of the punitive state through the lens of marginalized populations. Both methods offered me tools essential to understanding and documenting the lives of the young men I studied. Critical criminology, the study of crime in relation to power, which explicitly examines crime as a socially constructed phenomenon, allowed me to bring to light the mechanisms responsible for the plight of marginalized male youths in the new millennium. Urban ethnography, the systematic and meticulous method of examining culture unfolding in everyday life, allowed me to decipher the difficult and complex circumstances, social relations, and fabric of social life under which these young men lived.

Recruitment

I began recruiting participants at a youth leadership organization and a community center—which I refer to with the pseudonyms "Youth Leadership Project" (YLP) and "East Side Youth Center" (ESYC)—in Oakland, California. YLP was located in Oakland's Fruitvale District, where Latinos made up 49 percent and Blacks made up 20 percent of the population. ESYC was located in the Central East Oakland District, where Blacks made up 50 percent and Latinos made up 38 percent of the population. I told the community workers about the study and asked them to connect me with "at-promise" ("at-risk") young men, ages fourteen to seventeen, who had previously been arrested.[10] I was introduced to four Latino boys through community workers at YLP and three Black boys through community workers at ESYC. While both organizations focused on consciousness raising and politicizing young people as a means for transformation, I recruited young people who had spent less than one month working with these organizations. This way, I would gain insight from young men who had yet to be influenced by this approach.

After meeting with these young men, I asked them to refer me to other youths in similar situations, as well as to young men who they knew had not been arrested but who hung out with guys who had, a technique known as snowball sampling.[11] With snowball sampling, I was able to uncover a population of young men who were surrounded by or involved in crime and who had consistent interaction with police. Only the eight initial boys had contact with the youth organizations I initially contacted. The other thirty-two boys were not involved in any community programs at first contact. Although many of the boys ended up knowing each other and formed part of a social network, my goal was to understand how boys in these networks of crime, criminalization, and punishment made sense of these processes and to observe their interactions with authority figures.

The young men in this study were not representative of Black and Latino youths throughout the United States, in the inner city, in Oakland, or the criminal justice system. These were unique cases of young men from unique communities who reported and were seen to live in an environment where criminalization was an everyday part of their daily lives.[12] While many marginalized young people face the wrath of punitive social control and criminalization, it was difficult to generate an in-depth study that found a representative sample of young people in such a predicament. The alternative strategy was to utilize unique cases, young people who had already been marked by the system and who believed that they were being systematically criminalized. I ended up with a particular group of young people, those who were implicated in the regime of punishment in the inner city.

It is obvious that the majority of young people living in poverty are not delinquent. I specifically sought delinquent young people and their peers. This approach would help me to locate the mechanisms of control put in place to regulate this population, already formally labeled as deviant. Observing these young people might teach us more about the culture of punishment and criminalization prevalent in marginalized communities in the era of mass incarceration. After getting to know the boys and having them connect me with their friends, I began to interview them and gain enough trust to observe them. Field observations were carried out in three Oakland neighborhoods and eventually also in San Francisco and Berkeley, places where some of the young men in this study eventually moved. I also conducted observations at one continuation school—a school for students who had been expelled from "regular" high school—where eight of the boys in this study were eventually enrolled. Whereas traditionally urban ethnographers study a specific site as their case study, such as a neighborhood or a street corner,[13] I studied a group of young people, each of them representing a case.[14] This approach was crucial in order to keep track of the trajectories that developed for each of the young men in this study.

During the time I was in the field, the communities that these young men came from were becoming gentrified. Since the late 1990s, high rent increases and urban-development policies had forced many working-class families in the San Francisco Bay Area to constantly move between neighborhoods and cities in search of affordable housing. Many of the young men in my study consistently moved around because of this situation. This meant that I had to shadow participants wherever they ended up: sometimes to a neighboring city or neighborhood (and sometimes to juvenile facilities by way of their parents). Some of them I followed to their new neighborhoods. By the end of the study, I had lost track of eight of the forty youths I studied in-depth. Therefore, I ended up with thirty-two young men whom I studied in-depth for the entire three years.

Observing Masculinity

This study focuses on the experiences and stories of young men. Young women's experiences with punishment are unique and therefore may require a different methodological approach and conceptualization to understand their predicament. Researchers have shown that young women experience domestic abuse, criminal justice abuse, sexual abuse, and violence in qualitatively different ways than boys do.[15] Recent scholarship is finding that poor young women are heavily impacted by a "violent girl" trend in which young women who are considered violent are being incarcerated in record numbers.[16] I recognize the importance of gender in the experiences of youth, but analyzing the experiences of young women is beyond the scope of this current work.[17] I offer an in-depth analysis that deals with the ways that masculinity affects the lives of these boys and the way it spills over to impact the lives of young women—from expectations of violence to the enactment of sexism and misogyny. By interrogating the ways that gender, in this case masculinity, impacts the worlds of these youths, I hope to provide a more nuanced understanding of how gender norms are particularly affected by punishment.[18]

O.G. Sociology

When this study began, I was twenty-five years old. I had grown up in the flatlands of Oakland and had lived in two of the neighborhoods where these young men came from. These factors, along with the snowball sampling approach, in which the young men's friends vouched for me— often by saying, "He's cool; he's not with the five-o [police]"—allowed for most of the young men in the study to comfortably gain trust and develop a sense of camaraderie with me. Many of the boys acknowledged me as someone they could trust and look up to. The majority referred to me as "O.G. Vic." "O.G." stands for "original gangster." This label is often ascribed to older members of the neighborhood who have proven themselves and gained respect on the street and, as a result, are respected by younger residents. I told the young men not to consider me an O.G. since I believed, and still do, that I did not deserve the label. My belief was that any researcher who considered himself an O.G. was being deceptive. Although I grew up in most of the neighborhoods where I conducted this study, the reality was that at the time of the study I was a graduate student with many privileges that many of these young people did not have. I was an "outsider" as much as an "insider." This was important to recognize in a study that examined the lives of marginalized subjects. Throughout the study, I remained reflexive about my insider/outsider role and the power relations that emerged and solidified as I studied these young men.

At the same time, if the youths looked at me with the kind of respect that they gave to O.G.s, some who often led them in the wrong direction, I would guide them toward positive alternatives as much as I could. I often saw myself conducting "O.G. Sociology," similar to John Irwin's "Convict Criminology," where someone who had previously been incarcerated—in my case, someone who had also "put in work" (belonged to a street gang)—became an analyst of this very same experience.[19]

I wanted to avoid swaggering about my experiences gaining entrée, hanging out, witnessing violence, or "going rogue," as sociologist Sudhir

Venkatesh called it in his 2008 book, in which he claimed to have been allowed to "be a gang leader for a day" by a notorious Black gang in Chicago. Narratives such as Venkatesh's create what I call a "jungle-book trope." This very familiar colonial fairy-tale narrative in the Western imagination of the "Other" goes something like this: "I got lost in the wild, the wild people took me in and helped me, made me their king, and I lived to tell civilization about it!" Unfortunately, some of my colleagues who study the urban poor continue to perpetuate this self-aggrandizing narrative, perpetuating flawed policies and programs and a public understanding of the urban poor as creatures in need of pity and external salvation.

This book is not for those expecting to read about bravado, blood, and irrational violence—dominant allusions when discussing inner-city youths. In this study, I decided to normalize "dangerous settings" and discuss what happens on a routine basis—people living life, striving for dignity—and not what happens during extreme moments: people victimizing one another, often in response to marginalization. I discuss these extreme cases only when they apply to the production of knowledge and not when I think they will have some emotional appeal to the reader or when I feel like "going rogue." Sociologist Nikki Jones describes the process by which some ethnographers portray a false reality of marginalized populations: "In an attempt to explain the inner workings of one group of people to another, many contemporary ethnographic texts begin from a point of ignorance instead of from a point of understanding and commonality. . . . In an attempt to enlighten those with the power to effect change [these ethnographies] have the effect of making others under study more unintelligible than they ever really were."[20] Like Jones, I conducted this study with the assumption that the young people I studied were normal everyday people persisting in risky environments, striving for dignity, and organizing their social worlds despite a dearth of resources.

Sociology and feminism scholars Dorothy Smith and Patricia Hill Collins have argued that all knowledge is rooted in experience and that those who have lived on the margins may provide crucial insights to specific social problems.[21] I believe that my standpoint epistemology, the knowledge I have gained from my personal experiences, brings much insight to this conversation. However, it is my obligation as a social scientist to provide a road map for those who have not had my experience to be able to replicate a similar study and find the same patterns and processes I encountered. Although I brought my own social situation to this study, that was not enough to give me the insights I needed to develop an understanding of the conditions that marginalized young men from Oakland were facing. From my experience and from my reading of theories of crime, delinquency, race, and punishment, I had my own ideas about youth and punishment in Oakland. I wanted to go beyond my own experience. I wanted to create an empirical study that would uncover the process by which criminalization impacted the lives of young people.

One of my graduate-school professors warned me, "Go native, but make sure to come back." When I returned from the field, I told him, "I took your advice and went native in the academy, but I made sure to go back to the community where I come from." All quips aside, I acknowledge that my insider status limited my observations. As a researcher, participants' responses and my own assumptions may have resulted in "bias [of] the description to please the ethnographer."[22] In addition, my own assumptions and negative experiences with police may have shaped my view of observed events. However, I proceeded with caution and acknowledged that I was a participant in the creation of the stories that follow.[23] I became part of the study and part of the forces that both created and resisted the very power relations I sought to expose. The fact that I also encountered harassment by police and other community members for looking like the boys allowed me to embody a keen sense of what these young people were experiencing.[24] After all, as Erving Goffman put it, fieldwork requires "subjecting yourself, your own body and your own personality . . . to the set of contingencies that play upon a set of individuals, so that you can physically and ecologically penetrate their circle of response to their social situation, . . . so that you are close to them while you are responding to what life does to them."[25]

I was able to conduct an in-depth study on youth who saw me as an adult they could trust. With trust comes obligation—the obligation to give back by actively engaging in the lives of the youths I studied.[26] It became my obligation to address their questions in a world full of faulty answers. By the time I met them, many of their pathways were already set. They had already experienced a young life of adjudication and criminalization. Therefore, even if I represented the possibility of change in their lives, I could not negate the forces of criminalization and patterns of punishment already established. Helping a young person attain a job is a risk worth taking, even if we believe that this will change our findings. I think that it is naive to believe that one's subtle interventions in marginalized settings will change our findings. While I have power, privilege, and resources, my individual actions are not godly in any way to change structural conditions, entrenched processes that grind away, impacting the lives of abandoned populations on a day-to-day level.

My biases were very much part of this study. Howard Becker explains that "an observer unwittingly imposes normative judgments on what is observed."[27] These judgments are based on the observer's own politics and epistemologies. However, helping people and generating solid empirical research are not mutually exclusive in my view. Therefore, to ensure validity, I only bring out themes and cases that typify recurring patterns in my observations and interviews, and I also conduct a systematic search for disconfirming evidence.[28] In other words, every story that I tell in this book represents a reality that many other youths in the study experienced as well.

Youth Demographics

Of the forty youths I studied in-depth, thirty had previously been arrested when I met them. An additional ten had never been arrested but lived in a neighborhood with high violent-crime rates and had siblings or friends who had been previously involved with crime (see table 1.1). Most of the offenses committed by the delinquent youths were nonviolent; only three had been arrested for a violent act. All the youths in this study reported, at first contact, having persistent contact with police officers while growing up. Twenty-two had spent at least a week in juvenile facilities, and thirty were assigned a probation officer at the time that I met them. Nineteen of the youth I studied in-depth reported gang involvement. Out of seventy-eight others that I interviewed, met with in focus groups, and observed, fifty-two reported gang involvement. The neighborhoods in which these youths had grown up had at least four major Black gangs and four major Latino gangs.

TABLE 1.1

Criminal Justice Status at First Contact of Forty Youths Studied In-Depth

Previously arrested	30
Friend or relative of previously arrested youths	10
Reported negative interactions with police at first interview	40
One week or more spent in juvenile facility	22
Assigned a probation officer	30
Parent in jail or prison	14
Gang involved (confirmed through self-reports or observations)	19

TABLE 1.2

Class Status at First Contact of Forty Youths Studied In-Depth

Working Class:	*Working Poor:*	*Extreme Poverty:*
Two parent, low-wage incomes	Single parent, low-wage income	Unemployed single-parent household
Reported $16,000–$34,000 yearly household income	Reported $8,000–$16,000 yearly household income	Reported $0–$8,000 yearly household income.
12	16	12

Twenty-eight of the young men I studied in-depth came from single-parent households. Twelve of the boys were what I would define as working class: they had at least one parent who worked full-time in a viable and stable job, were able to afford a basic standard of living, and occasionally enjoyed some luxuries such as a family vacation or a new car. Sixteen boys were from working-poor families that had at least one working parent but were barely able to make ends meet, especially in an extremely expensive housing market, in which some families spent over 70 percent of their income on rent. Twelve boys came from extreme poverty, where they lived in an unemployed single-parent household, often in unhealthy living conditions, such as living with nine other people in a one-bedroom apartment or living in an apartment known to be used for drug use or drug sales.

Twenty of the boys were Black, and twenty were Latino. Because East Oakland was 40 percent Latino and 50 percent African American at the time that I began this study, I decided to focus on the experiences and perspectives of these two dominant groups. Although other cities or communities may host a majority African American population that experiences the brunt of punishment, Oakland, as I will demonstrate, criminalized Blacks and Latinos in similar ways. Boys from both of these racialized groups reported and were observed to encounter punishment almost identically, albeit to varying degrees. Oakland was one of the first traditionally Black cities in the United States to see an influx of Latino immigrants, which eventually transformed it into a Black/Latino city. Many other traditionally Black cities across the country continue to see an increase in the Latino population. What I found in Oakland was that the punitive patterns of punishment designed to historically control Black youths were also being applied to young Latinos. By understanding this process and the overall patterns of punishment in Oakland, we may be able to understand patterns of punishment among Blacks and Latinos in other multiracial urban settings.

In my observations, I found that Black youth encountered some of the worst criminalization in Oakland. One example is that light-skinned Latinos gained respect from teachers and police once they chose to dress more formally. Black youths, however, still faced criminalization, even when they dressed more formally.[29] Research on the impact of the criminal justice system and race continues to show that Blacks face the direst consequences and that Latinos are sandwiched in between Blacks and Whites. Latinos have a higher chance of being arrested, incarcerated, and convicted than Whites do for similar offenses, but they do not face the same severity as do Blacks. In Oakland, I found that both groups were criminalized in similar ways but that Black youths faced harsher sanctions than did Latino youths. I also found that both groups formed a common subculture which resisted punishment. I found that Black and Latino youths understood punitive social control as a collective racialization-criminalization process in which they saw themselves caught in the same web of punishment.

Consequences

Although parents, police officers, and school officials may have had good intentions, they were consistently understood by youths in this study as adversarial and excessive in their punishment.[30] Experiences with punishment led young people to develop a specific set of beliefs, thoughts, actions, and practices in order to survive the cruel treatment they encountered and to strive for their dignity.[31] But delinquent kids, those who had been arrested for breaking the law, were not the only young people who were criminalized. Young men who were not delinquent but lived in poor neighborhoods also encountered patterns of punishment. They were also, for example, pulled over by police officers, questioned by teachers and administrators, and looked at with suspicion by merchants and community members. Kids who were considered good, those who had not broken the law and did relatively well in school, experienced part of this stigma and punishment as well.[32] In order to avoid this punishment, they had to constantly prove that they were not guilty, that they were not criminals. These boys frequently felt that they were treated as guilty until they could prove themselves innocent, and much of their worldviews and actions were influenced by this process. Many of their social relations were structured by their attempts to prove their innocence, what I refer to as "acting lawful."

Although I focused my attention on a small number of young men in one American city, I believe, as many other scholars do, that this criminalization is occurring in other marginalized communities throughout the United States and in multiple institutional and community settings.[33] This study, while grounded in Oakland, California, may provide a deeper understanding of the punishment that other youth experience in other marginalized communities. For example, the Jena Six, who entered the national spotlight in 2007, encountered patterns of punishment and criminalization that are similar to those analyzed in this book. In the fall of 2006, two Black high school students in Jena, Louisiana, sat under the so-called White Tree at their high school. The White Tree was named by White students who specifically sought to exclude Black students from this space. The Black students asked their principal for permission to sit under the tree, despite its perceived status as belonging to White students. When the principal responded, "Sit wherever you want,"[34] and the Black students did, White students reacted by hanging nooses from the tree. When Black students protested the light punishment (a three-day suspension) given to the students who hung the nooses, District Attorney Reed Walters came to the school and told the Black students he could "take [their] lives away with a stroke of [his] pen."[35] Walters's statement proves true for many of the youths in this study; their life chances are impacted by the discretions of multiple authority figures in the community. A district attorney's intervention to solve a school conflict is indicative of the trend to use crime-control metaphors and material resources to solve non-criminal, everyday social problems. This was the trend in Oakland, and it seems that hypercriminalization has become a primary form of social control in several marginalized communities.

In Jena, in December 2007, a fight broke out between Black students and a White student who threatened them and called them "niggers." The White student sustained minor injuries from the fight. The Black students involved were arrested and charged with aggravated battery and second-degree attempted murder.[36] Mychal Bell, the first defendant to go to trial, was convicted as an adult, despite being sixteen years old when the event occurred. He faced up to twenty-two years in prison. The case produced protests around the nation against Bell's conviction and called national attention to the racism informing the punishment of these young Black men. As a result, *Dr. Phil, Oprah, Nightline,* and other major media outlets provided detailed coverage of the case. Most coverage emphasized the victimization of the White student who had been beaten by the Jena Six and the "racial demons" that haunted Jena. Few outlets, however, provided equal time to the extreme punitive treatment that the Jena Six students received. Jena showed how race matters in crime and how young Black people become criminalized. Media, political, and community explanations for these kinds of *personal troubles* often blame Black criminality, racial tensions, or White supremacy for events of this kind. However, it is time to find a systematic explanation for the *public issues* of punitive social control that affect poor marginalized youths in local settings, throughout the globe.[37]

Book Overview

What follows is a snapshot of the complicated world of some boys growing up in Oakland, California, in the midst of a system of punishment
which, from their perspective, maintains an ironclad grip on their everyday lives. I attempt to understand the processes by which marginalized
boys become enmeshed in punishment. Ultimately, I argue that a system of punitive social control held a grip on the minds and trajectories of
the boys in this study. What this study demonstrates is that the poor, at
least in this community, have not been abandoned by the state. Instead,
the state has become deeply embedded in their everyday lives, through
the auspices of punitive social control. Fieldwork allowed me to observe
firsthand the processes by which the state asserts itself into civil society
through various institutions, with the specific intent of regulating deviant behavior and maintaining social order. This punitive social control
becomes visible when we examine its consequences. These include oppositional culture, perilous masculinity, and other actions that attempt to
compensate for punitive treatment. But not all consequences of punitive
social control are detrimental. The mass and ubiquitous criminalization of
marginalized young people, what I refer to as hypercriminalization, brings
about a paradox. One response to criminalization is resistance. Some of
this resistance is self-defeating. However, other components of this resistance have the potential to radically alter the worldviews and trajectories
of the very marginalized young people that encounter criminalization.

Part 1 examines this system of punitive social control that has developed in Oakland, California. In chapter 2, Oakland is analyzed as a case
study in which young Black and Latino males have had a history of criminalization and punitive social control. Chapter 3 introduces the reader
to two young men who typify the recurring patterns I encountered with
most of the young men in this study. I delve into the life stories of these
boys, whose experiences provide the reader with an understanding of
the deeply embedded day-to-day criminalization that marks them from a
young age.[38] I discuss their perceptions of growing up in an environment
that renders them as criminals and the defiance that they develop to cope
with and resist the unresolved shame and stigma imposed on them by
punishment.

In chapter 4, I analyze the everyday cultural and institutional aspects of criminalization and provide a conceptual framework for understanding this system of punishment, which I call the *youth control complex*. Specifically, I examine the family, schools, police, and probation. I show how interactions with these different institutions of social control have a combined effect on youth which forces them to understand their social world as one where various institutions and individuals systematically criminalize them, generating ubiquitous punitive social control.

In part 2, I examine the consequences of this punitive treatment. I show how criminalization and punitive social control shapes young people's decision-making, actions, worldviews, and identities. Chapter 5 examines the significance that defiance and resistance have for inner-city boys. What types of resistance do they deploy? I argue that what some scholars have understood as "oppositional culture" and "self-defeating resistance" is often a form of resilience that, if channeled in the right way, is capable of transforming the lives of boys such as those in this study.

Chapter 6 examines how the criminal justice system is a gendered institution that heavily contributes to young men's understanding of manhood. I examine how these boys enter manhood in relation to patterns of punishment. Whether they comply with the system or resist it, these young men form specific types of masculinity that often lead them to enact symbolic and physical violence against young women.

Chapter 7 examines the lives of non-delinquent boys. I argue that the non-delinquent boys who lived in marginalized neighborhoods inhabited a double bind: they had to overcompensate to show authority figures that they were not criminal by rejecting their peers and family members who had been labeled as such. This rejection often led these "lawful" youths to be labeled as "sell-outs" or "snitches" by their peers, while at the same time authority figures continued to see them as suspects despite their extraneous efforts. This also rendered "lawful" young men as vulnerable to victimization for not being "man enough." Police told them to "man up" and provide information about their "criminal" friends and relatives, while the streets told them to "man up" and "don't snitch." I discuss how the "don't snitch campaign" became influential among these boys because of criminalization. In other words, "snitching" developed a new definition. "Snitching," for the young men in this study, meant collaborating with the youth control complex; it meant supporting the system in its endeavor to criminalize marginalized young people. "Don't snitch," for many of the boys, meant, "don't become part of the system that is criminalizing our community."

Finally, my conclusion discusses the types of alternative forms of social control that the young men who transformed their lives encountered. I show how resilience among the boys in this study was developed in relation to the social control they encountered. In other words, the more rehabilitative, reintegrative, and positive their interactions with authority figures, the more the boys believed in themselves and understood themselves to have a better future.

My ambition in this book is to show the failures of criminalization, the failures of using harsh, stigmatizing, and humiliating forms of punishment to "correct" and "manage" marginalized youths, as well as to highlight the consequences that these methods have on young people's trajectories. Ultimately, I believe that by understanding the lives of boys who are criminalized and pipelined through the criminal justice system, we can begin to develop empathic solutions which support these young men in their development and to eliminate the culture of criminalization that has become an overbearing part of their everyday lives.

2

The Flatlands of Oakland and the Youth Control Complex

The popular demonization and "dangerousation" of the young now justifies responses to youth that were unthinkable 20 years ago, including criminalization and imprisonment . . . and zero tolerance policies that model schools after prisons.
——Henry Giroux, *Youth in a Suspect Society,* 2009

It's like they put a bomb on my back, but I was the one that pulled the trigger.
——eighteen-year-old Flaco, 2003

The Flatlands

On any given sunny afternoon, one can find a concentration of hundreds of young people hanging out along an eighty-four-block span of International Boulevard, the main thoroughfare in Oakland, that streams through the four-mile heart of the poor and working-class districts of the city. This part of Oakland is known by some people as the "flatlands" and is associated by many with crime, violence, and drugs. A 2009 Discovery Channel documentary, *Gang Wars: Oakland,* claims that there are "ten thousand gang members here who rule with lethal force" and labels the neighborhoods that I studied as the "killing zone." In 2008, this part of Oakland made national headlines when a transit officer at a BART (subway) station was videotaped shooting and killing a young Black man named Oscar Grant. Grant was shot in the back while he was handcuffed and lying on the ground. Some in the community firmly believed that the killing of Oscar Grant was not an isolated incident. Many activists protested and claimed that the killing of Oscar Grant was a consequence of unchecked police harassment and brutality.

A few months later, Oakland again appeared on the national news: this time, a young Black man, by the name of Lovelle Mixon, shot and killed four police officers before police gunned him down, killing him as well. A few of the young men in this study, though they had never before participated in any form of social protest, took part in demonstrations that protested the killing of these two young Black men. Local and national news-media outlets reported these protests as "riots," delegitimizing their appeals for social justice and reinforcing images of wild, criminal youth.[1] Young people from Oakland, in the media and public imagination, seem to be synonymous with violence, poverty, drugs, gangs, and hopelessness. By 2010 an official from California's governor's office had declared Oakland to have a "dire" gang problem.[2]

But far from criminal "superpredators," most youths in Oakland are living productive, normal, everyday lives, surviving and persisting in a city that hosts the fourth-largest violent crime rate in the country. Some gather on street corners looking for excitement. They simply hang out on International Boulevard to pass the time, live, shop, court, work, or socialize. But some of them are active in the informal economy and are on the street to prostitute, sell drugs, or pirate stolen merchandise.[3] Traveling down this street, at the intersection of 14th Avenue and International Boulevard, we begin to find hallmarks representative of much of the flatlands: liquor stores, small businesses, mothers walking with small children, ethnic restaurants, and dilapidated buildings boarded up with plywood. In 2000, the U.S. Census conducted a "case study" in this part of Oakland and found that 33 percent of the population residing "near East 14th Street" (the former name for International Boulevard) lived below poverty.[4]

From 14th Avenue until about 19th Avenue, we find a large number of Southeast Asian businesses and residents. Some of the residents of this neighborhood are Cambodians who arrived in the United States as refugees of the Khmer Rogue and have since developed a strong ethnic enclave in the midst of a large Black and Latino/a presence. In this small community, young Asian men have formed gangs to protect themselves from larger Black and Latino gangs and to produce street-based alternatives to their parents' struggles to make ends meet.[5] One of the youths in the larger sample of this study, Sunny, grew up in this neighborhood. His story shows how Southeast Asian boys have also become criminalized when they don't fall into the expectations constructed by model-minority stereotypes.

From approximately 20th Avenue to 54th Avenue, the boulevard features mostly Mexican businesses and residents. This part of the flatlands is the most densely populated area in Oakland, and the level of heavy traffic up and down the boulevard reflects this. Buses pass by, constantly loaded with a multicultural array of passengers traveling to and from school and work. Paleteros, vendors pushing small shopping-cart-sized ice-cream containers on wheels, ring their bells to attract attention and, hopefully, a customer. "Scrapers," late-1980s and early-1990s Oldsmobile and Buick sedans with twenty-two-inch wheels and flashy paint jobs, make up part of the heavy traffic. Trucks and large SUVs, with even larger twenty-four- or twenty-six-inch chrome wheels, also cruise the boulevard. Most of the vehicles that we see are old and dented and appear ready to break down, perhaps explaining why a heavy concentration of mechanics, auto-body garages, and car-audio shops are littered across this section of the flatlands.

Latino/a and Black youth sit at bus stops, stand on corners, walk to and fro, and eat at the many taco trucks, mobile Mexican restaurants, which line the street. In this part of Oakland, the city has placed surveillance cameras on street corners. Police officers drive around on noisy Harley Davidson motorcycles and in patrol cars. The motorcycle officers often hide behind buildings, looking for drivers who appear "suspicious." The victims of these stops are typically nonwhite youths, who "match descriptions of criminal suspects," or undocumented immigrants, and their vehicles are confiscated until they can show up at the police station with a driver's license (which they cannot attain without papers proving citizenship or legal residency). The patrol-car officers stop and search young people, looking for drugs, weapons, or evidence of "gang activity."

A critical mass of Black residents begins to emerge after 55th Avenue and grows the further we travel into East Oakland through 98th Avenue. Black youths bustle through the boulevard in these parts. Some are walking to and from Heavenscourt Middle School, the only middle school located on International. Others make their way to Food King, a dilapidated nonfranchise supermarket which has been in business in this community for over twenty-five years; it is the only American-foods supermarket on International. Barbershops, a furniture store, a funeral home, beauty salons, and barbecue restaurants are some of the Black-owned businesses we find along this stretch. Black churches, some in large buildings which take up half the block and others in small storefronts, are scattered around. Liquor stores become larger and more numerous in this area. Recently remodeled, colorful public housing complexes face the boulevard. A large group of Black youths live in these complexes. We will later return to shadow Tyrell, who lived in this area.

An increase in the Latino/a population over the past twenty-five years is signaled by a handful of Mexican food stores and restaurants in the area. Police patrol cars drive around sporadically; young people are often stopped and searched here, as well. In 2009, I witnessed a Highway Patrol officer dragging a teenage Black girl out of a 1970s Chevrolet Caprice in front of Heavenscourt Middle School, over one mile away from the nearest highway. Even though she was in handcuffs and passive, the officer pulled her with enough force to make her scream in pain. As she fell to the ground, the officer continued to drag her as her arms and face scraped on the asphalt.

In this chapter, I argue that criminalization is embedded in Oakland's social order, that it is a fabric of everyday life. To understand why young people are policed, punished, and harassed in this city, we have to gain an understanding of Oakland's historical legacy of criminalizing young people. Oakland has been a pioneer in the criminalization of racialized youth. At one point, during the 1960s, many of the punitive criminal justice policies that would later be implemented throughout the country were created and put into practice in Oakland. Following the national advent of zero-tolerance policing, mandatory sentencing, gang enhancements (an added sentence to felony cases when the court finds a defendant guilty of committing a crime for the benefit of the gang), and mass incarceration, the city developed a powerful youth control complex, which continues to grip the lives of the young men in this study. The chapter concludes with a discussion of the youth control complex and its effects on young people.

Why Oakland?

Oakland's large Black and Latino/a communities, pervasive system of policing and surveillance, dynamic youth subcultures, and large working-class and poor populations make it a compelling place for the study of inner-city youth and punitive social control.[6] These factors combine to create a social landscape which epitomizes the sociological circumstances of other cities with large Black and Latino/a populations in the United States. Historian Chris Rhomberg argues in his book *No There There: Race, Class and Political Community in Oakland* that Oakland is an ideal city for the study of urban problems: "[Oakland] is large enough to feature problems of concentration, industrialization, and population change typical of American urban centers, yet small enough to permit observations of its social and political relations as a whole."[7]

Oakland is located in the sixth most populous metropolitan area in the United States, the San Francisco Bay Area. There are 460,000 people residing in Oakland and 7.4 million others living in the greater Bay Area.[8] Oakland is a young city, with 25 percent of its population under eighteen years old and 10 percent of its residents eighteen to twenty-four years old. As of 2006, Oakland's Whites made up 36 percent of its population; Blacks, 30 percent; and Latinos, 26 percent.[9] Despite these fairly equal numbers in population, youth of color are heavily segregated from White youth; over 70 percent of Black children and over 50 percent of Latino children live in neighborhoods which are segregated from Whites.[10] In the flatlands, White youths are a rare population. The majority of Oakland's Whites are middle class and live in the hills or foothills.[11] The city's poverty rates reflect some of this segregation: Black children in Oakland live in poverty at a rate of 30 percent; Latinos, 16 percent; and Whites, 5.2 percent.[12] Oakland has historically been known as the "Detroit of the West," because of its industrial economy in the mid-twentieth century.[13] More recently, since the 1980s, as in Detroit, Oakland residents have experienced massive job losses due to deindustrialization. As of 2010, the unemployment rate for Oakland was 17.7 percent.[14]

One can make a connection between the expansion of punitive social control and capitalist globalization. As industry fled, Oakland experienced massive job losses. This process became one of the contributing economic factors in the changing character of social control in the communities from which the young men in this study came. Sociologist William Robinson argues that capitalist globalization has resulted in a vast restructuring of the world economy, integrating all national economies into a transnational global economy.[15] Essentially, the proliferation of neoliberalism in the past three decades has erected a transnational global economy that frees capital to prey on vulnerable populations and resources and facilitates a transition from social-welfare to social-control, security societies. In order to understand the "trouble with young men" which takes place in the new millennium, we must understand how local troubles are often derived from global processes. In examining its effects on young, poor, racialized men in Oakland, neoliberalism has played a contributing role in producing marginalized populations abandoned by the left arm of the state (welfare) and gripped by the punitive right arm of the state (criminal justice). Today's working-class youths encounter a radically different world than they would have encountered just a few decades ago. These young people no longer "learn to labor"[16] but instead "prepare for prison."[17] Although it is well beyond the scope of this book to discuss global processes, the stories in this study may provide insight to how the global phenomenon of punishing the poor and deep investment in security industries have come to impact the everyday lives of marginalized young men, not just in Oakland but around the globe.[18]

Since the 1940s, Blacks have had a strong presence in Oakland. Blacks migrated from the South to Oakland during World War II, attracted by war-industry jobs on the shipping docks of the city. By the 1960s, Blacks in Oakland became heavily involved in the civil rights and Black Power movements.[19] By the 1980s, Oakland's Black communities began to experience an intensifying intersection of heavy unemployment, the "crack epidemic," punitive crime policies, and the influx of large numbers of Latino/a immigrants. Historically, young Blacks in Oakland have faced a lack of economic opportunities and excessive criminalization. Historian Donna Murch, who has written a book on the Black Panthers, demonstrates how this group of young people was criminalized and systematically attacked by the state, by way of crime-control tactics. She explains the impact of the combination of job loss and increased juvenile policing:

In contrast to their parents, who entered the San Francisco Bay Area in a time of economic boom, postwar youth faced a rapidly disappearing indus-trial base along with increased school, neighborhood, and job segrega-tion. . . . In response to the rapidly growing, and disproportionately young, migrant population, city and state government developed a program to combat "juvenile delinquency" that resulted in high rates of police harass-ment, arrest, and incarceration.[20]

Much of Oakland's Latino/a population arrived during the 1980s and 1990s as immigrants, primarily from Mexico. Attracted to low-income housing in traditionally Black neighborhoods, many Latino/as moved there. Today, many traditionally Black neighborhoods have Latino/a pop-ulations constituting up to 40 percent of their residents. These once-Black areas have now become "Blaxican," neighborhoods where Latino/a (spe-cifically Mexican) culture and Black culture continually meet and mesh. The close proximity of Black and Latino/a youth has created common subcultures, interracial relationships, and common institutional experi-ences, including similar punitive interactions with schools, police, and community members. The majority of the boys in this study analyzed their experiences as a process of collective criminalization and racialization. Young people believed that police, schools, and community members treated both Black and Latino/a youths in the very same ways. Oakland's history may provide an answer for why this belief is prevalent. Criminal-ization and punishment were practiced and perfected on Black popula-tions. By the time a critical mass of poor Latino/as arrived in Oakland, the community and its institutions had a clear system by which to incorporate this new population: criminalization and punitive social control.

A History of Racialized Social Control in Oakland

Oakland has a long history of controlling racialized populations through punitive force. Criminologist Geoff Ward defines racialized social control as the regulation and repression of a population based on its race.[21] Ward argues that social control becomes a negotiated racial order. In other words, the primary way by which racialized populations are regulated is through punitive social control, which in turn establishes social control as a race-creating system.[22] Murch connects race and class with punitive social control in Oakland:

> In Oakland . . . racial anxieties about the city's rapidly changing demograph-
> ics led to an increasing integration of school and recreational programs
> with police and penal authorities. In this context, the discourse of "juvenile
> delinquency" took on a clear racial caste, leading to wide-scale policing
> and criminalization of Black youth. While extensive police harassment and
> arrest of Black migrants started during the population influx of World War
> II, it vastly intensified in the period of economic decline that ensued.[23]

Many noted scholars have argued that today's U.S. criminal justice system has become a central mechanism for controlling and managing unemployed and racialized "surplus" populations.[24] Scholars contend that the civil rights movement, economic crises, and other structural shifts in contemporary society have facilitated the expansion of the criminal justice system and punitive crime-control policies.[25] The civil rights movement of the 1960s provoked mass fear in mainstream America about urban ghettos. Sporadic "race riots" sparked white fright and flight. The call for "law and order" was a response to rising crime rates in the 1960s and signaled opposition to the ongoing civil rights and antiwar movements.[26] The law-and-order campaign of the late 1960s laid the foundation for a "tough on crime" movement in the 1970s and '80s, which became the philosophy of the American criminal justice system for decades thereafter.[27] Ronald Reagan's "War on Drugs" solidified this movement into a mass-incarceration machine.[28]

Also wrapped up in the law-and-order movement was the subtle message to citizens about the supposed rise in Black criminal behavior. By 1969, a Harris poll reported that 81 percent of the public believed that law and order had broken down, with a majority blaming "Negroes, who start riots, and communists."[29] The *New York Times,* analyzing Richard Nixon's law-and-order panacea, announced, "[Nixon] undoubtedly will emphasize order in the cities, for that is his best issue. . . . He thinks he can tame the ghettos and then reconstruct them."[30] Because Oakland was one of the nation's hubs for the Black Power movement, it became a target for politicians such as Nixon and government agencies such as the CIA. The Black

Panthers—a Black youth organization started in Oakland, California, that worked for justice in the Black community—was labeled a "criminal enterprise" by the CIA and the Oakland police, and, as a result, its members were harassed, brutalized, and incarcerated.[31] Eventually, the CIA developed a sophisticated program known as COINTELPRO, designed to spy on, entrap, sabotage, and incarcerate members of the Black Panther Party.

In Oakland, the person responsible for "taming the ghetto," and specifically the Black Panthers, was Edwin Meese. Meese infamously implemented some of the city's harshest policing policies as Oakland's district attorney during the 1960s. His policies sent many Black Panther members to prison. Meese was also responsible for the infamous crackdown at People's Park in Berkeley, California, in 1969. People's Park was a park near the University of California campus that had been taken over by student and community activists. Governor Ronald Reagan denounced this takeover and chastised UC-Berkeley students, stating that UC-Berkeley was "a haven for communist sympathizers, protesters and sex deviants."[32] Under Meese's advice, Reagan declared a state of emergency and sent in the National Guard. One student was killed by police-inflicted shotgun wounds. Many others were severely injured.[33] Meese later served as Reagan's attorney general during the 1980s, implementing the same criminalization and repression tactics that he developed in Oakland in other Black communities throughout the nation. Practices and discourses of criminalization and punishment of young people in the new millennium could be directly traced to the state repression of social movements of the 1960s.

Given the passion with which the Panthers were pursued, it's easy to forget they were primarily a youth organization. Most members were still in their teens, a neglected fact that emphasizes Oakland's long history of targeting youth of color. The Black Panthers began because Black youth in Oakland grew frustrated with being criminalized in the late 1960s.[34] Ironically, the founding of the Black Panther Party sparked some of the most intense criminalization of Black youth. The FBI, for example, declared the Black Panthers "the greatest threat to the internal security of the country" and used COINTELPRO to set up Black Panther Party members for conflict and incarceration.[35] Such programs effectively diminished the Black Panthers' influence by the 1970s. Left without resources for mobilization amid punitive securitization, deindustrialization and the decline of social-welfare programs, gangs and drug dealing became a new modality for some marginalized young people in Oakland.[36]

By the 1970s, conservatives such as Meese latched onto a few studies arguing that rehabilitation did not work and pushed for incapacitation through zero-tolerance policing and longer prison terms.[37] Incapacitation proponents argued that as long as an offender was locked up, he could not commit crimes on the streets.[38] The Reagan administration solidified the "tough on crime" campaign by emphasizing "just deserts" and eradicating what was left of rehabilitation programs. Funding for social programs which focused on rehabilitating convicted offenders or preventing the emergence of new offenders was eliminated.[39]

By 1987, the California legislature declared a "state of crisis caused by violent street gangs whose members threaten, terrorize, and commit a multitude of crimes against the peaceful citizens of their neighborhoods."[40] The legislature claimed that there were nearly six hundred criminal street gangs operating in California; Los Angeles alone saw 328 gang-related murders in 1986.[41] By 1988, California had passed the Street Terrorism Enforcement and Prevention Act, which required longer sentences for offenders recognized as gang members. Black and Latino youths made up the vast majority of people labeled gang members in California.[42]

Following the tough-on-youth crime trend, California voters passed Proposition 21 in 2000. Among other strict reforms, this measure made it a felony to cause more than four hundred dollars worth of graffiti damage (before 2000, a felony charge for property damage required fifty thousand dollars or more of damage). Prop. 21 also targeted youth gang members specifically, allowing youth to be prosecuted for crimes committed by peers if the defendant was deemed to be part of the gang. Many of the boys in this study had been sentenced more severely under Prop. 21. These boys, along with many others in the community, had come to use Prop. 21 as a verb. They would say, "I got Prop. 21'd" or "My brother got Prop. 21'd," referring to the added sentence to their transgression. To compound the problem, sloppy gang labeling by law enforcement—which will include young men in the database on the slightest provocation, such as wearing a certain color, dressing a certain way, or associating with known gang members— has become a serious danger for racialized youth.[43] Being placed in this database increases a young person's chances of being tried as a gang member and given an enhanced sentence for committing any crime thereafter. This labeling leads to harsher punishment, a higher likelihood of being tried as an adult, increased surveillance, and a permanent criminal record.

From 2002 to 2005 Oakland continued to focus on punitive social control in attempts to reduce the crime rate. The city prioritized funding for law enforcement, resulting in declines in spending for educational and social programs. In 2002, Oakland spent $128,331 per law-enforcement employee; by 2005, this rate had increased to $190,140.[44] This approach was further evident in the demands made by the Oakland City Council to the city's new chief of police: "You said you can't arrest our way out of this problem. Well, you sure better try. We all have our jobs to do, and your job is to arrest people."[45] As this book went to press in 2010, Oakland's district attorney imposed its first gang injunction on a neighborhood in north Oakland. A gang injunction allows prosecutors and police to impose sanctions on people labeled as gang members for noncriminal acts, such as associating with other labeled gang members or visiting a neighborhood.

Mass Incarceration

Since the 1970s, the incarcerated population in the United States has increased fourfold to over 2.3 million. As of 2007, one out of every one hundred Americans was behind bars.[46] Massive race and age disparities are prevalent in this incarcerated population. One of every nine Black males aged twenty to thirty-four is incarcerated. One of every twenty-five Latino males and one of every fifty-six White males aged twenty to thirty-four are also incarcerated in the United States. Roughly 27 percent of the incarcerated population is Latino, while it represents 15 percent of the total U.S. population. For Blacks, the statistics demonstrate even deeper disparities: roughly 50 percent of the incarcerated population is Black, while it represents 14 percent of the total U.S. population. In 2007, about 16.6 percent of all Black males were or had previously been incarcerated; 7.7 percent of all Latino males and 2.6 percent of White males had the same status. The chance of a Black male going to prison sometime in his lifetime is one in three, compared to one in six for Latino men and one in seventeen for White men.[47] Thirty percent of juveniles arrested for crime are youth of color, yet they make up 58 percent of those sentenced as adults.[48]

Explanations for why these kinds of punitive and racialized social-control disparities developed are abundant. Sociologist Loïc Wacquant argues that the practices of the punitive state, which have led to mass incarceration, have become the fourth stage of racial domination for African Americans. Following slavery, the Jim Crow South, and the ghetto, the prison, according to Wacquant, has become a central pillar of racial inequality and a space in which to house poor, disreputable, racialized populations.[49] Other scholars argue that conservative politics and a fear of crime led to a "culture of control" whereby mass incarceration became a possibility.[50] Still others argue that economic restructuring and the failure of markets in local and global contexts led to punitive policies and a boom in prison building.[51]

Bridging the material and cultural, Christian Parenti explains that both economic and social crises are responsible for the development of mass incarceration.[52] Wacquant also bridges paradigms by arguing that mass incarceration is a system by which the state deals with the urban disorders brought about by economic deregulation, imposing specific kinds of unsecure and underpaid jobs on racialized and poor populations.[53] In addition, he contends that a "moral theater" is performed by politicians who demonize the poor in order to disguise the state's inability to provide everyday citizens with economic and social protection.[54] Ultimately, Wacquant argues, incarceration has become a core political institution by which poverty has become penalized and a punitive state has developed.[55]

I argue that punitive social control is embedded in the everyday lives of marginalized young males and that the state has not abandoned the poor but instead has punitively asserted itself into various institutions in the community. Ironically, this system of punitive social control, historically developed to control dissent, ends up developing the conditions by which some of these young people become politically conscious and politicized.

Collateral Consequences

While there are many sophisticated explanations for why unprecedented punitive policies and incarceration rates have developed in the United States over the past forty years, few scholars have examined the everyday effects of this phenomenon on marginalized populations.[56] Mass incarceration was an everyday reality for the boys I studied in Oakland.[57]

Fourteen of the boys in this study had parents in prison or jail during the three-year span that I studied them.[58] Many of the older men in the neighborhood—who often had considerable influence on the youth—were convicts. Often, they would return from prison to the neighborhood, attempt to change, find few alternatives, and eventually prey on young people to make money. This would inevitably lead many of them to return to jail or prison or to influence young people to commit crimes that would lead them to incarceration.[59]

When the forty boys in the main group were asked to write down the names of close friends and family members who were currently incarcerated, all of them knew at least six people. One of them, Spider, knew thirty-two. He wrote down their name and age and rated, from 1 to 5, how close he felt to them. When the boys were asked to respond to the question "From 1 to 5, 5 being the highest and 1 being the lowest, how likely do you think you are to get incarcerated in the next few months?" all of them responded with at least a 4, meaning that they all felt that their chances of being incarcerated were high or extremely high. Many of the boys held the same belief that criminologists Mark Mauer and Meda Chesney-Lind have articulated: "It is not difficult to imagine that neighborhoods beset by social ills are not well served when boys and girls perceive that going to prison may be a more likely prospect than going to college."[60] The young men in this study discussed prison as a familiar place. Since many of the adults they looked up to were convicts, as opposed to college graduates, and police and school personnel often treated them like prisoners, the youths became familiar with the culture and rules of prison life and even attached a sense of glamour and admiration to it, before ever serving a day in an adult jail or prison.[61]

The effects of punitive social-control policies and mass incarceration are so widespread that scholars have come up with the term "collateral consequences" to describe them.[62] The collateral consequences of mass incarceration are those negative predicaments in which families, communities, and individuals find themselves as a result of their incarceration or the incarceration of their family members or neighbors. Mauer and Chesney-Lind argue that "with the unprecedented expansion of the prison system over three decades has come a complex network of invisible punishments affecting families and communities nationwide."[63]

Studies have found that the children of the incarcerated suffer psychologically, their families suffer economically, their communities lose adults who would otherwise contribute to incomes and families, and former inmates lose the right to vote.[64] The aftereffects of incarceration include permanent stigma, the loss of opportunities to receive federal and state assistance (e.g., public housing and student loans) or accredited certification in several trades (e.g., automotive, construction, and plumbing), and the loss of one of the fundamental rights of citizenship, the right to vote. These consequences lead to the preclusion of released inmates from positive social networks and to chronic unemployment.[65] Other, more residual collateral consequences are uncovered when we study these marginalized populations at a more in-depth, social relational level.

Very few urban ethnographies have examined punishment as a system that grips the lives of inner-city, street-oriented youths.[66] Sociologist Alice Goffman notes that, "although ethnographic accounts should arguably capture what enhanced policing and supervision has meant for the dynamics of daily life in poor minority communities, most ethnographies were written before the criminal justice system became such a prevalent institution in the life of the poor."[67] In the past, ethnographers reported that police had a minimal presence in the inner city.[68] One exception is sociologist Elijah Anderson's 1990 study "The Police and the Black Male," in which he found young black males encountering constant surveillance and overpolicing: "The police appear to engage in an informal policy of monitoring young black men as a means of controlling crime, and often they seem to go beyond the bounds of duty."[69] In Oakland, policing, surveillance, and criminalization played a major role in the lives of black and Latino street-oriented youths. Street-oriented youths were equally as concerned and impacted by punishment as they were by violence, drugs, crime, and gangs. Not only had the criminal justice system become a prevalent part of the lives of these young people, it had also embedded its logic and practices into other institutions in the community, which then also stigmatized and criminalized the youths. Various institutions in the community became part of a ubiquitous system of punishment that impacted the boys on a daily basis.

These consequences are best understood by taking into account that the criminal justice system has been used as a template for solving other social problems, such as poverty, school truancy, school failure, family conflict, and youth delinquency.[70] Legal scholar Jonathan Simon argues that this punitive shift has resulted in a society that is governed through crime.[71] He contends that crime is no longer regulated solely by the criminal justice system but that policing has been extended to other institutions such as schools, welfare offices, workplaces, and domestic spheres. For example, schools deal with "problem students" as potential criminals, sometimes referring them to police before they have even committed a crime. Thus, teachers become like prison guards, monitoring potential threats and making sure students follow strict orders. In fact, Simon argues, the role of government in the new millennium is to govern through crime. From this perspective, the government appeases citizens by giving them a sense of security through harsh criminal sanctions and strict school and workplace regulations. Private companies bolster such arrangements by developing state-of-the-art auto, home, personal, and business security systems. Simon argues that when we govern through crime, ideas about dealing with criminals become embedded in everyday life. Citizens and government alike use these ideas to "frame all social action as a problem of governance."[72]

According to Simon, the language of the criminal justice system has so permeated all aspects of social life that we have come to believe that crime control is the solution to all social ills. He argues that the "technologies, discourses, and metaphors of crime and criminal justice have become more visible features of all kinds of institutions, where they can easily gravitate into new opportunities for governance."[73] One concrete example of this is zero-tolerance policies in schools. Zero-tolerance policies derive from policing strategies, developed in the 1980s, that were designed to crack down on serious crime by punishing small offenses which were thought to lead to more serious crimes. Some schools in my study have implemented "three strikes" programs, in which students are referred to police after their third disciplinary infraction. This policy is modeled on California's "three strikes" law, which requires a mandatory sentence of twenty-five years to life for anyone convicted of a third felony. Simon concludes that "social problems of all varieties are now treated as a crime problem: poverty, adolescent deviance, and workplace and school conflict."[74] In this book, I build on Simon's work by empirically demonstrating how governing through crime functions on an everyday level and how this new form of governance creates blocked opportunity, negative credentials, and, paradoxically, a political conscious for the boys in this study.

Sociologist Devah Pager argues that the state serves as a "credentializing institution, providing official and public certification of those among us who have been convicted of wrongdoing."[75] Scores of young Black and Latino men receive credentials from the state that permanently mark them as incompetent and dangerous citizens. Further, Pager argues that "the credential of a criminal record, like educational or professional credentials, constitutes a formal and enduring classification of social status, which can be used to regulate access and opportunity across numerous social, economic, and political domains."[76] I found that the boys in this study experienced the process of receiving negative credentials, even prior to having a criminal record. In the era of mass incarceration, negative credentials go beyond a criminal record; some young and poor Black and Latino boys are conferred with negative credentials from a young age. Negative credentials in this sense come in the form of the criminalization of style and behaviors labeled as deviant at school, by police, and in the community. Institutions in the community coalesce to mark young people as dangerous risks for noncriminal deviant behavior and, as such, deny them affirmation and dignified treatment through stigmatizing and exclusionary practices. As a result, young people strive for dignity, so that their social relations, interactions, and everyday activities become organized around maintaining their freedom and feeling empowered in a social landscape that seems to deny them basic human acknowledgment.[77] While some scholars believe that these kinds of young people are aggressively searching for respect, for others to pay them homage and help them earn their "stripes," I find that these young men are, at a more basic level, striving for dignity, demanding to be treated as fellow citizens who are innocent until proven guilty. Working for dignity has to do more with a sense of humanity than a sense of power. Social psychologists who study the law have found that the way that people experience the legal system has much more to do with whether they feel they have been treated fairly than with the actual legal outcome. "Procedures and procedural behavior that violate basic norms of politeness will be seen as unfair both because the basic normative rules that are violated are valued in their own right and because impolite behavior denies the recipient's dignity as a full-status member of the group."[78] In other words, marginalized Black and Latino young men's actions must be understood in the context of wanting to be acknowledged, to feel accepted, to feel human, instead of the typical assessment that they are power-hungry, preemptive, respect-seeking individuals, as most accounts make them out to be. In the era of mass incarceration, when marginalized young people are governed through crime and marked with negative credentials, many strive to maintain their dignity and persist in a social ecology where they are managed by a youth control complex.

The Youth Control Complex

The youth control complex is a ubiquitous system of criminalization molded by the synchronized, systematic punishment meted out by socializing and social control institutions. This complex is the unique whole derived from the sum of the punitive parts that young people encounter. While being called a "thug" by a random adult may seem trivial to some people, when a young person is called a "thug" by a random adult, told by a teacher that he or she will never amount to anything, and frisked by a police officer, all in the same day, this combination becomes greater than the sum of its parts. It becomes a unique formation—the youth control complex—taking a toll on the mind and future outcomes of this young person. This complex is the combined effect of the web of institutions, schools, families, businesses, residents, media, community centers, and the criminal justice system, that collectively punish, stigmatize, monitor, and criminalize young people in an attempt to control them.

The youth control complex is composed of material and symbolic criminalization. Material criminalization includes police harassment, exclusion from businesses and public recreation spaces, and the enforcement of zero-tolerance policies that lead to detention rooms, school suspensions, and incarceration. Symbolic criminalization includes the surveillance, profiling, stigma, and degrading interactions that young people regularly endure. Symbolic punishment, as it relates to race, can be understood as "racial microaggressions."[79] Racial microaggressions are those subtle acts of racism that people of color experience on a daily basis, such as being followed by security at a store, being stopped by police for matching the description of a criminal gang member, or being ignored at school by counselors because they are not expected to make it to college. These are microaggressions because at any given moment, the police, security, and counselors can justify their behavior by saying something like, "That was not racist; I was following the law." If a young person complains and calls this racism, authorities often retort by claiming the youth "is playing the race card." Although a few occasional encounters with these racial microaggressions may not prove to be harmful, consistent negative encounters lead young people to become adversarial toward the system, to lose faith in it, to resist against it, or to build resilience skills to cope. As nineteen-year-old Emiliano, a former gang member who became politically active, told me, "Racism makes some people break, but it makes others break records." Emiliano believed that punitive policing, zero-tolerance school policies, and the criminalization of Black and Brown youth in the media are all part of a system of racism that is intentionally attempting to incapacitate young people of color. One result, for example, was Emiliano's understanding of punishment as a central struggle for young, poor people of color and his belief that this is one of the central mechanisms by which they became politically active.

Emiliano and many of the other youths developed political identities based on their resistance to criminalization and the youth control complex. Marginalized young people who encounter racialized punitive treatment are "not just humans-in-the-making, but resourceful social actors who take an active role in shaping their daily experiences."[80] I found that the young men in this study recognized, had a clear analysis of, and were resisting the criminalization they encountered. This resistance came in different forms. Some resisted by committing violent crime, others by organizing themselves and blocking off their streets with stolen cars and concrete slabs so police cars were unable to access them; and others resisted by becoming political organizers and returning to school. Much of the literature on mass incarceration has not been able to account for agency and resistance in the people most impacted by the punitive state. Furthermore, some scholars have assumed that people in the ghetto are socially disorganized and are not able to persist and create their own social efficacy—the ability to take control of their social settings in order to solve social problems they encounter.[81] Agency is lost and the ghetto incapacitated. In contrast, the young people in this study were constantly resisting. Some of their deviance was a form of resistance to punitive social control.

Whereas some of the young men attempted to overcome their criminalization by resisting, others embraced the support they received from the few institutional actors who acknowledged them. Youths who encountered less punitive forms of control were able to see themselves overcoming the youth control complex. In this sense, those who desisted did so because they encountered an alternative form of social control, one that was "informal, decentralized, inclusive and non-stigmatic, lying somewhere outside the tentacles of the organized state systems of criminal law, criminal justice, imprisonment, and punishment."[82] But while most adults in the community might attempt to support young people, they may be limited by inadequate policies, philosophies, programming, or financial resources to provide deviant youths with successful alternatives that might allow them to reform. As such, these often well-intended adults often fall back on the dominant resources available to them: zero-tolerance policies, punitive policing, and criminal justice discourses and programs. Oakland has a long history of managing marginalized young people through punitive social control, criminalization, and marking them with negative credentials.

3

The Labeling Hype

Coming of Age in the Era of Mass Incarceration

The disparaging view of young people has promulgated the rise of a punishing and (in)security industry whose discourses, technologies, and practices have become visible across a wide range of spaces and institutions.
> —Henry Giroux, *Youth in a Suspect Society*, 2009

Overall, ethnic minority youths, gang or non-gang, resent the "dissing" (disrespect) meted out by patrol officers. . . . Once youths have begun to reject the law and its underlying values, they often develop a resistance orientation and take a defiant and destructive stance.
> —James Diego Vigil, *A Rainbow of Gangs*, 2002

Tyrell, a Black youth, and Jose, a Latino youth, both sixteen years old, sat on a splintered wood bench at the bus stop on the corner of 35th and International, in front of Hernandez Meat Market. Right above them, a pig and the head of a cow, painted on the meat-market wall, stared straight down at them. A street sign, adjacent to the bus stop, read, "All activity on this block is being recorded." I leaned back on the sign, as I observed and listened to Tyrell and Jose. They looked around: Jose stared at people in cars, while Tyrell looked at a group of four teenage Black boys walking across the street.

I was shadowing Tyrell and Jose as they made their way home from school. Tyrell lived close to 65th Avenue; and Jose, past 80th Avenue. They were having a conversation about their principal. "Man! Mr. Schwartz is an asshole! He be on one, man [gets crazy]!" Tyrell told Jose. Jose rubbed his head and replied, "Dude just called the police on me today." When I asked why, he answered, "'Cause he said I was threatening him. But all I did was tell him that if he called the police, they had nothing on me. . . . He said, 'Oh, yeah, all right. Let's see.' And then he called them." Jose dug into the baggy black jeans' pocket that sat close to his knee and handed me a yellow citation given to him by the police officer. At the top it read, "Notice to Appear," with the number 0188546XX. In the middle was Jose's violation: "CPC 647 Dist. Peace." "Dude [police officer] came by and just started writing me a ticket. He said he would arrest me, but he had some other shit to do."

"What did you do?" I asked.

"Shit, disturbed the peace at school. . . . I talked back to the principal. That's what I get."

Tyrell responded, "Homey, that's nothing. You should see all the times they've stopped me for little shit, like looking at them crazy or walking down the street."

During three years of observations I counted forty-two citations imposed on the boys. Loitering, disturbing the peace, drinking in public, not wearing a properly fitted bicycle helmet, and violating curfew were among the violations they received citations for. Minor citations for "little shit" played a crucial role in pipelining many of the young men in this study deeper into the criminal justice system. Some of the boys missed their court dates; others appeared in court but could not pay their citations. This led to warrants for arrest or probation. Warrants and probationary status marked the young men for further criminalization. Police, school personnel, and probation officers would graduate the boys to a new level of policing and harassment. Being on probation, for instance, meant that the boys could be stopped, searched, or reported, at any given moment. Probation status provided the youth control complex a carte blanche in its endeavor to stigmatize, punish, and exclude young people. When a young person is on probation, he is left with few rights; he can be stopped and searched for no reason, and he can be arrested for noncriminal transgressions such as hanging out with his friends or walking in the wrong part of the neighborhood.

In this chapter, I argue that labeling is not just a process whereby schools, police, probation officers, and families stigmatize the boys, and, in turn, their delinquency persists or increases.[1] In the era of mass incarceration, labeling is also a process by which agencies of social control further stigmatize and mark the boys in response to their original label.[2] This in turn creates a vicious cycle that multiplies the boys' experiences with criminalization, what I call a labeling hype. I found that the boys in this study felt outcast, shamed, and unaccepted, sometimes leading them to a sense of hopelessness and a "deviant self-concept."[3] In addition, I also found that the young men were caught in a spiral of punitive responses imposed by institutions which labeled them as deviant. Being labeled or marked for minor transgressions would place the boys at risk for being granted additional, more serious labels.

Institutions became involved in a spiral of criminalization that began with informal, trivial labels, such as "This kid comes from a bad family and is at-risk." This label alone would sometimes lead to more detrimental labels, such as "This kid is delinquent, and he is a risk." Criminologist Paul Hirschfield argues that labels have little impact on the individual identities of marginalized black males, but they have a big effect on young people's social mobility. He posits that "mass criminalization" is responsible for "social exclusion" and "diminished social expectations."[4] In the era of mass incarceration, labeling not only generates criminality; it also perpetuates criminalization.

Previous studies in urban ethnography have done an exceptional job at describing blocked opportunity and its consequences.[5] However, criminalization as a system that contributes to this blocked opportunity has yet to be analyzed. This system had such an extensive influence on the lives of the boys in this study that many of them were criminalized even when they were victims of crime. Criminalization became internalized by many of the boys, even leading some to believe that they did not deserve protection from the police. Tyrell's and Jose's life stories show the process by which young men come of age in Oakland being labeled as deviant and eventually being treated like criminals. In this respect, they are representative of many of the other boys in this study.

Historian Robin Kelley argues that academics have contributed to society's understanding of poor Black populations as pathological and nihilistic, by creating stories that only focus on compensatory behaviors. Sometimes, Kelley argues, researchers overemphasize and exaggerate the resistant and adaptive strategies of the poor and present them to the mainstream world as indicators of pathologies or as negative responses to a system that victimizes them.[6] By focusing on the boys' worldviews about their negative encounters with social control agents and by looking at the creative responses they develop, I hope to move beyond understanding marginalized populations as only victims, or pathological, or compensatory conduct driven. This endeavor begins by paying close attention to the life stories of these young people and their perspectives on the structural predicaments in which they live.

The bus arrived. Tyrell and Jose changed their conversation about police and citations. Tyrell asked me, "So you still wanna go to the Ville?" I told him I did. The "Ville" was a low-income housing project located on 66th Avenue and International. Tyrell spent most of his childhood there. Although he had recently moved out, he hung out there every day with his friends, in an alley that residents refer to as "Death Alley." We got on the bus and remained silent, observing the twenty or so other teenagers sardined inside. Tyrell and I got off the bus and silently nodded to Jose, who remained on the bus heading further down International. When we arrived at the Ville, I asked Tyrell to give me a tour, from his perspective, and tell me about growing up in this environment.

Tyrell's Too Tall

Since the late 1980s, the Ville housing project has been notorious for its crime rate.[7] Famous former residents include Felix Mitchell, who established one of the most influential crack-cocaine gang empires in the country there during the '80s. Mitchell was killed in prison in 1986, but he is still a legend in this community. The 1991 film *New Jack City* used Mitchell's life as the basis for one of its main characters, Nino Brown.

Tyrell and his friends still talk about Mitchell: "Mitchell was a true G [gangster]. . . . He is like the only role model we got," said Tyrell. This statement is indicative of the lack of programs in schools or in the community, which could have exposed young people to professional and college-educated role models.

The Ville, notorious for its drug trafficking and violence, consisted of rows and rows of two-story, shoebox-shaped apartment buildings, with metal window and door gates—the epitome of West Coast housing projects. The new two-tone light-beige and pink paint and fancy geometric trim on the top of some of the recently remodeled buildings belied the bullet holes in apartment windows, the homemade tin-foil crack pipes laying on the lawns, and the dire poverty of little kids fighting to ride the only neighborhood bike. The city had recently demolished similar buildings down the street and in their place developed modern townhouse-style projects, shaped like squares, with attractive geometrical rooftops and three-tone light-beige, yellow, and green paint jobs. These new housing developments were juxtaposed with drug dealers standing at the corner, with middle-aged crack addicts pacing about in desperation and the bloody street fights that constantly took place in the Ville. The millions of dollars spent on physical upgrades could not bandage the persistence of violence, crime, and criminalization that could only be transformed by implementing programs which could change the social order and social control of the neighborhood, not just its physical appearance.[8] If certain social contexts breed criminality, then certain social contexts breed criminalization. The cycle of crime and violence cannot be addressed by changing the appearance of a place and incarcerating its denizens; we must start by changing the social contexts that provide actors the resources for partaking in specific behaviors and by transforming the ways in which we perceive and treat—criminalize or incorporate—these populations.

As we walked around the Ville, Tyrell pointed to different locations that ignited his memory: where he first got high, where he first witnessed a murder in Death Alley, and where the police brutalized him for the very first time. Tyrell looked at me when we got to "death alley," an alley that residents understood as a space where deadly violence was a regular presence, and asked, "What do you want to know?" The space seemed to spark a desire in Tyrell to share his story. We sat on a giant piece of broken concrete which was used to form a retaining wall between the alley and a now-abandoned house.

Tyrell was raised by his father, John. According to Tyrell, his mother had left them for a man who made a good living selling crack. "She told my dad, 'You ain't shit, can't even get a job,' so she bounced." Soon after, she became addicted to crack. According to Tyrell, his mother's boyfriend was also a crack user and passed the addiction on to her. Tyrell's mother showed up sporadically, asking him and his grandmother for money to support her addiction. "She smokes so much crack, she calls herself 'Bubbles,'" Tyrell told me. On another day, when I was hanging out with Tyrell in Death Alley, where he and his friends would convene every afternoon, Tyrell's mother came around the corner. She asked him, "Have you seen Mo?" Tyrell nodded, looking embarrassed. She asked me for money, and I told her I would give Tyrell some money on her behalf. She thanked me for what she perceived as my helping her son and walked off, through an alley onto an adjacent block. This situation was not unique to Tyrell: eighteen of the boys in the study reported having at least one parent who had problems with drugs or alcohol.

Tyrell was homeless for part of his childhood, sleeping in cars, shelters, crack houses, and in the parking lot of the Ville. In Tyrell's account, the housing authority did not want to provide his father housing. "Because he was not a woman . . . they told him that he had no reason for not having a job." Tyrell's dad was a mechanic but could not find work at the time:

> He worked on other people's cars, but they were broke too. They gave him five, ten dollars, but he couldn't pay rent with this. So we ended up at other people's houses or in our car most of the time. . . . One day a crack head [addict] told us she was moving back to Atlanta. She said that we could live in her apartment if we wanted, but we had to pay rent. This is when we got our own place. I was hella happy knowing that I would have my own place. That's crazy, I was happy, 'cause I was gonna live in the projects. . . . It was hella fun living there.

Despite the surrounding violence, drug abuse, and poverty—as well as the consequential trauma, homelessness, and hunger—Tyrell remembers having a fun childhood. His father taught him about being respectful to others and obeying the law no matter how poor they were. "Pops wouldn't steal from nobody. He would rather starve than steal," Tyrell told me. John attempted to keep Tyrell sheltered from the effects of poverty; sometimes it worked. John taught him that some police officers were good and encouraged him to be the cop when he played cops and robbers. By the second or third grade, all his friends made fun of him for playing the cop. By then, most of his peers believed that the police were a negative force in the community, but Tyrell still believed that police had the power to "take the bad people away from the Ville."

Despite not having the resources to provide "proper" parenting, such as help with homework or money for school trips or work clothes, the majority of the boys' parents attempted to instill positive values in their children, even if some of them did not have a standard definition of mainstream values. Often, parents became desperate in their failed attempts to guide their children. This led some parents to ask probation, police, or school officials to teach them strategies for parenting their children. As these institutions advised desperate individuals on how to parent their children, they passed on their punitive approaches to treating deviant and delinquent behavior. In a sense, they taught parents how to criminalize their own children.

Sociologist Ross Matsueda finds that informal labels, negative treatment, and stigma derived from a perception of criminality are imposed on individuals who have committed crime but also are imposed on individuals who are from a group or community perceived to be criminogenic. Matsueda finds that these informal labels have an effect on the labeled individual's perceptions of how others see him. Matsueda also finds that some parents actively participate in the process of labeling their children.[9] In chapter 4, I discuss the ways in which some parents label and criminalize their children, often under the influence of the criminal justice system.

In fourth grade, an older Tyrell and his homies would walk a few miles to the Oakland Coliseum, located two miles from the Ville, when the Oakland Athletics or Oakland Raiders played games. "We would walk like twenty blocks to the Coliseum to watch the games. They wouldn't let us in, so we stood outside on the very top and looked through the cracks between the fence. The guys [players] were this little [he measures about an inch with his thumb and index finger], but we still got to see 'em, they hit a homerun." Police chased Tyrell and his friends off the Coliseum grounds. He could not understand why they were so aggressive toward him, when he was "just trying to watch a game." According to Tyrell, police threatened him and his friends with arrest if they continued to loiter at the Coliseum.

By the sixth grade, Tyrell felt that he could no longer exist outside the violence that defined the Ville. "Sixth grade is where it all went down. Cops started beating on me, fools [peers] started getting hyphy [crazy] with me. I had to get into, um, lots of fights," Tyrell said. He told me that his height contributed to his forced entry into street life. In the sixth grade, Tyrell was the tallest student in school. He remembered going into class on the first day of sixth grade, and his teacher, Mrs. Turpin, would not stop staring at him. Tyrell became bothered and asked her, "What you lookin' at?" She used his comment as a lesson to the class that everyone was to respect the teacher. She kicked him out of class and told the principal she was "threatened" by Tyrell. Twenty-two of the boys reported feeling as if their teachers were scared of them.

Tyrell believes that the teacher was not the only person who saw him as a threat, because of his height, when he was younger. In his account, because he looked like a man by age twelve, he also became a target of constant police surveillance and random checks for drugs or criminal suspicions:

> The five-o [police] stopped me all the time. They checked me for drugs and guns most of the time. At first I was scared and told them I was only twelve. They didn't believe me and kept asking me where I was hiding the drugs. That made me hella mad 'cause I wasn't slanging [selling drugs] or anything. On mama's [I promise] I wasn't slanging. I said, fuck it. So a few months later I started selling weed.

Tyrell's perspective was that he could not control his height, physical appearance, or the perceptions that others had of him. The one thing he could control was making the choice to sell drugs to support himself. Tyrell's decision to sell drugs is representative of the patterns that I found among all the boys during their first arrest. They chose to commit a crime, consciously calculating the potential risk of arrest and incarceration. Many of the boys came to this assessment after believing that they had no other choice, that they had nothing to lose.

In my observations, I noticed that Tyrell had a compelling presence. Police officers whom he had never encountered before targeted Tyrell more often than the other Black and Latino youths I hung out with. Over the course of three years, I watched or heard from Tyrell about being stopped by police twenty-one times, more than any other youth in this study. Most of the time, these stops ended with just a short conversation. But sometimes, police officers seemed threatened by Tyrell, and they either handcuffed him, pulled a gun on him, or put him in the patrol car.

Meanwhile, according to Tyrell, his father increasingly took his stress and anger out on Tyrell. John grew frustrated at his inability to find a steady job. Despite his charisma and exceptional mechanic skills, he could not find regular work. He was only able to find employment in the local informal economy: poor local residents would bring their cars to him for repairs but were not able to pay enough for him to make a living. In the Ville, no matter what time of day, I always saw John working on someone's car. He was always cheerful and joked around with everyone in the neighborhood. While John had all the characteristics of a supportive father, his lack of economic resources led Tyrell to realize that he would have to "hustle" for his own money:

> I told him I had a little money, and he knew where I got it from. He got hella mad and beat me down. He told me he did not want me selling that shit. I told him it was only weed, but he didn't care. He told me that I would end up selling crack. I think he didn't want me to start smoking that. . . . I stopped selling it for a while, but we both were broke. This is when I started selling at school again but just didn't tell him.

In Tyrell's worldview, he made a conscious choice to commit crime within the context of the limited resources available to him and the vilification he encountered at school and with police. To the extent that material resources became scarce, and he became constructed as a deviant, he calculated that his only choice was to sell drugs. His father's inability to provide for him, and the stigma that school officials and police officers imposed on him, left Tyrell feeling trapped. In this constricted location, Tyrell's options were few, and one of the only lucrative options available at the time was to sell drugs. He dropped out of school and dedicated

himself to making money on the streets. Breaking the law was his decision, yet his hand was largely forced by overdetermined structural conditions. In Tyrell's perspective, poverty and criminalization "pushed" him
into selling drugs, but he also consciously took this "jump," knowing that
this was one of the only ways he could make some money.[10]

Tyrell had agency to decide whether he would commit crime or not.
But a system of punitive social control established a context for Tyrell in
which he felt disconnected from his community, stigmatized, and socially
outcast, leading him to see criminality as almost inevitable. As such,
Tyrell was punished into believing something external to his sense of self:
that he was a criminal, that he had nothing at stake, and that he "might
as well handle business"—sell drugs and victimize others—since he has
"nothing to lose." All the young men in this study believed that they were
inherently criminal: their interactions with the world around them had
led them to internalize a foreign concept, that criminality was part of
their persona. Tyrell, like many other marginalized youth, experienced a
life-course process in which he was systematically punished into believing that he had nothing to lose. In the context of punitive social control,
some marginalized boys are fostered by punishment, at every stage in
their development, encountering a social world that, in their account,
treats them as suspects and criminals.

Although I was not present during the boys' various stages of childhood development, the three years I spent in the field taught me that their
perceptions of a punitive social order were rational and reasonable. One
only needs to spend a few hours with marginalized young people in their
everyday settings to realize how much they are policed, stigmatized, and
treated differently from other citizens. Their stories were corroborated by
observations of similar events that took place during my time in the field.

Jose Learns the Code

Three days after that day with Tyrell, I repeated my bus-stop routine of
catching up with Jose and Tyrell. I met them at the same bus stop, con-
versed with them, and rode the bus. This time, I got off the bus with Jose. We
walked to a liquor store on the corner of 80th and International, purchased
two Coca-Colas and two bags of Flamin' Hot Fries, and leaned against the

store's wall outside, staring at a 1980s white delivery truck that had been used as a canvas by the neighborhood youth to tag their street names and territories. Jose proudly stared at his tag name, "Topo," written in black spray paint on the belly of the delivery truck. We walked a few blocks to his apartment complex, where we sat on the concrete steps. After we sat idly for about twenty minutes, I asked Jose to tell me about growing up there.

Jose had lived his whole life in the heart of the neighborhood that hosted one of Oakland's largest gangs, which I will call the East Side Gangsters (ESG). A few times in his early teenage years, his mother attempted to move him to Berkeley, a neighboring city she thought might be safer. However, the high rent prices always forced the family to return to the same apartment in Oakland. Their apartment complex was the main hangout for the gang. The complex sat adjacent to a neighborhood liquor store, where drug dealers, drug addicts, and gang members congregated. The apartment complex was shaped like a horseshoe, with three floors on each of the three sides. Clothes were hung to dry on the building's loose metal rails; old tennis shoes hung from the electric lines that ran in front of the complex; and the small parking lot served as a soccer field for little kids, a car-repair area for unemployed men, a drug-stashing area for dealers, and, on the weekends, a dance ballroom for families celebrating baptisms, birthday parties, and quinceaneras.[11] For as long as Jose could remember, the gang loitered in the parking lot of his apartment complex, often blocking the steps that led to Jose's apartment. "They would, like, just do stupid stuff, like scare us [the apartment-building families], like shoot their guns and break shit and fight. I used to be hella scared of them," explained Jose.

Jose remembered being terrified of the gang at age six or seven. He yearned for the police to protect him and his family from the gang. One day, when he was about ten years old, a teenage gang member pushed him as he returned home from buying a gallon of milk from the liquor store for his family. Jose fell back, landing on the gallon of milk. White fluid splattered everywhere. The teenage boys laughed at him. He began to cry. Soaked, he returned home to tell his mother. She yelled at him, "Pendejo [idiot], don't you know we don't have money for more milk?" Jose wanted the gang members to pay for another gallon of milk. He left the house and walked the neighborhood, looking for a police officer. When he found a patrol car, he told the officer about the incident and wanted the officer to talk to the gang members and ask them to buy his family another gallon of milk. According to Jose, the officer laughed at him and told him, "I got better things to do."

In my observations, I counted twenty-two instances when police were called to solve "minor" community problems such as disputes, bullying, harassment, and vandalism. In these twenty-two instances, police were only able or willing to intervene in these "minor" issues one time. In the other twenty-one cases, the officers either ignored residents who called or took down information and left the scene. This is indicative of the underpolicing that I found in this study. It may seem contradictory to say that young people are hypercriminalized by law enforcement but that their communities are also underpoliced. However, Jose's experience and my observations confirm what many of the other boys reported: officers consistently police certain kinds of deviance and crime, while neglecting or ignoring other instances when their help is needed. One reason for this may be that officers follow the path of least resistance. They police easy targets, such as youth who visibly display their deviance and delinquency. These kids, whom police have come to criminalize, are sometimes the same ones who need help when they are victimized. Officers may be less sympathetic to those populations that they have rendered criminal. This process I refer to as the overpolicing-underpolicing paradox. Policing seemed to be a ubiquitous part of the lives of many of these marginalized young people; however, the law was rarely there to protect them when they encountered victimization.

Jose remembered the milk incident as a moment when he decided he would begin to take justice into his own hands.[12] Jose recounted that after this incident, he began to develop a tough demeanor and increasingly turned to violence in an attempt to prevent victimization.[13] He even joined the same gang that harassed him as a child.

> VR: Being tough at a young age, did that protect you from being attacked?
>
> JOSE: [Smacks his lips] You know, Vic, I tried to be hella hard, and I ended up getting beat down even more.
>
> VR: Like, what were some things that you remember happening to you after trying to be tough?

JOSE: So, that one time with the milk, I went and got a bat and went up to the dude that pushed me. He grabbed the bat from me and pushed me to the ground. I thought he was gonna crack me in the head. But he thought I was too little. I went home hella pissed off.

Sociologist Elijah Anderson finds that appearing aggressive and willing to commit violence is a self-defense process for some inner-city residents, part of what he calls "the code of the street." This code offers individuals a way to protect themselves from victimization in violent communities and to build respect from others: "In service to this ethic, repeated displays of 'nerve' and 'heart' build or reinforce a credible reputation for vengeance that works to deter aggression and disrespect, which are sources of great anxiety on the inner-city street."[14] Anderson goes on to show that the code of the street is embedded in everyday interaction across various institutions in the community: "The 'code of the street' is not the goal or product of any individual's actions but is the fabric of everyday life, a vivid and pressing milieu within which all local residents must shape their personal routines, income strategies, and orientations to schooling, as well as their mating, parenting, and neighbor relations."[15] Preemptively attacking an enemy to prevent future victimization is a key element of the code.[16] Jose's story is representative of the other boys who reported using the code in attempts to protect themselves. The code became amplified when Jose joined the gang, because now he became part of a group whose central motive was to collectively attack others to prevent and avenge victimization. Jose joined because he wanted to prevent being victimized by the neighborhood gang. A double bind became apparent in Jose's endeavor to protect himself: while the gang protected Jose from specific kinds of victimization, such as being attacked by non-gang members, he experienced more victimization by rival gang members after joining the gang. The boys seemed to understand that preemptively attacking others would lead to further victimization. However, they chose to do so as a means of feeling a sense of justice for crimes that had been committed against them and gone unresolved. The code of the street was used as a form of street justice when the formal justice system had failed them.

Some of this victimization was at best ignored and at worst condoned by the police. Jose explained, for instance, that when he was a child he could not understand why the police wouldn't just take all the gang members to jail since they all carried weapons. When he became a gang member, he came to his own conclusion. Jose explained that the police allowed them to loiter and sell drugs within the confines of their apartment complex because they were not visible to the public and therefore were not a problem the police would be held accountable for. During my time observing the complex while hanging out with Jose and his friends, I found a pattern that affirmed this assumption. Police were often stationed at the street corner but would never enter the complex, even when fights and drug use were clearly visible. However, once young people walked to the street corner, police would proceed to harass and arrest them, as is evident in the following story from one of the forty boys in the study, J.T., whom I met through Jose and who lived in the same complex: "When I was young, we didn't know nothing about the laws, so they always tried to scare us when we were little, telling us they would take us to juvenile hall. 'Cause, like, we would throw rocks at cars or do lil' things or even just hanging out on the corner. They would tell us to go home, and they would handcuff us if we didn't listen. . . . We were like six [years old]." Thus, in this apartment complex, young boys, as early as age six, learned from police the spatial terrain in which they could be deviant and commit crime. Criminalization created spatial demarcation; police set parameters for where individuals could loiter or commit crime. The consequences of "playing" or "hanging out" beyond the established limits of invisible and marginalized spaces included brutalization, harassment, and arrest. For the older boys, this spatial demarcation structured the rules governing the code of the street: gang members were allowed to commit violence and victimize others, as long as the acts were committed within the confines of the apartment complex, which law enforcement underpoliced.

Residents suffered from the concentration of gang members who had been contained in these invisible spaces by police.[17] Often, families—women and children—became the victims of a small handful of predatory gang members whom police neglected to apprehend. In this apartment complex, out of a group of about thirty boys, two of them were the ones that incited, provoked, and caused most of the assaults and crimes that occurred while I was there. Everyone in the complex knew who they were, and many residents seemed anxious when these two boys came around. A mother who lived in the complex told me one day, as one of the boys, nicknamed Psycho, greeted us and walked up the street with a sharpened, broken metal table leg in his hand, "When that boy is locked up, the whole neighborhood is at peace. But now that he is out, all the boys have gone crazy." The only party that did not seem to know that these two boys were responsible for most of the havoc in the complex was the police. By criminalizing all of the boys, the police, it seemed, could not tell the difference between predatory criminals and innocent young people trying to live their lives. By policing and harassing youth who stepped into the public sphere looking like a "gang member" or a "drug dealer," and not learning from the community about the small group responsible for most crimes, police allowed a few predatory criminals to reign inside the marginalized space of the apartment complex. Police failed to intervene in crime that took place on the property, as if this area were outside their purview.

Police in School

For all the boys in the study, negative encounters with police were not restricted to the streets. When asked "What was your first experience with police?" all the boys commented that their first encounters with police took place in or near school. In Oakland, probation and police officers were stationed at or near many schools. A few of the boys attended a middle school that I visited while I shadowed them. On a few occasions, when I was invited to talk to some students about college, I noticed a police officer advising parents and students on academic matters, including courses to choose in preparation for high school, studying strategies, and career options. This example is representative of some of the many ways in which police and probation officers became involved in non-criminal-justice matters at school and in the community.

For Jose, police seemed to always be part of his school experience. His first encounter happened at school when he was eight years old. "The first time was in third grade. I had set the bathroom garbage can on fire. We ran away, and they caught us and handcuffed us. . . . I was just trying to do something funny. Police came and arrested me and my friends.

They only had a pair of handcuffs, and they handcuffed me and my friend together. This is the first time I got arrested. I also flunked that year." Jose was not taken to jail; instead, his mother picked him up from the custody of the police office. However, his parents, his friends, and the school staff started to view him as a kid who had been arrested. Jose returned to school after the incident and remembers being treated differently by teachers and friends: "Teachers would tell me that if I kept messing up, they would have to call the cops again. I was really scared, so I tried to do good, but then [long pause] I don't know what happened. I just started messing up anyway. . . . My friends started to respect me more, and they looked up to me. That kinda felt good. . . . That is probably why I messed up even more."[18] From fourth to sixth grade, Jose consistently failed in his academic endeavors. He spent most of his time in detention rooms and "opportunity" classes designed to house the most disruptive students at school: "I would just sit there and stare at the wall or lay my head down to rest. The teacher would give me good grades just as long as I didn't flash [go crazy]." The school-stationed police officer regularly checked on Jose. Over time, Jose says, school began to serve as a site of punishment and control, a space where teachers, police, probation officers, and administrators alike "just waited" for him "to fuck up."

Jose believed that school served as a space that systematically denied him what sociologists call a "positive rite"—the universal human need to be perceived by others in a positive light, with consideration instead of degradation.[19] In other words, in Jose's account, school functioned as a space where his personal need to feel acknowledged and respected was systematically denied, and instead he was treated with indignity and disdain. In the context of juvenile crime, researchers have found that shame is an integral component of criminalization and is part of the vicious cycle that creates lifelong lawbreakers.[20] Being shamed and feeling stigmatized often leads young people into crime.[21] For Jose, this cycle may have begun when he was taken through the ritual of being handcuffed and walked out of school at eight years of age, an event that publicly identified him as a criminal. The stigma produced by this ritual helped to generate a self-fulfilling prophecy that shaped his ensuing relationships with teachers, police, and probation officers. Because Jose believed they were all collaborating to criminalize and punish him, he treated them with hostility, an attitude that led adults to act punitively toward him. I noticed similar events countless times during my observations at Jose's middle school and continuation high school.

I observed Jose react to teachers, school security officers, and police with defiance, and in return they responded by intensifying their punitive treatment of him. One day, I asked a school security supervisor why she treated Jose so "tough." She replied, "Listen, man, when these kids get to the point where they start talking back, you gotta regulate. You gotta make sure they know that you're in command—no matter what it takes." I later asked Jose what he thought about this statement. Jose was not surprised. He told me that most security guards, school police, and school officials had treated him with this attitude. In this context, Jose recalls losing interest in school by the time he started fifth grade.[22] He stopped wearing a backpack, stopped actively participating in class, and eventually received an "age promotion" into middle school. Jose failed fourth and fifth grade, but the school promoted him because he was too old to stay in elementary school.

Jose recounted being beaten by police a week after he started middle school. He was twelve years old. The same police that patrolled his neighborhood since he was a small child, the same officer who had refused to help him recover his family's gallon of milk, gave him his first police beating:

> Sometimes, they be trying to jack me and stuff. Like they be trying to mess with us, like play around. They'll . . . they'll try to play around with us: "We got calls saying that you guys are doing this and that." 'Cause sometimes we wouldn't be doing nothing; they would just blurb us [light and siren signals of police vehicles]. One day they just got me for doing too much [messing around]. I was looking at the cop like crazy and stuck my tongue out him. He got out and whipped my ass.

By sixth grade Jose began to flirt with gang life. Middle school provided him with the resources to become a "wannabe," a youth who has displayed interest in becoming part of the gang. A major reason for wanting to join the gang, at least initially, was for protection from violence.

> I was . . . was by the house. . . . So some, uhh, Sureños [Southerners—rival gang members] . . .—I seen them when they were in the car—they had a gun. I was walking. I was by my house [apartment], and I see my lil' sister in

front of the house; my older sister, she was walking on the other side. And
then out of nowhere they just like started shooting. And I told my sisters
to duck. I started ducking. And then I . . . I . . . I hopped over the fence, and
they left. I wasn't really scared to get shot, but I was scared for my sisters.

No one was hurt that day. Jose, however, knew that, based solely on the
apartment building he lived in, he had become a target for other gangs.
Based on previous experience with the police, he believed they were not
going to find the shooters. When officers asked him for information, he
did not say a word. Jose explained that he was afraid that telling the officers
would lead to the people who shot at him finding out and retaliating. Jose
had good reason for these suspicions, as many young men in this study
provided stories of police officers giving them information about rival
gang members. I myself witnessed this process three times. During one
observation, an officer arrived at the street corner where we were standing. He called us over and got out of the car. He told the boys, "You know,
the Scraps [derogatory name for Sureños] just ratted one of your boys out.
They say that he was involved in a shooting on Friday night. Where is he?"

The culture of criminalization that affects many communities of color
has created a corresponding culture that forbids "snitching." In this study,
the sense that community members and homies were regularly incarcerated through false accusations, police "setups," entrapment, and forced
testimonies led many of the boys to declare a vow against ever providing information to police, even when they were the victims. The "don't
snitch" campaign among the boys in this study was not a commitment to
allow murderers to remain free; it was an attempt to avoid further criminalization and unjust arrests and sentencing and to protect themselves
from being "ratted out" by police. One can make sense of the perceiv-
ably senseless "don't snitch campaign" as a collective attempt to resist the
overpolicing-underpolicing paradox and mass incarceration. At such a
young age, Jose already had a keen sense that the police would do more
harm than good with the information he provided. Meanwhile, another
cast of characters provided Jose with the support denied by law enforcement that he felt he needed: the neighborhood gang members.

The older gang members from the neighborhood acknowledged Jose
for having experienced an attack on his family. They told him that they

would back him up. "Even though I was little, they was like, 'You got a lot of heart.' I told them, 'Yeah,' and they said, 'All right then, you gotta put in work.'" For Jose, putting in work meant attacking rival gang members to avenge the attack on his family. At the time, Jose was fourteen years old and had unofficially been accepted into the gang for taking a hit from rivals. Jose went on "missions" with his homeboys to find and beat up rival gang members. He also began to smoke marijuana and to "love it." This led to his first stint in juvenile hall.

One day, an officer stopped him in front of the neighborhood liquor store, searched him, and arrested him for a ten-dollar bag of marijuana he had in his pocket. After two days in "juvy," Jose returned to his neighborhood. This time, he figured that if he was going to take risks and be arrested for minor drug possession, he "might as well grind big thangs and make some money." He attempted to become a crack-cocaine dealer.[23] He had big dreams that he would become rich and buy his mother a house so that he could move away from the apartment complex. He learned how to cook up powder cocaine with baking soda to produce crack rocks. He learned how to wrap the rocks in balloons and keep them in his mouth. This way, if the police stopped him, he would swallow the rocks to hide the evidence. Jose even shadowed a group of older guys from six in the morning to three the next morning, twenty-one entire hours, just to learn how "business was handled." Sixteen of the youths in this study had sold drugs at one point, and all these boys described making a lot of money while they sold drugs. After more probing, I realized that their notion of "lots of money" was relative. Some of them made five hundred dollars in one day. However, there were also days when they only made twenty dollars. Overall, their "salaries" averaged out to less than forty dollars a day. However, their working day sometimes lasted up to twenty-one hours. In other words, it is quite possible that the majority of drug-dealing young people in Oakland make less than minimum wage, all while risking incarceration, violence, and addiction by selling drugs on the street.[24] Despite all Jose's hard work and training, on his first day selling crack, the police arrested him.

> I was about like at East 15th, and five-o [police] blurbed me. And . . . I was by myself before they grabbed me by my neck. And, like, they tried to make me spit out the, um, rocks. And, like, I didn't want to spit them out.

They, like—he was holding my neck for like . . . for like twenty seconds or less. And after that, I spit them out myself. 'Cause, I thought he was gonna choke me, hard, harder.

The police arrested Jose and placed him in a gang database, CalGang, a statewide documentation system that officers use to maintain information on people they deem gang members.[25] I later verified that Jose was in the database when he and I were stopped and they conducted a search on our records. One of the officers said to another, "Yeah, he's in the database." He turned to Jose and, referring to his nickname, "Topo," said, "Tapo, Tipo, Taco? What is your nickname?" Jose ignored him, knowing that he was being mocked. The officer turned to me and told me, "Jose is a crazy little dude. He's been a player ever since he was little, . . . no trouble, but we got him in the gang database just in case."[26] Being placed on the gang database can add five, ten, fifteen, and even twenty-five years to a felony sentence, since under the 1988 Street Terrorism Enforcement and Prevention Act, a prosecutor can charge a youth for committing a crime to further a gang's criminal activity. Six of the boys in this study were eventually charged with gang enhancements.

Soon after I met Jose and interviewed him about his life story, he was arrested again. This time the police spotted him in the middle of a street fight and found a knife on him. Jose explained that while he was fighting, his opponent pulled out a knife, and he knocked the knife out of the other kid's hand and grabbed it, with no intention of using it. He claimed that he had the knife on him for a long time before the police arrived, just trying to keep it off the street. Jose spent three weeks in juvenile hall following this arrest.

A few months later, Jose was arrested again for stealing a bicycle. The officer arrested him even though Jose did not have the bicycle in his possession. According to Jose, he knew the group of Black youths who had stolen the bicycle, but he did not want to "snitch" on them. When the judge told Jose that he was not going to lock him up but that he would have to follow a strict program with his probation officer, Jose thought that he might get help and turn his life around. His main concern was to stay away from the people he associated with on the street, because he wanted to escape the pressures to prove himself through violence and criminality:

I just wanted to start doing better, so I told my probation officer to help me. He said that I had to stay away from all those crazy kids I hung around with. He also told me that if I got caught with them, I would go back to jail. He told me to tell them that I would go to jail if I talked to them, but they didn't believe me. . . . I think that for Mr. Bryan [his probation officer] it is easy to tell me to change, but I hella try and he doesn't see what happens when I try.

At first glance, one might believe that Jose was a violent, drug-pushing thief. However, when we take a closer look at Jose's understanding of his environment, we uncover the process by which Jose was criminalized; his interactions with authority figures set part of the stage on which he performed illicit activity, and this illicit activity generated further punitive treatment. Jose's criminal trajectory may have been instrumentally determined by his negative interactions with agents of social control.

Tyrell Gets Marked

Eventually, Jose and Tyrell became marked as criminals. When Tyrell was fourteen, he was caught with an ounce of marijuana and spent three weeks in juvenile hall. When he returned home after release, his father attempted to beat him. Tyrell fought back, wrestling his father to the ground. After the fight, his father disregarded him, saying that if Tyrell thought he was a man, he should take care of himself. He refused to speak to Tyrell for weeks at a time, and, as a consequence, their relationship more or less shifted to that of roommates: "I do my own thing, and he does his own thing. He can't say shit to me anymore, and I don't trip off of him."

The combination of stigma at school, harassment from police on the street, and Tyrell's resentment of his defunct relationship with his father may have led him to develop the attitude to "not give a fuck." In Tyrell's frame of reference, the implications of breaking the law were imposed on him daily. In such situations, getting incarcerated might begin to feel like a viable option. The irony of Tyrell's mentality was that the stress of being criminalized in the neighborhood led him to believe that juvenile hall might serve as an escape. In some sense, he was willing to trade one punitive community for another: "In juvy," Tyrell explained, "at least if I follow the rules, I'll be left alone."[27] When incarcerated, Tyrell could predict when he would be treated punitively: if he broke the rules. On the street, however, even if he followed the rules, he felt he would still be punished. For Tyrell and many of the boys, detention facilities became preferred social contexts because they provided structure, discipline, and predictability—rare attributes in the punitive context of the streets. Although the boys did not want to be incarcerated, detention facilities were the only spaces where they felt that they could predict cause and effect. Tyrell described it this way: "If I do my program, then I know I will be straight [good]. . . . If I don't follow directions, then I'll be stuck." We can make sense of why many young people who decide to violate their probation or parole do so, to seek shelter from a punitive social order, a youth control complex, that to many is worse than being incarcerated.

Hypercriminalization creates conditions in which young people actually seek more predictable, albeit more restrictive, forms of punishment. Many of the boys talked about liking the structure of incarceration because it dictated a clear set of rules. In the community, police, probation officers, schools, businesses, and families were perceived as unpredictable; the youths reported frustration with not knowing when their teachers, parents, or police would criminalize them.

Compelled to become a man on his own, to act and maneuver as an adult, and to take responsibility for himself, Tyrell faced the wrath of peer violence and police oppression. By the time he was fifteen, Tyrell became a bona-fide target for police. The police could pick him out easily because of his height, and they harassed him every time they saw him: "Man, they wouldn't stop messing with me. One day I pushed a cop, and he fell. They grabbed me and whooped my ass. They beat me so bad that they let me go. They felt bad for me. I have a scar here and here [he points to two small scars on his scalp and forehead]." Instead of dealing drugs in fear of being arrested again, Tyrell chose a different specialization. He went to the drug dealers in the neighborhood and offered to collect from people who owed them money. The drug dealers began paying him to recover debts. With this work Tyrell became extremely violent, as he recovered amounts owed that ranged from ten to five hundred dollars:

I had to send the message that I was not fucking around, so I ran into a crack head that owed my nigga [friend] some money. I grabbed his ass and whooped him so hard he's been limping ever since. . . . That was all I had to do. Most of the time people paid me what they owed. One day, though, I had to whoop some fool's ass. I hit him on the leg with a golf club, so they charged me with aggravated assault and assault with a deadly weapon, but they dropped the deadly weapon charge. I still did three months in juvy.

At sixteen, Tyrell was placed on two years' probation. He was also placed on electronic monitoring (EM) as a condition of his release. EM is a program that probation officers use to keep track of juvenile offenders. A black, square-shaped device, about the size of a large cellular phone, is strapped around the youth's ankle. Whenever Tyrell went over a few hundred feet from his house, the device would send a message to his probation officer. The probation officer then could arrest him for violating probation. In the beginning, Tyrell was arrested and held for two days for going outside his area limit. Afterward, however, he got the hang of the monitoring device and completed his six-month program:

I did it, but it was hecka hard. I couldn't leave home, and then that shit started itching me all the time. [He shows me his leg, scarred from the scratching.] My boys thought that shit was tight [appealing], but I told them it wasn't cool at all. They would come visit me and kick it at my house, since I couldn't go anywhere. We set up shop [a hangout space] there and just chilled there until they let me off.

Tyrell and his friends were confined to a small apartment because of his requirement to remain at home. The consequence of the electronic monitoring device was that it created a new "kick-it spot" for the boys in Tyrell's apartment building. This new hangout concentrated a large group of delinquent boys in a private space where they became invisible. The possibility of their receiving support or services from adults in the public sphere who wanted to help them was now diminished. Yet Tyrell and his friends believed this to be a safe haven from the criminalizing interactions they endured in the public sphere: suspicion in stores, automatic searches by police and probation officers, denial of employment for having a criminal record, and stigma imposed by school authorities and other adults.

Jose Internalizes Violence

One day I caught up with Jose at his apartment. When I arrived, his mother told me that he had taken off to the Indoor Flea Market, a popular warehouse with twenty or so booths, where residents found cheap clothing, expensive tennis shoes, and jewelry. I drove down International to go look for Jose. Halfway to the "Indoor," I noticed Jose standing at the corner of International Boulevard and High Street, one of the busiest intersections in Oakland. I parked my car and walked over to Jose. Smacking meat out of his teeth, Jose told me he stopped there to get a taco from his favorite truck, El Taco Zamorano. We sat on a cement divider in front of All Mufflers, a mechanic shop situated on the corner. The hot yellow color of the square concrete building served as a canvas for Black and Latino bodies, painting a picture of local residents as they stood waiting for the bus to make their way through town. An old, white pickup truck, with an open hood and a Latino mechanic hunched over the engine trying to fix it, sat adjacent to us.

I started asking Jose about his week. He seemed distracted. He looked around and ignored my questions. And then it dawned on me: we were in the heart of rival gang territory. As I started asking him another question, he interrupted me and said, "Hold up, hold up, man!" I turned in the direction he was looking and noticed another young man walking toward us. Jose ran up to him and, without warning, punched him in the face and knocked him down. When he hit the ground, Jose started kicking him in the stomach. I yelled at Jose, "Get off!" but he did not listen. The young man on the ground looked at me with despair, his head leaning on the concrete. I wrapped my arms around Jose and pulled him back. He forcefully shook me off and went back to kick his rival. I rolled my wrists into the kid's XXL-size white T-shirt and yanked him up from the ground and away from Jose, who followed us, shouting, "You little bitch! . . . Punk-ass coward!" I told Jose to go home, and I drove the beaten kid home. The boy refused to answer any more questions after telling me, "I'm okay."

I found Jose a few days later and asked him about the assault. He told me that the other kid, Puppet, a member of a rival gang, 37th Street, lived in Jose's neighborhood. Jose and the rest of his gang were upset about this and were determined to drive Puppet out of their neighborhood. Every time Jose or his friends saw Puppet, they immediately attacked him. Jose was also upset because Puppet had, in his view, caused him to go to jail.

> Like, we were on International [Boulevard], and we seen Puppet. I chased him on a bike and pulled him off the bike. And, uh, he started running; he got away. I guess the Black dudes that kick it at the corner, they took his bike. And I got, like, at the park, 'cause I ran to the park because I seen a lotta po-police! So I ran to the park, and they got me at the park for robbery, me and another homey.

Jose served two weeks in juvenile hall and afterward was sent to a group home (a reform program managed from a private residence) for six months. Some of the youth at the group home did not like him, and Jose made more enemies during his stay there. Jose described getting into a fight with two youths from San Francisco because they picked on him.

> So I'm not no punk. I just told them I went to the garage, and they told me it was gonna be a one-on-one [fight]. And I was winning, so they jumped me. . . . The people from the group home, they called the police. They was like, "You gonna . . . you gonna do a couple months in the hall." This is just a punishment. I didn't want to do that. So I just grabbed my stuff, and I left. And it's a regular house; you can just leave from the front door. So I just grabbed my stuff, and I ran out. And I got caught a month later.

Jose served two months in juvenile hall and then was sent to another group home. He ran away once more. I checked on Jose a few weeks later. His mother told me he'd been arrested and was facing six months in the California Youth Authority (the state prison for minors) for carrying an unloaded gun.

Jose's mother, Rosario, was in despair. She was an undocumented, single mother of two, Jose and his thirteen-year-old sister, Rosa. Rosario worked as a maid in Walnut Creek, an affluent suburb on the other side of the hill from Oakland. She was paid sixty dollars a day, working ten- to twelve-hour shifts. Her employer officially paid her as a part-time worker but pressured her to work more hours for no pay. She left home at six in the morning, and after taking a BART train and two buses—a three-hour commute in all—she arrived at work at nine. By the time she returned home, it was eight o'clock at night. Rosario had received welfare to help her with the rent. However, after being pressured to obtain a job by her social worker at the welfare office, she took the house-cleaning job. The family continued to struggle financially, despite Rosario's employment. Rosario told me that she made less money when working than when she was receiving welfare. She was stressed because she could no longer be there to watch over her children. During my observations at the apartment complex, I often found Rosa sitting on the steps talking to a nineteen-year-old gang member.[28] Rosario's absence exposed Rosa and Jose, even more, to the vulnerabilities and vices of the streets. Punished and abandoned by the welfare state for being poor, Rosa was forced to work and abandon her own children, leaving them vulnerable to the violence of the streets and criminalization of the state (and civil society).

I went to Jose's court date with Rosario. The judge made it clear to Jose that if the gun had been loaded, he would have sent him to be tried as an adult, where he would face a minimum of five years in prison. The judge said to Jose, "You are living on the brink of self-destruction. This is probably your last chance in life. If you don't follow your program at camp, and I see you in here again, I will make sure you never get out again. You understand?" Jose nodded and looked down. He looked ashamed and scared. After the judge's statement, Jose turned and looked at his mother and me with a slight smile, celebrating the fact that his fear of being sent to adult court did not materialize.

Jose's Life at Age Seventeen

By age seventeen, Jose had served time at Camp Sweeney, an Alameda County juvenile justice facility which detained young offenders during the week and attempted to provide them with a structured, camp-style program that included academic courses, counseling, and health-awareness workshops. Despite Camp Sweeney's ideal of rehabilitating nonviolent criminals, Jose understood it this way: as a place where they "put all the crazy fools together and makes us fight or plot some shit that will get us in hella even more trouble."

Jose was allowed to leave the camp on weekends and return to his family, as long as he did not leave home. When I visited him over the weekend, Jose told me he felt ashamed of himself. He said that he wanted to change but did not know how. "Being locked up, even at camp," he explained, "was making me have to do crazy shit to put my name out [to gain a reputation] even more." Jose felt that he had to prove himself to his peers at camp or become a victim. If he did not act tough and get into fights, he might be seen as a punk and face attacks from the rest of his camp mates. Three of the boys in this study had been to this same camp. They all reported that the guards at camp did not protect them from victimization, that the guards even encouraged a culture of street justice in which young men who were victimized had to learn, as Jose described one of the guards saying, to "be a grown man and defend yourself."

Once released, Jose inhabited the same streets; this time, however, he claimed to have an understanding of his environment. He now articulated a deep desire to change his life around, whereas in the past, he saw his environment only as a place in which to prove his manhood. But the streets were not forgiving, and Jose had to pretend that he was still street oriented and that he was willing to continue to put in work: "If I go out there and pretend to be someone else, they [friends and peers] won't look at me the same way. They will see weakness in me and try to take advantage. That's why its hella hard to change." I followed Jose as he attempted to find support for his endeavor to change, and I witnessed as school and community centers were unable to provide him the support he believed he needed: help looking for a job, a mentoring program, and somewhere to hang out where he did not have to feel forced to prove himself.

Jose's probation officer served as the only possible source of support for change. Mr. Bryan talked to Jose repeatedly about finding a nonviolent way to manage conflict and told him that only "silly little punks" folded to the pressure of peers. According to Jose, Mr. Bryan expected positive behavior from him regardless of the situation he was in. "What if I get messed with, and other kids try to beat me up?" Jose asked. "You just tell them that your PO is gonna kick your and their ass," Mr. Bryan responded. Jose realized that this kind of response was unrealistic and that it did not help him. Not having a realistic and viable alternative to resolving conflict on the street, Jose defaulted to the only skills he believed were proven to work in the past in managing conflict: posturing as if he was ready to commit violence and "flash" in response to any threats posed by peers. Although Jose reasoned that he no longer wanted to participate in this ritual, the streets reminded him that following the "code of the street," despite its many drawbacks, was the only problem-solving and survival strategy available to him. For many of the boys in this study, using the "code of the street" was like flipping a coin. Sometimes their gamble paid off, and the code would protect them and make them feel protected. Other times, the wrong side of the coin appeared, and their confrontational demeanor would render them victims.

Many of the young people in this study said that they expected probation and police officers to help them find alternative ways of coping with violence but that these adults did not realize their advice had little practical application on the street, as Mr. Bryan's perspective on Jose suggested: "Jose is a good kid, but he folds to peer pressure really easy. As soon as one of his friends tells him to do something, he does it. He just has to be strong and tell his little friends that he is not messing with negativity anymore. He needs to be responsible for himself and show his friends that he can be a man and not fold to peer pressure." When I asked Jose about peer pressure, he told me that it had an influence but that he was his "own man." He articulated a desire to change yet acknowledged that his friends would be an obstacle. I asked him, "What would you do if you had all the resources you needed to change?" He replied,

> If I could, I would finish my diploma and go to community college and get some kind of certificate to work on cars. I want to own my own shop one day. I am already good with cars, and I think I would be a good mechanic. But I don't know, I still got a long ways to go. . . . Maybe a lawyer, maybe helping the community, those in my position now or those who will be in my position. People who get in trouble, I like to help them. I wouldn't be doing half of the shit I'm doing now, if I had a better environment. . . . I think I need a program that comes to me, you know, like, you—like, people that call you and come over and check up on you. Sometimes I don't have money to take the bus to go to a program, or the programs they have are whack [inadequate or boring]. You know, like, "Don't do drugs—this is your brain on drugs—just say no" type of shit.

The disjuncture between Jose's expectations of a supportive, nurturing, resource-savvy probation officer and his negative interactions with his probation officer's unrealistic expectations of him resulted in a belief that resources to change were not available, despite his aspiration to do so.

To make matters worse, Jose's commentary on wanting to change and his actions sometimes did not correspond with one another. For example, one afternoon Jose told me that he would no longer hang out with his homies; later that night, he called a few of his friends to visit him at his house, despite being prohibited to hang out with them, according to the terms of his probation. Sociologist Elliot Liebow calls the difference between what people say and what they do a "half-truth."[29] Jose's half-truth was this articulation of wanting to change but acting in ways that would limit his ability to do so. I don't believe that Jose was attempting to "play the system" when he began to articulate that he was ready to change. Instead, Jose had developed an illusion of change in which he thought that wanting to change would translate into real change. Jose's belief in change did not necessarily mean that he would receive the necessary resources—help with job applications, help reenrolling in school, mentoring, counseling, and so on—to change his life around.

Sociologist Alice Goffman argues that young, Black, male felons "maintain self respect in the face of failure" by telling "half-truths," by using their wanted status as an excuse not to provide for their families or show responsibility: "Being wanted serves as an excuse for a variety of unfulfilled obligations and expectations."[30] I did not find this to be true with the boys in my study, even when they were "on the run." The boys in my study did not blame the system to maintain self-respect or to create excuses for their unfulfilled obligations and expectations. These boys were more than willing to confess that they had "fucked up," that they were responsible for their social conditions. While the boys believed that the police beatings, excessive sentences, harassment, and heavy surveillance were unjust, they also acknowledged that they had made some wrong choices and that they were accountable for not completing school, not providing for their children (six of the boys were fathers), or not having a job. In an era of "personal responsibility" when schools, police, and community members could not guarantee the boys success, nurturing, or security, the one thing that these agencies of social control could do was to inculcate in the boys a sense of self-blame. The boys were taught that poverty, victimization, criminalization, and neglect were products of their own actions. The boys internalized these messages, and in turn they all reported feeling personally responsible for their plight.

Code of the Street, Code of the State

Schools, police, and probation officers helped to perpetuate the code of the street. They did so either by assuming that all the boys were actively engaged in criminal and violent activity or by providing the boys little choice but to engage in the code. In refusing to protect residents, and in encouraging young men to take care of themselves, authority figures, including police and probation officers, explicitly encouraged young men to engage in the code. In Oakland, police officers encouraged young men to apply the code of the street in two main ways. First, officers purposely refused to provide protection. Second, the police diverted resources to policing youths who were easy targets in the public sphere and often ignored predatory criminal activity that happened right below the surface, in areas that they had chosen not to police, such as apartment complexes, parks, and "death alleys" that they might have perceived as dangerous. Police operated under a demographic rather than a criminological model of threat. In doing so, they missed countless opportunities to protect innocent people from being victimized.

Many events in this study demonstrated that police were involved in magnifying the code of the street. Another example is Slick, who, like Jose, reported that police encouraged residents to take justice into their own hands. Slick was brutally attacked by a group of gang members during the time when he became a "wannabe." When the police showed up to conduct an investigation, Slick and his friends told the officer the name of the gang members who attacked them: "The pigs told us where we could find them. They told us they had just seen them hanging out at the corner of 9th and e-one-four (East 14th). They said to us, 'You gotta do what you gotta do.' So we did."

The code of the street allowed the police to justify harassment and arrest, schools to punish and suspend students for defiance, and community members to fear young people. In responding to the code of the street, authority figures in Oakland created a labeling hype and culture of punishment that criminalized young people's everyday style and pursuit of happiness, even when these did not involve breaking the law. I found that it was not only important to understand how the boys used the code of the street but also to understand how the community responded to young people who were associated with the code of the street. Seeing how others responded to the code of the street allowed me to understand how institutions such as the criminal justice system and schools were also responsible for creating a social order, a code of conduct that inculcated criminality and victimization among marginalized youths.[31] By operating in the belief that the code of the street was rampant among marginalized youths, despite the fact that a minority of these youths lived by this code, institutions created a social order that managed every young person it encountered as a threat who followed a code that victimized others. Alford Young argues that social scientists have focused too much of their attention on marginalized black men's behaviors on the streets.[32] This has enabled schools, law enforcement, and policy makers to treat marginalized young black men as if the streets determine all of their codes of conduct and worldviews. The boys in this study believed that some agents of social control, the family, school administrators, and police, interacted with them as if at any given moment they would engage in crime or violence. As the boys came of age, they experienced being treated as criminal risks in need of constant, ubiquitous surveillance and control across social contexts.

4

The Coupling of Criminal Justice
and Community Institutions

No public safety officer shall be prohibited from seeking election to, or serving as a member of, the governing board of a school district.
—California Government Code, "Police Officers Bill of
Rights," 1977

In its function, the power to punish is not essentially different from that of curing or educating.
—Michel Foucault, *Discipline and Punish*, 1977

I drove to Spider's house late one afternoon after a long day of discussing inequality with urban sociologists at the University of California, Berkeley. Some claimed to have found answers to the problematic questions they asked: "Why do African Americans commit disproportionate crime?" "Why does the inner city produce a culture of violence?" and "Why do immigrants become involved in gangs?" As these, primarily White, male, and middle-class, graduate students and faculty continued to dissect the ghetto from the comfort of the university, it dawned on me that I had to hit the streets and catch up with Spider, who had recently been stabbed. While I would be asking Spider about violence and gangs, an equally pressing topic, in his mind, was that of criminalization and police misconduct. I knew I had a short window before Spider decided to leave his house. I grabbed my backpack, ran to my car, and drove to his house. As I left Berkeley, majestic oak and redwood trees faded from my rearview mirror, replaced by old cars, dilapidated Victorians, and track houses that had been turned into multiple apartments by slumlords.

So far, from youth accounts and my observations, I had discovered that school personnel, police officers, and other adults in the community had created an environment that made these young people feel criminalized from a young age. Although I had encountered a few racist cops and even a few racist teachers, I knew that most people in the community were well intentioned and had a genuine interest in the well-being of boys. How was it possible that all the young men whom I followed believed wholeheartedly that most adults in the community worked to ubiquitously punish them? In the minds of these young men, the community had conspired to impose detrimental sanctions on them. My observations led me to uncover a complex process by which even well-intentioned adults participated in the criminalization of the boys. Some people in the community did believe that the boys were irreparable criminals and needed to be locked away. But others, those who cared dearly for these boys, did not conspire to criminalize them. Instead, these caring adults were caught up in a system of imposing punitive social control, which influenced their actions despite their having a genuine interest in the well-being of the boys.

Criminologist David Garland reminds us that "punishment does not just restrain or discipline 'society'—punishment helps create it." He contends that punishment is one of the many institutions which helps construct and support the social world by producing the shared categories and authoritative classifications through which individuals understand each other and themselves.[1] I use Garland's analysis of punishment as an institution to understand the role that criminalization, as a form of punishment, plays in the lives of the boys in this study. Garland argues, "Like all social institutions, punishment interacts with its environment, forming part of the mutually constructing configuration of elements which make up the social world."[2] If Garland is correct, the workings of punitive social control set the stage for the development of specific meaning-making and cultural practices among youths who encounter criminalization. Their subjectivities are partially constructed by punishment. But young people also have agency and develop systems of interaction and resistance to cope with these patterns of punishment and to create an alternative world, an escape from their punitive reality.

Labor historian Robin Kelley argues that young people become involved in "play"—the seeking of personal enjoyment despite their detrimental circumstances. Social scientists, according to Kelley, have confused this "play" for a form of social disorder: "The growing numbers of young brown bodies engaged in 'play' rather than work (from street-corner bantering, to 'mailing' [hanging out at shopping malls], to basketball) have contributed to popular constructions of the 'underclass' as a threat and shaped urban police practices. The invention of terms such as *wilding*, as Houston Baker points out, reveal a discourse of black male youth out of control, rampaging teenagers free of the disciplinary structures of school, work, and prison."[3] In 2010, groups of Black youths in Philadelphia were placed in the national media spotlight when the city called in the FBI, made student transportation passes invalid after 4 p.m., and implemented a policy to cite parents when their children broke curfew laws. This crackdown occurred in response to "flash mobs," large numbers of people who gather after being organized through text messaging.[4] Although the majority of these gatherings did not involve delinquency, a few events, where violence and vandalism took place, led to the criminalization of young Black people gathering in groups in downtown Philadelphia. These flash mobs can be analyzed as creative responses to social isolation and a lack of recreation spaces. According to Kelley and consistent with my findings, marginalized young people's "play" has become criminalized.

Criminalizing the Victim

I pulled up to Spider's house, a two-story Victorian. The house looked as if it had not been maintained since it was first built in the early 1900s. Bare, splintered wood protruded through the flaking khaki paint. The gutterless roof had allowed rainwater to seep through the wooden paneling on the house, creating warps and cracks on the surface as if an earthquake had shaken the house from its foundation and dragged it from its original location. His mother rented a one-bedroom apartment conversion in the rear of the house. The side of the house had a driveway that had been fenced off. This is where Spider kept two dogs he owned, a red-nose pit bull and a small mutt. Both dogs looked malnourished, with their ribs visibly showing and their stomachs tucked deep into their hind legs. I knocked on Slick's metal gate door. After a few knocks, Slick answered the door. "Wassup, Vic?" "Wassup, Slick?" I replied. I had not seen him in two weeks, and the last time I saw him he was in a hospital bed.

Spider was fifteen years young when he was brutally attacked by gang members on a night when he sat on his front door steps talking with friends.

> I was kicking it in front of my house with some homies and stuff, and then a few of them were wearing red. And they thought we were claiming [members of a gang]. And they rolled by and passed once and came a second time. And we was fighting. And I was running by myself, and my brother went that way [pointing to the right]. Then I came down this way [pointing to the left], and they caught me. And they just shanked [stabbed] me. They shanked me four in the stomach, one in the chest, and eight in the leg. They were like twenty-five years old. . . . You don't feel nothing, but then, after, I just blacked out and woke up at the hospital. My mom came, and I told her I was OK and blacked out.

Spider nearly died. He was hospitalized for three weeks. The detectives who investigated his case paid him a visit a few hours after the incident:

> When I woke up, that's when they came, the detectives I mean. Molina [the detective investigating his case] and shit came to the hospital. And they tried to see if it was Sureños that stabbed me and tried to label me as a Norteño [rival gang to Sureños]. No! But I am not Norteño, I don't gang bang, but when I was there, they tried to make me say that I was Norteño and stuff. I couldn't remember who stabbed me. I just know it was Sureños 'cause they kept yelling MS [Mara Salvatrucha, the name of another gang]. Yeah, and, you know, you gotta make a police report and shit. But they arrested a juvenile, and then they tried to make me testify, but I didn't want to go to court. I already know they didn't got the dudes that got me 'cause those dudes were grown men and stuff. And I wanted to be left alone. And then that's why we dropped the charges, and all that. And then the DA wanted me to go to court.

After this near-death experience, Spider was registered by the Oakland police as an active gang member. Prior to this event, he had never been arrested or registered by police as a gang member. During his stay at the hospital, one of the gang detectives asked his mother for his personal information and asked her how long he had been in the gang. His mother insisted that he was not in the gang. The officer told her, "That's the reason your son got stabbed. You're ignoring his gang involvement."

During my time in the field, I verified that Spider was not in the gang. It was not difficult to find out who was actively gang involved. There were many indicators: whom the young person hung out with, who self-identified as a gang member, and how the young person interacted with known gang members. Community workers were also good sources. Most gang members were honest, because if their homies found out that they had negated the gang, the consequences could be devastating. I had found no signs that indicated that Spider was involved in the gang. However, the gang detective came to a different conclusion and placed him in the gang database.

The rampant use of the gang database was an additional factor which accentuated the criminalization process. Police officers constantly placed young men in this database, allowing any other officer who came into contact with the boys to have detailed information about what "turf" they belonged to or where they were last stopped or when they were last questioned. It appeared that the police classified young people as gang members in order to benefit from the ability to keep track of them and impose harsher restrictions and policing on them. This categorization later affected Spider during a criminal case, in which he was charged with assault with a deadly weapon, for the benefit of the gang, after he got into a fight with a guy who was making fun of him for getting stabbed. The gang enhancement carried an added five-year sentence.

When the police classified Spider as a gang member, school staff, community workers, and other adults in the community also adopted this categorization. The punishment that Spider encountered, after being viciously attacked, was not an isolated case of individual rogue gang detectives: there was a recurring pattern of criminalizing the victim in the lives of these young men. Meanwhile, police officers, school personnel, probation officers, and even community workers supported the labeling of Spider as a culprit, despite his being the victim who had been stabbed.

Spider's School

Two months before Spider was stabbed, I visited the East Oakland Continuation School (EOCS),[5] which Spider and six other boys in this study attended. The EOCS was a school for those students who had already been officially labeled as deviant and delinquent by the Oakland Unified School District and who were no longer allowed to attend the "regular" high school. The school welcomed me in as a community member who could mentor some of the youth at the school. The first person at the entrance of the school was a security guard named Shirley, a short, chubby Black woman who looked about thirty-five years old. She spoke with a deep voice and always seemed to stand on her toes. Her modus operandi was to "mean mug" (stare down) every student who walked in through the gate, as if to remind them whom they would have to face if they were defiant that day. Once the students were inside the school, another security guard checked them with a handheld metal detector to make sure they did not bring a weapon to school. As Spider dragged his left leg across the school yard to keep his baggy pants from falling, the middle-aged, six-foot-tall, White, male school principal walked by us. "Mr. Juarez!" he called in a deep voice. "You're not going to give us any trouble today. Right?" "I'm cool, Mr. Ellis," replied Spider. The school was small, made up of three dilapidated World War II–era bungalows placed perpendicular to one another to form a courtyard. The courtyard was all cement, with a few benches and two basketball hoops. On rainy days, Spider and the other students wore their hoods in class, in case the roof started leaking on their heads.

Spider and I walked into class. Although class had already started, the teacher was missing. Students sat in groups of four, facing each other. The class was composed of seven Latinos and eight Blacks. One of the students played a rap song on his cell phone's speaker: "I'm raw, I'm raw, I'm raw . . ." the song continued, then the sound was interrupted by a young Black lady who talked on her cell phone: "Yeah, bitch. You crazy bitch . . . Yeah, bitch . . ." One of the Latino males, Julio, looked at his Black classmate, Jason, and said, "You got some coke?" "Coke? Nigga! Is you crazy? You do it all?" replied Jason. Julio looked at him with a serious look and said, "Everything: pills, crystal, smoke, drank. Tienes de la negrita? [You got some little black stuff?] You know, heroin?" I found that the boys I observed often pre-

[79]

tended to use more drugs than they were really using. Julio was always at school, and rarely on the streets, during the times I conducted my observations. He was headed for graduation and never displayed any signs of major drug use such as being on the streets, not attending school, or being distracted in the classroom. I believe Julio was pretending to use various drugs in order to appear "crazy" around the other boys and possibly to gain their respect. The school later suspended Julio and reported him to the local police officer for asking other students if they had drugs to offer.

The teacher finally walked into the classroom. He was a substitute. The school had trouble finding permanent teachers. One possible reason was the school's notoriety: recently a student had placed a chokehold on the principal. As the substitute, a fifty-year-old, light-skinned Black male, walked in, a seventeen-year-old Black male, Deandre, said to him, "Hey, bra [bro], what's up with it, bra." The substitute ignored him and turned to the girl who was using her cell phone: "Hang that up." She told her friend, "I'll call you back, bitch. My teacher wants me." The teacher told the students to open their Earth Science books to page 223. "Today's lesson is about rocks," he told the students. Deandre grunted, "I don't care 'bout no rock." The substitute responded, "You will when it starts shaking!" Deandre replied, "That's when niggas start running!" The teacher dropped the book and scolded the students, "You know where you are headed? . . . Narcissism is gonna lead you to prison." The students all looked down. At this point, I turned to Spider. He gave me a look, raising his right eyebrow, as if to tell me, "I told you so." I looked down. The teacher finally convinced another student to read to the class.

A few minutes later the bell rang. I asked the substitute about his narcissism remark. He replied, "You know, these students have some internalized nihilism [sic]. They are just here out of the rain from the streets. They come here wanting you to bring them up-to-date. What causes unconformity? That is what we have a lot of here." Spider walked into the classroom to check on me and overheard the last part of the teacher's remarks. "You saying I'm slow?" he asked. "No, I'm saying that if you keep acting slow and continue gang banging, you going to prison," the teacher replied. Spider insisted, "I ain't no gang member. You trippin', cuz." The school had a high turnover rate with teachers and substitutes. When new teachers arrived, they attempted to use their unique pedagogical approaches to connect with students; some of them were really nice, others really mean, and many in-between. But all the teachers had one practice in common: whenever any student misbehaved, the teachers would threaten either to call the police, to send them to jail, or to call a probation officer (sometimes, even for those students who were not on probation). In the school's attempt to maintain order, it used the full force of criminal justice institutions to regulate students' behavior. Although this school was for students already labeled delinquents, these boys reported receiving the same treatment at the "regular" schools they attended as well.

Later on in the day, Spider and I walked outside the school gate. As we walked past the security guard, I heard a walkie-talkie buzz, and the guard said, "Officer Miles, we have a few of them walking your way." We walked a few blocks to International Boulevard, and an all-black patrol car, with no police markings—what the kids referred to as a "Narc"—turned the corner. The officer stared us down. He drove down the street, made a U-turn, and drove slowly right behind us. "Shit! That's the mothafucker that beat down Marquill the other day in front of McDonald's, remember?" I remembered: two weeks before, a Black male student walked into the school at the end of the lunch period, his extra-long white T-shirt soiled with black tar and his lip busted open, with red flesh showing. One of his friends asked him, "What happened?" "The Narcs, they beat my ass." He replied in monotone, with little emotion as he walked, head bowed, to the boys' bathroom. Slick had witnessed the beating. According to Slick, Marquill had talked back to the police officer. The officer got out of the car, grabbed Marquill by his T-shirt, and slammed him onto the grunge-covered cement parking lot of the McDonald's. The White officer stood over Marquill for a few minutes. Then Marquill was released and returned to school.

I had never seen Slick display so much fear, even when he recounted his stabbing story. I turned to Slick and told him, "Let's just keep walking. We'll be fine." The officer continued to follow us, driving slowly behind us. Slick became paranoid, turned around, and gave the officer a dirty look. I turned to look. The officer, a White man with a shaved head in his late thirties, looked at us, grinned, and drove off. Police officers played a crafty cat-and-mouse game in which the boys remained in constant fear of being humiliated, brutalized, or arrested.

This officer often stationed himself at the McDonald's parking lot. Most of his work appeared to revolve around looking for traffic violations or waiting for the school to call when a student misbehaved. The school had impeccable communication between the security officer, the administrators, and this police officer. I witnessed eight events when police were called by the security officer for students talking back, cursing, or other minor school-rule transgressions. At EOCS, stigma, labeling, detention, harassment, and humiliation were just about the only consistent experiences that young people could count on as they entered the school. If students attempted to resist this criminalization by acting up, a violent police officer lurked.

For the boys, the school represented just another space where they were criminalized for their style and culture. The school, in the eyes of the boys, was indistinguishable from the police officer stationed at McDonald's, the adults in the community who called the police on them, or the community-center staff who ousted them. Jose, who also attended the school, put it into perspective: "Man, it's like every day, teachers gotta sweat me, police gotta pocket-check me, mom's gotta trip on me, and my PO's gotta stress me. . . . It's like having a zookeeper watching us at all times. We walk home, and we see them [probation officers and police]; we shoot some hoops, and we see them; we take a shit at school, and we see them."[6]

After school, Jose would take a two-hour bus ride to Berkeley to visit his cousins and attend a court-mandated community-center program facilitated by his probation officer. Since Jose lived in Berkeley at the time of his last court hearing, he was assigned a probation officer stationed at a Berkeley community center. Jose was required to check in with him once a week.

Parents

The young people I interviewed also perceived themselves to be criminalized by parents. School personnel, police, and probation officers provided the boys' parents with "courtesy stigmas." A "courtesy stigma" is a stigma that develops as a result of being related to a person with a stigma.[7] The conversations that school personnel, police, and probation officers had with one another about troubled youths almost always followed the same trajectory: "These parents need to learn how to discipline these kids"; "It's their parents' fault for letting them do whatever they want"; "It's no surprise that they're this way—look at their parents." These are just a few examples of countless depictions of parents as deviants, like their children. Authority figures often attempted to intervene and teach parents the "right way" to parent. For instance, a probation officer periodically visited Jose's mother in Oakland and attempted to influence how she parented. Jose's mother, Rosario, explained, "The [probation officer], he frightens me. He comes over and tells me, 'Why don't you learn to be a mother? Take away all this gangster stuff from Jose. You are at fault for what he does.'" This process sometimes changed the relationship that youths had with their parents. Some parents came to have similar perspectives as police and probation officers. Fourteen of the boys reported not having trusting relationships with their parents and believed that their parents would turn them in to authorities for arguing with them. Parents felt compelled to obey the discourse provided by the youth control complex: "Your child is a deviant, your child needs to be scrutinized and policed, and when your child acts negatively in any kind of way, such as dressing like a 'thug,' you need to call probation and police."

For Jose and most of the other boys, their perceptions of being watched, managed, and treated as criminals began at a young age and became exacerbated after their first offense, in most cases, a misdemeanor. Their minor transgressions branded them with a mark that would make their one-time criminal act into a permanent criminal identity. Part of the process of making Jose feel that he was constructed as a criminal was his mother's participation in his criminalization. He believed that she was forced to listen to school and criminal justice authorities' agendas on how to parent, especially after his first arrest. According to Jose and his mother, he was first arrested for carrying a ten-dollar bag of marijuana. They found that everyone in the community treated Jose differently after his first arrest. Jose began to feel watched, police began to randomly stop and search him, and his teachers would threaten him with calling his probation officer if he disobeyed at school. And, despite his mother's empathizing with the negative treatment he was now receiving, she constantly reminded him that he would end up in jail if he misbehaved, and she used these threats as a means to discipline him.[8]

Probation

According to the boys I interviewed, probation officers served the purpose of punishing them by branding them criminals in front of the rest of the community and by marking their territory in the settings through which the boys navigated. Community centers made office space available for probation officers.[9] Parents were constantly interacting with probation officers and were often being chastised and influenced by them. Teachers had direct contact with probation officers, in order to inform them when boys misbehaved. Schools also provided office space for police and probation officers to check in with trouble students.

The probation experience varied for the boys. Some of the boys had probation officers that required them to check in once a week. Others knocked on doors at 7:45 in the morning once a week to make sure the youngster was getting ready and planning to go to school. Most, however, had high and unrealistic expectations of the boys but did not play a role in aiding them in meeting these expectations. For example, Deandre's probation officer, Ms. Moore, wrote a contract for him, full of unreachable goals, which he showed me soon after meeting with her: "Find a job. Pass all your classes. Do not get caught hanging out with your old friends." Weeks went by, and Ms. Moore did not check in with Deandre. Although he attempted to "stay legit," he found no work. I watched and helped him apply to twelve jobs. After a few weeks, he had not received one call. Meanwhile, he did not pass all his classes because the two weeks he spent in juvenile hall led to a failed semester at school, and he could not stay away from his old friends because they all lived in the same apartment complex and went to the same school he attended.

While Deandre seemed like a victim of his circumstances, I also noticed that he developed creative ways to walk the tightrope between the contradictory expectations of the streets and those of his probation officer. I observed Deandre's crafty strategy to avoid trouble around his friends. After being placed on probation, Deandre took a passive role in his "crew." He shied away from partaking in visible activities, such as walking in a large group or playing dice on the sidewalk. Instead, he "chilled," mostly on his front steps, and avoided joining the crew when they talked about fighting. Despite strategic attempts to stay out of trouble, the system caught up with him, as it does with the majority of youths on probation. No matter how crafty a young person was at attempting to stay away from trouble, his probation officer found a way to "violate" him, arrest him again for the smallest of infractions. While probation generated a desire to change in many young people's minds, the resources to produce outcomes in their attempts to change were not provided. Probation was successful at forcing young people to discuss personal responsibility and reflect on their own actions, but it completely failed at providing young men the resources necessary for desisting from crime. The criminalization process was already in motion, leading probation officers to overlook this desire to change and instead to focus on minor transgressions, such as violating curfew or hanging out with known gang members, many of whom were family or next-door neighbors.

It would have taken consistent case-management work to help Deandre meet Ms. Moore's requirements; however, she did not meet with Deandre again until three months after his release. When she finally met with him, she arrested him because he had violated his probation: a police officer had caught him hanging out with his friends, and he had failed all his classes. After being released, Deandre believed that his probation officer was teaching him a lesson. "She be doing too much, man. She don't help a nigga out, but then she lock a nigga up for stupid shit, yadadamean [you know what I mean]?"

Probation meetings are one-on-one meetings, often mandated at least once per month, in which a young person is asked by his or her probation officer a series of questions centered on desisting or "staying straight." According to the boys, a good probation officer could provide access and connections to programs and jobs. Out of thirty boys on probation, only five believed that their probation officers were helpful. The other twenty-five boys reported having probation officers who spent less than twenty minutes talking to them and who were obsessed with hearing a confession of the boy's violation of probation. I rode the bus to downtown Oakland with three of the boys on three different occasions. All three of the boys were in and out of their appointments within fifteen minutes. "What did he tell you?" I asked. "Nothing," they responded and proceeded to describe the probation officer's lecturing them about doing well in school. At community centers, this also seemed to be the case.

While probation officers did not give good advice or connect youths to programs, they did maintain close contact with police and community workers. The overpolicing-underpolicing paradox existed here: probation officers were rarely around to help young men through the process of staying free but were consistently there to chastise or arrest them when they were purported to have violated the law.

At the end of the boys' initial arrest, all of them were placed on probation and required to report to their probation officers. The meetings would sometimes take place at neighborhood community centers located near the youngsters' homes. The boys did not like the community-center arrangement because everyone knew when they were checking in with their probation officer. Although at one point, some of the boys believed this to be "cool," after a while, boys such as Deandre became frustrated and felt stigmatized by the reality of having to walk into a community center to check in with a probation officer in front of the entire community. Theoretically, this kind of shame might help someone like Deandre "reintegrate" into the community, by feeling ashamed to have committed a crime due to the public shaming, which held him accountable to the entire community for his misdeeds. However, the community seemed to respond to Deandre and the other boys not through an "I will help you learn your lesson," "tough love" perspective but through an "I hope you get arrested again" punitive perspective.

From the perspective of juvenile probation and many school personnel, the point of the probation officer's being present at community centers and schools was to make sure that youths who were on probation did not commit another crime. Often, the probation officer served as a coercive force, which constantly reminded youngsters that a pair of handcuffs was waiting for them as soon as they committed their first infraction. Fourteen of the boys were released from probation during the three-year study. Twelve of the boys were arrested soon after. Their violations, all minor, included being drunk in public, violating curfew, being suspended at school, and hanging out with old friends. Despite being off of probation, the boys continued to be tracked.

Probation officer–youth relations were overwhelmingly negative and punitive, with probation officers being a disruptive control force in the boys' lives, waiting for them to, as Jose put it, "fuck up."[10] By being present in all aspects of the youths' lives, probation officers could potentially have a positive impact on the boys' rehabilitation and reintegration into society. Often, the boys did follow the strict orders of the probation officer, but only in the direct presence of the officer. Probation officers' punitive approach failed to teach young people how to desist on their own, through self-control instead of through external threat. This threat often developed resentment in the boys and led to resistance, which was sometimes articulated through deviance and criminality.

While direct punitive control kept many of the young men from committing crime, many of them ended up being arrested anyway, for the most minor of infractions, which were no longer independent crimes but "crimes" of violating a probation contract. This occurred because the young men resisted many of the unrealistic expectations which probation imposed, including being home by 8 p.m. and checking in with the probation officer at the local community center, where peers would see them interacting with law enforcement and sometimes ask them if they were "snitches." Probation placed the boys between a rock and a hard place; if they followed their probation program, they ran the risk of being victimized by others who saw them as snitches. This, in turn, led many of the boys to be rearrested for simple infractions. Probation created a magnifying-glass effect for the boys, which led them deeper into the criminal justice system for the most minor of infractions, violations which were often outside of criminal code and fell under the purview of school or community rules and norms, such as being suspended, having an argument with parents, or cursing at a store clerk.

Slick's probation officer, Mr. Johnson, a Black man in his forties, always wore a cowboy hat and cowboy boots. He was about six feet tall. His demeanor was gruff. He reminded me of characters that actor Clint Eastwood played in vigilante Wild West movies. When I first introduced myself to him, he asked me what I was going to do to keep Slick off the street. "Either you are helping him, or you are in his way," he told me. On another occasion, I was at Slick's home talking with him and his mother. Mr. Johnson paid a surprise visit, pounding Slick's metal door gate. Slick knew it was Mr. Johnson by the way he knocked. As he heard the pounding he turned to his mom and said, "Ese cabron ya llego a cagar el palo. Me va querer llevar a la carcel." [That asshole is here to harass me. He is going to want to take me to jail.] Slick had been scared into following his probation program by Mr. Johnson. However, fear tactics generally did not work with the boys, since the effects of such tactics were short-lived. Sure, Slick was afraid of being arrested the first few times that Mr. Johnson yelled at him. But after a while, Slick began to resist this punitive treatment, sometimes even purposely breaking probation rules.

Philosopher Michel Foucault argues that the practices and architecture of constant surveillance, what he calls "panopticism," makes individuals internalize their punishment and become self-disciplined, docile bodies.[11] But in Oakland, young men were not being taught this self-discipline. Instead, the criminalization which existed in this context led the boys to manipulate the system, by agreeing to obey under coercion and, at the same time, resisting this coercion by breaking the rules which they had agreed to follow. In Foucault's formulation, the disciplined subject sits at the periphery of the panopticon, with the disciplinarian power at the center, keeping a constant gaze on the subject. This soft surveillance is intended to reform the soul and produce an obedient subject. The ultimate goal of the panopticon, according to Foucault, is to create self-discipline in the prisoner. This process is scientific, neat, and controlled. The kind of discipline I found in the streets of Oakland differs drastically. The boys in Oakland were placed at the center of the panopticon. Punitive treatment surrounded them, beaming itself in high intensity, from multiple directions. Different from Foucault's panopticon, the punishment I found in Oakland was aimed at controlling and containing the young men who were seen as risks, threats, and culprits. The boys in Oakland were not seen as souls that needed to be disciplined but as irreparable risks and threats that needed to be controlled and ultimately contained. The discipline imposed on the boys in Oakland did not do much to reform the soul. Instead it incapacitated them as social subjects; it stripped them of their dignity and humanity by systematically marking them and denying them the ability to function in school, in the labor market, and as law-abiding citizens. The boys did not learn to self-discipline; instead, they resisted, became incapacitated, or both. The boys knew they were being watched, and so they resisted; they created a spectacle of the system, exposing its flaws and contradictions, which in turn led to an altered sense of having recovered some dignity. In a securitized Oakland, Foucault's panopticon had been flipped on its head: it had become inverted, placing the boys at the center of the complex, with forces of punitive social control surrounding them, delivering them constant ubiquitous punishment and criminalization, leading many to resist.

Although direct threat and coercion from probation officers worked well in changing youth behaviors, it was only a temporary fix. As soon as the boys were taken off the intensive probation program of electronic monitoring, weekly meetings, and home arrest, they began to commit acts which further criminalized them and which often led to a second arrest. They often expressed that being contained, monitored, and threatened for so long made them unable to control themselves when the direct authoritative treatment was removed. They had been trained to live under forceful supervision and sanctions from the state, and, now, there was no other mechanism by which to regulate their behavior or to teach them how to function as healthy young adults.

The boys had not been able to find positive, informal social control based on nurturing, guidance, and support; instead, they had encountered a system of control which disciplined them through punitive force.[12] The system may have been fooled by the fact that the boys followed orders when they were under direct supervision. In Slick's case, the immediate threat of violence and incarceration led to short-term desistance. However, once the threat was removed, Slick was left with no guidance to continue to avoid crime. This punitive approach did not work, because the boys did not develop navigational skills necessary for becoming productive citizens. The boys needed to learn how to desist on their own behalf, through internal controls, so that a punitive and highly expensive system of control would no longer be necessary. Criminologists John Hagan and Bill McCarthy explain the difference between debilitating social control and rehabilitative social control: "Normal shame and shaming produce social solidarity, whereas pathological shame and shaming produce alienation."[13] Normal shame is the process by which a community member is held accountable for his or her transgressions by way of shaming, so that he or she learns, makes amends, and becomes reintegrated into the group or society. Pathological shaming is the process by which the transgressor is permanently stigmatized, shamed into feeling like a permanent outsider, and perpetually humiliated for his or her negative behavior. This in turn leads the transgressor to become disintegrated from the group or society. When young people are integrated back into society and "taught a lesson" through self-reflection and the development of internal controls, they see themselves as part of the community and hence hold themselves accountable. When they are shamed through criminalization, young people resist and lose hope, often leading to more crime or criminalization.

Eighteen of the youths in this study had probation officers who placed the burden on them to immediately change their social worlds by avoiding their friends or to face further punishment and criminalization. They all felt that their probation officers had given them advice which did not work on the streets with their peers. And many of the youths did attempt to use the threat of probation or juvenile hall as an excuse to stay away from some of their old peers, in order to avoid being stigmatized for attempting to improve in school, avoid drugs and alcohol, and avoid committing violence. However, because many of their friends had already been to jail, they knew the storyline: probation officers exaggerated their threats, and youths who began to hang out again with old friends did not immediately go back to jail. Probation officers had minimal credibility with the boys. Peers who had been to jail would simply explain to their friends that the probation officer was exaggerating and that most of the time they would not get caught if they broke probation. "Come on, fool, just kick it with us," I heard Slick's friends tell him one day at the park, "That busta' ain't gonna arrest you. They just tell you that to scare you." Because probation officers often tested the boys for marijuana use through a urine test, some of the boys became cocaine users after they were placed on probation. "Cocaine," as Slick described, "stays in your system for two days. Dank [marijuana] stays in your system for thirty days." This obsession with finding marijuana use in young people is indicative of how cracking down on less harmful offenses often led young people to "graduate" into more harmful yet less targeted offenses.

Police and probation officers often communicated with shopkeepers and community members about the "criminals" whom they should look out for. Ronny, a Black youth who moved back and forth between Oakland and Berkeley, began to realize a few weeks after being placed on probation that everyone in the community knew about his arrest and probation program. "I walked into the liquor store, and the Arab told me, 'I know the police are after you, so if you do anything, I'm gonna call them.'" I asked him, "Did you steal anything? Had you ever stolen anything there?" "No. I just talk shit to him because he won't front me a soda when I'm broke."

Community Centers

Eight of the boys who had been previously arrested and four of the boys who had not been arrested were enrolled in community-center programs. Two were enrolled in a community center in Berkeley, because they had previously lived there. The rest of the youths were enrolled in two different organizations in Oakland. Each center claimed to serve between two hundred and seven hundred youths per year. Community workers estimated that over ten thousand young people lived in the neighborhoods which their centers serviced. The lack of community programs for young people, in all the neighborhoods where the boys lived, was observable. When the boys were asked, "Would you join a program that took you on field trips or where you could play sports or talk to a mentor or get a job?" all of them responded, "Yes." However, only four of them were able to enroll in community programs without any strings attached. The other eight enrolled because they were mandated by probation. This was a common pattern: criminal justice institutions sometimes held a stake in youth programs. During the three years of this study, I noticed that funding for case workers from foundations and non-criminal-justice government agencies declined, and funding from criminal justice entities became available. At one point, a former gang member turned community worker, Joey, had been funded through various grants to provide mentoring for gang youths in the community. As the money for this position expired, the community center turned to the county probation department to continue to fund the position. The county agreed but wanted direct oversight of Joey. Over time, youths who had grown to trust Joey and respect him came to see him as a "snitch" for the probation department and the police. Eventually, Joey lost the boys' respect, became ineffective in the community, and was laid off by the community center.

Although these organizations claimed to serve "at-risk" youths, very few of the boys in this study were accepted or invited to enroll in programs. Instead, the community centers focused on youths who they thought would respond to their programming. This made sense, because their funding was dependent on their "numbers." Angelo, a youth-programs director at Communities Organizing Youth (COY), explained:

ANGELO: You see, I try to help the at-risk ones, you know, the ones that are on the street. But they [his boss] tell me, 'If you help them, we won't get funded,' because, as you know, when you put time into the crazy youth, they take up a lot of time.

VR: So, are you able to give programming to any of the street youth?

ANGELO: The one, two programs we have for them come from probation. One is anger management, and the other is life skills.

VR: What do they do?

ANGELO: They learn about controlling their anger and about living a healthy lifestyle.

VR: Who runs the programs? Counselors? Community members?

ANGELO: POs [probation officers] mostly.

Although the community centers hired some charismatic individuals with transformational skills, people who in the past had helped to transform the lives of some of the toughest youths in the community, their hard work and youth-development approach was rarely institutionalized. Charismatic individuals were given a large caseload and were burdened with high expectations from many people in the community. This led many of them to burn out. Nene, another former gang member turned charismatic youth worker, explained, "Man! I like working with the youngsters, but this red-tape bullshit of having to feel like a snitch for probation is getting to me. . . . The other day I caught myself threatening one of the boys to call the police if they kept talking in my workshop." Although many youth workers did not use this approach—to contact a police officer or to report an incident to a probation officer—many of the boys reported having this experience when the community center called probation or police for non-criminal activity.

In recent years, an influential program known as Cease-Fire has been implemented in communities across the country, including in Oakland. The Cease-Fire project calls for identifying hard-core community members who may potentially commit violence, calling them in for a meeting with law enforcement and community workers, threatening the potential transgressors that they will be watched and punished if they commit a crime, and offering programs to them if they choose to "go legit." Although this study did not document Cease-Fire because it started after I left the field, a program such as this may pose the risk of entangling law enforcement with community workers even further. Dire consequences result from this process. Community centers sometimes seemed like criminal justice centers to some of the boys, places where programming was provided by law-enforcement officials, instead of youth-development workers. However, if police stick to their terrain to protect the community, and programs are created to help young people who have expressed an interest in change, then a program like Cease-Fire may prove promising. The key is to invest enough resources in social programs which are independent from, and set clear parameters between, themselves and criminal justice institutions. Otherwise, young people perceive the various institutions in the community as accomplices in a plot to criminalize them. The young men in this study compared encounters with police, probation officers, and prosecutors with interactions they had with school administrators and teachers who placed them in detention rooms; community centers that attempted to exorcise their criminality; and even parents, who felt ashamed or dishonored and relinquished their relationship with their own children altogether. It seemed, in the accounts of the boys, that various institutions were collaborating to form a system that degraded them on an everyday basis. As such, these young men's understanding of their environment as a punitive one, where they were not given a second chance, led them to believe that they had no choice but to resist.

These institutions, though independently operated with their own practices, policies, and logics, intersected with one another to provide a consistent flow of criminalization. The consequences of this formation were often brutal. Young Ronny explained,

We are not trusted. Even if we try to change, it's us against the world. It's almost like they don't want us to change. They rather we stay crazy than to try to pick ourselves up. Why they gotta send us to the ghetto alternative high school? We don't deserve to go to the same school down the street? . . . And when we try to apply for a job, we just get looked at like we crazy. If we do get an interview, the first question is, "Have you been arrested before?" . . . We got little choice.

Ronny understood his actions as responses to this system of punishment, which restricted his ability to survive, work, play, and learn. As such, he developed coping skills that were often seen as deviant and criminal by the system. Sociologist Elijah Anderson reminds us that young men, in these kinds of situations, react by demonstrating mistrust of the system: "Highly alienated and embittered, they exude generalized contempt for the wider scheme of things, and for a system they are sure has nothing but contempt for them."[14] Spider's experiences with police not protecting him and instead marking him as a gang member solidified his mistrust and contempt for the police. In addition, his experiences in a school where teachers warned him about his inevitable entry into the criminal justice system and where security guards reported students to police for minimal transgressions led Spider to believe that he was caught in the center of a web of punishment, which consistently and ubiquitously constrained him. This web of punishment, the youth control complex, added to the boys' blocked opportunities but also generated creative responses, which allowed the boys to feel dignified. Sometimes these responses even led to informal and formal political resistance.

PART II

Consequences

5

"Dummy Smart"

Misrecognition, Acting Out, and "Going Dumb"

In attempting to maintain the existing order, the powerful commit crimes of control. . . . At the same time, oppressed people engage in . . . crimes of resistance.
> —Meda Chesney-Lind and Randall G. Shelden, *Girls, Delinquency, and Juvenile Justice*, 1992

It's a war going on
The ghetto is a cage
They only give you two choices
Be a rebel or a slave
> —Dead Prez, "Turn off the Radio," 2002

Ronny was called in for a job interview at Carrows, a chain restaurant that served $9.99 sirloin steak and shrimp. He called me up, asking for help.[1] I lent him a crisp white dress shirt, which I had purchased at a discount store when I worked as a server at a steak house during my undergraduate years. I convinced Ronny to wear fitted khakis, rather than his customary baggy jeans. He agreed, with the condition that he would wear his white Nike Air Force Ones, a popular basketball shoe at the time. These shoes had been in and out of style in the urban setting since the early 1980s. By 2002, a famous rapper, Nelly, created a popular song named "Air Force Ones." Around this time, famous basketball players such as Kobe Bryant wore these shoes during games and advertised for Nike. Black and Latino youths in Oakland gravitated to these shoes, sometimes even wearing them to more formal events such as high school proms, quinceañeras (coming-of-age parties for girls turning fifteen, celebrated in many Latino cultures), and weddings. I asked Ronny why he insisted on wearing these shoes in a professional setting. He replied, "Because professionals wear them."

Many of the boys believed that they had a clear sense of what courteous, professional, and "good" behavior was. Despite their attempts to present themselves with good manners and good morals, their idea of professional behavior did not match mainstream ideas of professional behavior. This in turn created what I refer to as *misrecognition*. When the boys displayed a genuine interest in "going legit," getting a job or doing well in school, adults often could not recognize their positive attempts and sometimes interpreted them as rude or malicious acts and therefore criminalized them.

The boys had grown up in an environment which had deprived them of the social and cultural capital that they needed to progress in school and the labor market. Therefore, they developed their own alternative social and cultural capital, which they used to survive poverty, persist in a violent and punitive social ecology, prevent violence, avoid incarceration, and attempt to fit into mainstream institutions. Borrowing from philosopher Antonio Gramsci's notion of "organic intellectuals"[2]—those individuals who come from the marginalized conditions that they write about and study—I call the creative social and cultural capital that the boys developed in response to being prevented from acquiring capital to succeed in mainstream institutions *organic capital*. This organic capital was often misunderstood and misrecognized by mainstream institutions and was, in turn, criminalized. On the other hand, young people often used organic capital as a resilience strategy that allowed them to persist through neglect and exclusionary experiences. Education scholar Tara Yosso develops a framework for understanding and using the capital that marginalized communities develop, what she calls "community cultural wealth."[3] She argues that marginalized communities have always generated certain kinds of capital that have allowed them to survive and resist. Sociologist Martín Sánchez-Jankowski has recently discussed poor people's ability to organize their social world and maintain social order as "persistence."[4] According to Sánchez-Jankowski, contrary to the popular academic belief that poor people live in a disorganized world where they have a limited capacity to generate "collective efficacy"—the ability of a community to solve its own social problems—the urban poor shape their behaviors around making sense of and creating social order within a marginal context. Organic capital is the creative response that the boys in this study developed in the midst of blocked opportunity and criminalization. However, these creative responses, despite being well intentioned, were often not well received by mainstream institutions.

The paradox that these marginalized young people faced was that the organic capital that they developed to negotiate conflict and organize their survival on the streets often did not translate well in a school or labor-market setting. Criminologist Yasser Payne argues that some marginalized Black youths, who have been excluded from mainstream institutions, find affirmation, fulfillment, and resilience in practices associated with street life. These practices, according to Payne, provide young men with "sites of resilience," spaces where they feel empowered and affirmed.[5] Some boys in this study wholeheartedly believed that they were making a formidable attempt to tap into mainstream institutions, using every possible resource to do so, but, in return, they would often receive negative responses.

The boys attempted to use the resilience skills they had learned on the streets, their organic capital, in spaces that could not value the respectability and morals that they brought to the table. These morals and values were often rendered deviant, and the boys were excluded or criminalized. One of their responses was to manifest a resistance to this perceived exclusion and criminalization, a stance that could place value on their self-developed survival skills. This resistance developed in the form of deviance, "irrational behavior," breaking rules, or committing crime. The resistance became more methodical for some of the boys, as they turned to more formal ways of organizing and resisting punitive social control.

Ronny's story is indicative of how many of the boys attempted to tap into mainstream institutions but failed. As they encountered rejection, they returned to the resilience and survival strategies that they had developed in their neighborhoods. I continued to prepare Ronny for his interview, to help him develop "acceptable" cultural capital. We prepared for the interview with some mock questions. "Why do you want to work for us?" I asked him. He responded, "I am a hard worker." "That's a good start," I said. "How about expanding that and telling them that you're also a team player and that you enjoy the restaurant atmosphere?" Ronny nodded. The day of the interview, I walked into the restaurant separately from Ronny. To calm his nerves I told him, "You look great, man. This job is yours!" He looked sharp: a professionally dressed, athletically built, charismatic, tall, African American young man with a charming dimple on his face every time he smiled. I was certain he would get the job. I sat down for lunch at a booth, in an attempt to observe Ronny being interviewed. I looked at the menu and, with a knot in my gut, nervous for Ronny, ordered what I knew would eventually give me a stomachache: a Mile-High Chipotle Southwest Burger. I sat about twenty feet away from the table where Ronny had been asked to wait. A manager appeared and sat with him.

Ronny tried to use his charisma to connect with the manager, but she kept her distance and did not look at Ronny the entire time he answered questions, seemingly uninterested in what he had to say. At the end of the interview, Ronny abruptly stood up and walked away from the manager, with no handshake or smile. He went outside. I ordered my burger to go, paid my bill, and met him in the parking lot. As I headed to the door, I turned to look in the manager's direction, and she was greeting a White male youth. She smiled, gave him her hand, and offered him a place to sit down. Ronny's first contact with her was not this friendly.[6] I walked outside to meet Ronny, who sat on the hood of my car.

I asked Ronny to give me a debriefing. He told me that he had a good feeling and that the manager had seemed to like him. I asked him to walk me through the interview. He had followed the plan flawlessly. I was proud of him. "You followed the plan. You did a great job," I told him. "Why didn't you shake her hand when you left?" I asked. "'Cause," Ronny replied. "Why not?" I scolded. "Because it was a White lady. You not supposed to shake a White lady's hand. They be scared of a nigga. They think I'ma try to take their shit or fuck 'em. I just said thanks and walked out." Ronny did not get the job.

Ronny had been socialized from a young age, according to him, by his White female teachers to overcompensate around White women and to go the extra mile to show that he was not attempting to harm or disrespect them. This behavior may have been a result of the stereotyped expectations of Black men as criminals and sexual aggressors, which is deeply rooted in American culture and which Ronny had to contend with as a young Black man. The history of lynching and hate crimes against Black men in the United States has often been the result of accusations of attacks by Black men on White women, a fact well documented by historians.[7] It seemed that the longue-durée idea that Black males are a threat to White females had become embedded in the socialization of Black boys in Oakland.

Ronny did all he could to land the job, but the limited resources that he had at his disposal for showing respect may have kept him from getting the position. In this case, he believed that not shaking the manager's hand would show respect; instead, Ronny may have been perceived as a rude kid not able to hold employment in a restaurant environment. I asked Ronny to tell me how he learned about not shaking White women's hands. He told me that White teachers and White women in public had always been intimidated by him.[8] His White female teachers had asked him to keep his distance from them, White women on the street would clasp their purses when they saw him walking by, and White female store clerks would nervously watch him when he walked into an establishment.

Anthropologist Philippe Bourgois found that poor Puerto Rican young men living in New York had a difficult time making it in the labor market because of the cultural collision that took place. He showed that corporate culture was organized around humiliating low-skilled workers and that these workers were supposed to tolerate this hazing process until they were able to move up the corporate ladder. The boys in his study came from a world where they gave and expected respect and honor.[9] This conflict led young men to become isolated and forced them out of work. Similarly, I found that the boys in my study organized their worlds around dignity, respect, and empathic treatment (among friends and homies). Tyrell's comment is representative: "My little Gs [friends] all respect me, watch my back, and give me love. They's all I got." The boys often found themselves fighting for dignity. They constantly worked at feeling worthy of honor and respect from the institutions they interacted with. This dignity work often led them to fall further into criminalization and, in turn, impacted their ability to effectuate social mobility or to remain free.

Ronny applied for multiple jobs. After about a dozen applications and three failed interviews, he became discouraged. He reported being asked by other managers about his "drug habits" and "criminal background." Ronny decided to abandon the job-search process and instead invested twenty dollars in pirated DVDs; a few hours later, he made fifty dollars from the illegally copied movies. He reinvested the fifty dollars in a back-pack full of pirated DVDs. After a few weeks, Ronny made enough to buy a few new pairs of glossy Nike Air Force One tennis shoes. However, the six to ten hours that he spent in front of Albertson's grocery store, waiting for customers for his DVDs, made him a measly twenty to thirty dollars a day—certainly not worth the risk of getting arrested for a federal offense, the classification that DVD pirating receives in the United States.

Still, Ronny preferred to take on the risk of incarceration and the low wages that this underground entrepreneurship granted him, in order to avoid the stigma, shame, and feeling of failure that the job-application process produced for him. This feeling the young men had of being racially stigmatized and being punished for their well-intended actions made some of them reject the mainstream job-application process and develop their own underground economies.[10] Misrecognition of genuine attempts to do well in school, the labor market, or their probation program led many of the boys to grow frustrated and to produce alternatives in which their organic capital could be put to productive use.

Resistance Identities

Resistance identities, according to sociologist Manuel Castells, are those identities created by subordinated populations in response to oppression. These identities operate by "excluding the excluder."[11] In feeling excluded from a network of positive credentials, education, and employment opportunities, young people develop creative responses that provide them with the necessary tools to survive in an environment where they have been left behind and where they are consistently criminalized.[12] They develop practices that seem to embrace criminality as a means of contesting a system that sees them as criminals.[13] Sociologist Richard Quinney argues that poor people engage in crimes such as stealing, robbing, and pirating as "acts of survival," in an economic system where they have been left behind and where their well-being is not fulfilled by other collective means. He further argues that some poor and working-class people engage in "crimes of resistance," such as sabotaging workplace equipment and destroying public property, as a form of protest against their economic conditions.[14] Sociologist John Hagedorn argues that one promising avenue for transforming the lives of marginalized young people is to embrace their resistance: "Encouraging cultural resistance identities and linking them to social movements, like those in the United States opposing gentrification, police brutality, or deportations, may present the best opportunity to reach out to our alienated youth."[15] Sociologist Felix Padilla finds that gang-involved youths hold a "conscious understanding of the workings of social institutions."[16] Padilla quotes education scholar Henry Giroux to frame his analysis of the critical consciousness developed by marginalized young people:

> In some cases . . . youngsters may not be fully aware of the political grounds of the position toward the conventional society, except for a general awareness of its dominating nature and the need to somehow escape from it without relegating themselves to a future they do not want. Even this vague understanding and its attendant behavior portend a politically progressive logic.[17]

I build on this work by demonstrating how the young men in this study engaged in acts of survival and crimes of resistance. Further, I argue that some of their non-serious offenses were committed as acts of resistance to being criminalized. The boys in this study were clearly aware of, recognized, and had an analysis of the system that criminalized them. Consequently, youth labeled as deviants participated in everyday practices of resistance. This approach is different from the one adopted by Philippe Bourgois, described in the preceding section, in that young men commit crime not just in search of respect and honor but also as a conscious revolt against a system of exclusion and punitive control that they clearly understand. Sociologist Howard Becker finds that labeled youths resist by internalizing their label and committing more crime.[18] My study finds a missing link in this analysis: the internalization of criminality is only one outcome in the labeling process; another outcome that young people who are labeled partake in is resistance: they internalize criminalization, flip it on its head, and generate action that seeks to change the very system that oppresses them.

The young men in this study constantly participated in everyday acts of resistance that did not make sense to adults. Teachers, police officers, and community-center workers were often baffled by the deviant acts committed by the boys. From the perspective of adults, these transgressions and small crimes were ridiculous and irrational because the risk of being caught was high and the benefit derived from committing the deviant act was minuscule. This frustration led adults to abandon empathy for the boys and to apply the toughest sanctions on them. "If they're going to act like idiots, I am going to have to give them the axe," explained one of the gang task-force officers.

Many of the adults I interviewed believed that the boys' defiance was, as some called it, "stupid." Sarcastic remarks such as "that was smart" often followed when a youth purposely broke a simple rule, leading him to be ostracized, kicked out of class, or even arrested. Why would the boys break the simplest of rules knowing that there would be grave consequences? From the perspective of the boys, they were breaking the rules in order to resist a system that seemed stacked against them. In many ways, breaking the rules was one of the few resources that the boys could use in response to criminalization.

Why would these boys steal a twenty-five-cent bag of chips when they had money in their pocket? Curse out a police officer who was trying to befriend them? Act indifferent to a potential employer? Or purposely not answer their probation officer's call during curfew time, even though they were sitting next to the phone? These seemingly irrational transgressions often created meaning that gave these youngsters dignity in an environment that already saw them as criminal prior to their committing the act. But working for dignity does not necessarily translate to working for freedom. In other words, when the boys sought out dignity, they were often at risk of losing their freedom; when they worked for freedom, they were making an attempt to stay out of jail or prison but often felt that they had lost their dignity in the process.

Patterns of behavior that are often misrecognized as ignorant, stupid, and self-defeating by authority figures, policymakers, and scholars are often young people's attempt to use the resources provided by their environment to transform their social conditions. Sociologist Ann Swidler's concept of "culture as repertoire" contends that individuals deploy different, often contradicting actions in the social world based on the needs demanded by specific social situations. For Swidler, culture influences action by providing a tool kit of actions to choose from. This notion of culture is important in the study of working-class populations, because it provides a space for scholars to "study culture and poverty without blaming the victim."[19]

The boys used the resources around them to develop a response to what they perceived as punitive treatment. Their responses where often misinterpreted by authority figures. Ronny, for example, responded to his potential employer's cold gestures by using the tools he had learned from others in the community: to avoid being perceived as aggressive toward White women. Whereas the protocols of mainstream culture would have provided him with the understanding that he should shake a potential employer's hand, his racialization had conditioned him to remain passive and avoid physical contact of any kind, even a seemingly innocuous handshake. The youths in this study demonstrated a yearning for being accepted by mainstream society and used the resources available to them in an attempt to do so. However, their actions were misinterpreted as acts of deviance, and at times even their phenotypes were seen as indicating deviance. This in turn led the system to further criminalize them. The boys had utilized the resources available to them to show the system that they were worthy of being treated as young people with promise, as potential good students, and as hardworking, honest employees. However, the misrecognition of these actions not only denied the boys access; it interpreted their well-intended acts as deviant and even criminal activity.

The Stolen Bag of Chips

One fall afternoon, I met with fifteen-year-old Flaco, a Latino gang-associated young man from east Oakland. We joined three of his friends as they walked to their usual afterschool hang out, Walnut Park. They decided to make a stop at Sam's Liquor Store. I walked in with them, noticing a sign on the outside that read, "Only two kids allowed in store at one time." I realized that they were breaking the store rule by entering in a group of four. I pretended to walk in separately from the group to see how the store clerk would respond to their transgression. I stood in the back of the store next to the soft-drink and beer refrigerators. Flaco walked up to the candy-bar aisle—keeping a good distance between himself and the Snickers, Twix, and Skittles, to show the clerk, who was already staring him down, that he was not attempting to steal. He grabbed a candy bar, held it far away from his body, walked a few steps, and placed it on the counter. Many of the boys in this study often maintained their distance in the candy or soda aisles at stores. This may have been a way for them to show the store that they were not attempting to steal. Store clerks in the neighborhoods I studied were always apprehensive of customers. They watched people from the moment they walked in and had surveillance cameras set up; one clerk had taped on his counter personal pictures of himself holding an AK-47 rifle to indicate to customers that he was prepared. This particular clerk may have been concerned that too many kids in his store meant that he could not keep an eye on all of them at the same time.

The store clerk, a balding, middle-aged, Asian American male, pointed to the door and yelled, "Only two kids allowed in the store at a time!" The three youths who were in line to pay for their items looked at the store clerk and at each other. I could see in their faces the look of despair as their most pleasurable moment of the day, to bite into a delicious candy bar, fell apart. Mike, who stood closest to the entrance of the door, responded, "We ain't doing shit." The store clerk looked at him and replied, "I am going to call the police!" Mike grabbed a twenty-five-cent bag of Fritos Flamin' Hot chips, lifted it up in front of the clerk's face, and said, "You see this? I was gonna pay for it, but now I ain't paying for shit, stupid mothafucka." He rushed out of the store with the bag of chips. The clerk picked up the phone and called the police. The rest of the youngsters dropped the snacks they were in line to purchase and ran out of the store. I walked up to the store clerk and gave him a quarter for Mike, who had stolen the chips. With an infuriated look, the clerk responded, "It's too late. The police are on their way to get the robbers."

When I walked out of the store, the boys had all disappeared. I was not able to track them down until a few days later. When I ran into Flaco, he informed me that the police had arrested Mike that day for stealing the twenty-five-cent bag of chips. After interviewing the boys and observing the store clerk's interactions with them soon after this event, I found that Mike's "irrational" behavior had changed the way the store clerk interacted with the boys. The boys believed that the store clerk had begun to treat them with more respect. The store clerk avoided provoking negative interactions with the boys, even if it meant allowing a few more boys into the store than his store policy demanded. While even Mike's peers believed that his actions were "crazy," they also acknowledged that something significant had changed in their interactions with the store clerk. For example, Flaco thought that Mike had overreacted, but he also rationalized Mike's actions. Because of Mike, Flaco felt respected by the store clerk the next time he went in the store: "Mike fucked up. He was acting hyphy [crazy] that day. He should have paid the guy. . . . But because of what he did, me and my dogs go into the sto', and the guy don't say shit. We all go in like five deep—like 'what?'—and dude [the store clerk] don't say shit no more." When I asked Mike why he had stolen the bag of chips, he responded, "That fool was trippin'. He should've come correct. I was gonna pay him. You saw, I had the money in my hand. . . . That fool knows not to fuck with us anymore. . . . I did get taken in for that, but it don't matter. They gave me probation and shit. I'll just keep it cool now since that fool will keep it cool now too." In Mike's worldview, his strategy of fighting for dignity at the cost of giving up his freedom had paid off. Mike's actions resulted in his commitment to the criminal justice system. According to him, he was very aware of this risk when he stole the bag of chips. He had grown frustrated at the treatment he had received at school, by police, and then culminating at the store. This frustration, and a deep desire to feel respected, led Mike to willfully expose himself to incarceration. In the end, Mike lost his freedom, becoming supervised by the criminal justice system. Nonetheless, Mike gained a sense of dignity for himself and his peers, which, in his mind, made it worth exchanging his freedom. This scenario is representative of many of the crimes that the other boys committed. Demanding dignity from the system generated a paradox for the boys: they all indicated wanting to be free of incarceration, policing, and surveillance, while, at the same time, punitive surveillance, policing, and discipline led many of them to consciously seek their dignity and act in a way that pipelined them into the criminal justice system. Nonetheless, striving for dignity led some of the boys deeper into the system.

The boys took control of their criminalization by using the few resources they had at hand. In this example, Mike and his friends changed the interactional dynamic between themselves and the store clerk. The store clerk would no longer yell or enforce the rule of no more than two boys in the store at a time, which the youths perceived as ridiculous. Instead, he adjusted his practices by allowing the boys into the store, as long as they did not steal. However, the price that Mike paid was steep. This arrest later led him deeper into the criminal justice system.

I asked Mike, "Why didn't you steal something more expensive?" He told me that he thought about it, but, in the moment, he didn't care what he took. He wanted to prove a point to the clerk: "not to fuck with me." For Mike, stealing the bag of chips wasn't about saving the quarter he had to pay for the chips; it wasn't about accumulating the most valuable commodity he could get his hands on; it wasn't about stealing because he was poor and wanted to eat a bag of chips. Although he may have had a desire for all of the above, the purpose of stealing the bag of chips was to redeem himself for being shamed and feeling disrespected.[20] In the end, despite facing further punishment, Mike and his friends felt that their actions were not in vain; they had won a small battle in a war they were so tired of losing. While authority figures expected the boys to desist and follow the rules, and while the boys expressed a deep desire "to be left alone" and remain free, one of the only resources they had to feel respected within the system was to actively engage in behaviors that defied the rules of the game. This in turn led to further misrecognition and criminalization.

The Probation Officer

Like Mike's store incident, other youths often broke rules that they could have easily followed. Examples of this rule breaking were taunting and cursing at police officers when they were simply trying to say hello, purposely breaking a rule in front of a teacher or principal, and breaking an 8 p.m. curfew with the probation officer by not walking inside the house to answer the officer's phone call at 8:01 p.m. Flaco's and Spider's probation officer, Ms. Lawrence, discussed this nonsense rule breaking with me.

v.r.: Ms. Lawrence, why do these young men continue to get violated [arrested for violating their probation agreement]?

MS. LAWRENCE: I don't know what is wrong with these kids. It's simple. Do
your program, do good, and act right. Eighty percent of my
kids recidivate, and it's for the dumbest things. They spit on
a teacher and get kicked out of school, or they won't cooper-
ate when a cop pulls them over. The other day one of the boys
was arrested for talking back to the principal. He told her that
the police could not go into his house without a warrant, after
the principal threatened to call the cops on him. The principal
dialed the school officer, and he arrested him for threatening
his teacher. Why did he have to talk back to the principal?
They act like they want to go back to the hall [juvenile hall].

Ms. Lawrence spoke of many more youths who did not follow simple
directions. She could not figure out why these young men were risking
so much by disobeying basic rules. It seemed that no matter what reper-
cussion was placed in front of them—loss of educational or employment
opportunities, loss of freedom, or six months in jail—they continued to
break the rules. I asked her if she knew why the boys acted this way if they
knew the repercussions. She replied,

> I could see them not wanting to do something, but we all have to follow
> the rules in society. If we all were to break even the smallest of rules, the
> world would be chaotic. There would be crime everywhere. . . . We [proba-
> tion officers] aren't assigned to them because the kids are good. They did
> the crime, and they have to prove to society that they can stop committing
> crimes. . . . They have to learn to follow basic rules at some point in life, . . .
> even if they have to learn the hard way.

Sociologist Thomas Scheff argues that the combination of alienation
(being an outcast at school and shamed on the street) with the repression
of emotions (in this case, the boys' need to hide their feelings and put up
a tough front to prove themselves on the street) leads to violence.[21] The
boys consistently expressed feeling emotional alienation. In addition,
expectations of manhood on the street, and in other institutional settings,

dictated to the boys that their emotions be repressed. This combination of emotional alienation and repression of emotions may have led some of the boys to commit "crimes of resistance." When probation officers attempted to "teach" the boys by using punitive measures, the boys felt alienated. They then normalized this negative treatment, believing that it might be treatment they deserved and that this treatment might help them to rehabilitate. When the boys realized that the punitive treatment failed as a reform tool, they rejected it, pushing back, often through the only means they had, crimes of resistance.

Slick and the Policeman

In the middle of a warm, spring school day, I drove up to the boys' hangout, "Wino Park," to look for Slick. They had named the park after all the drug addicts and alcoholics who practically lived there. On regular occasions, I spotted men sleeping on the lawn, homeless women with shopping carts full of trinkets they had collected in an attempt to sell them, and half a dozen or so middle-aged crack- or heroin-addicted men sitting on the old and splintered wood tables, which sat adjacent to solid metal, rusted-out barbeque grills. Some of the grills had a fire burning, but never any food. A group of about eight teenage boys stood in a circle talking with one another. Some of them were leaning on a tree, others were sitting on a bench, and one of them was squatting on the ground in the classic *cholo* (gangster) pose, sitting on one leg with the other leg extended, foot pointing straight ahead. They talked about common topics: girls, enemies, and police. They told stories about being brutalized by the police. A common practice, as had been experienced by Ronny with his probation officer, had to do with being taken to the ground by the collarbone. One of the boys, who did not want me to mention his personal information or name or even to assign him a pseudonym, explained the process: "That fool stuck his fingers inside my neck [points to the collarbone area] and slammed me to the ground. Then he made me get up and [pulled] me for half a block, with one hand inside my fucking neck!" Many other stories of brutality followed from the rest of the boys. "You 'member the time Russ got knocked the fuck out by the task force for talking shit? We were standing in front of KFC [Kentucky Fried

Chicken], and task [force] was looking at us crazy, so Russ said, 'Wassup?' And the cop ran up and scraped his ass." This officer, Officer Sweeney, a White man in his forties with a shaved bald head, was infamous for beating down young Black and Latino boys.

I asked them, "Why do you keep getting attacked by cops?" "We make them get mad. We like it when they get mad. It makes us know that we did our part." "Even if you get beat up and go to jail?" I asked. The response, and agreement, from the rest of the group was, "Don't matter what happens to us, as long as we make them respect us the next time they see us." Slick explained: "One of the cops almost broke my leg the other day. He slammed the door on my foot, and he knew my foot was sticking out. That shit still hurts, but I know that he won't fuck with me like that next time, 'cause I gave him a hard time for fucking with me." I asked him what made him certain that the police officer would give him respect the next time he saw him. Slick responded, "Because I saw him again, a week later, and he just looked at me crazy, and I looked at him crazy, but he didn't stop me anymore like he used to." Slick took the risk of undergoing immediate physical punishment, rather than suffer ongoing systematic harassment. His gamble paid off. The officer no longer harassed him. Slick felt good about being able to gain respect from the police officer, since this was the same officer who had beat him when he was still a child. In Slick's perspective, more defiance could lead to less harassment. Although I witnessed police officers "back down" when young men defied them, I also witnessed the strategy backfire on the boys, as, eventually, this resistance led officers to call in backup, and then a group of officers would suppress the entire group. On two encounters I observed, a police officer called in backup: a group of officers arrived, assault rifles in hands, and handcuffed and searched all the boys. Some of the boys, who had not been placed into the gang database, were placed into it on these occasions. Others were arrested for the smallest of infractions.

Defiance as Resistance

It seemed that defiance constituted a temporary success to the boys. Watching interactions between the boys and authority figures was often like watching a life-sized game of chess in action, with a rook strategically moving in response to a queen's movement. A police officer would get out of his car, the boys would posture, an officer would grab a young man, his friends would prepare to run, an officer would humiliate one of the boys, and the boy would respond by not cooperating or by cursing back. As one side moved its pieces to repress, another moved its pieces to resist. The boys were almost always captured and eliminated from the chess board, but not before they had encroached into the opponent's territory, throwing the system off and influencing the rules and movements of the game.

Returning to the stolen bag of chips, we can see how adults and the boys perceived specific acts of defiance in completely different terms. I mentioned the incident to Ms. Stanley, the probation officer, and she responded, "Any normal person would have paid the cashier. This kid must be crazy. . . . Shoo, it gets me mad just thinking about it. Let's not talk about it." It is this "craziness"—as understood by the dominant group, adults attempting to enact social control—which the boys found productive to their resistance. For Mike, it was more important to claim his dignity than to follow the rules and pay for the chips. He was convinced that three days in juvenile hall, the stigma he received in the community, the trouble he got into with his parents, and the year of probation he received were all worth making a statement to the store clerk.

Mike and Ronny were searching for something beyond immediate gratification. They did not want to follow the rules in order to gain the social rewards—a good grade, a legitimate bag of chips, completing a probation program, and becoming a "normal" citizen—for being rule followers. Instead, the boys chose a road that at first seemed futile and ignorant, a self-defeating path that led them into more trouble but eventually provided them with a sense of agency and dignity against criminalization.

"Dummy Smart" and "Going Dumb"

Darius was a sixteen-year-old African American young man. He understood his social world to be a place in which he was a suspect. His strategy was to devise actions for fooling the system into believing what it expected of him, to break the law. In school, for example, he acted out, even though he was one of the smartest students in the class, what he called "dummy smart":

DARIUS: 'Cause, it's like—you feel me [you understand]? It's like, I still hung out with good people, but, like, there was, you know, like, that kid in class that was hecka bad, but he is dummy smart, feel me? That's how my partners and me is. We was the kids that the teacher be like, "Oh, what's the answer to this?" She try to play us like we don't know what we talking about, but we'll still be able to answer, without hearing nothing she say.

V.R.: Did this get you into trouble?

DARIUS: I got suspended [in ninth grade].

Darius's suspension made him vulnerable to further sanctions, both in school and in the community.

V.R.: How did you do after you started getting suspended, and, like, how did you do in school?

DARIUS: After I got suspended, I came back to school and told the teacher I wanted to do good, or else . . . She thought I was threatening her, but what I meant was that I wanted to change, or else I would be very upset at myself. She sent me out [of school] again. I got angry. I ran into this dude [on the street] that I did not like, but I had kept it cool. I got mad, so I fought him. After that fight, uh, I went to juvenile, 'cause it was a one-on-one fight with me and him. And then, like, my family, I told them to let me fight him on my own, but they thought I wanted them to help me. So we all came together and whooped his ass. Dude came home with a black eye and busted lips, pressed charges. I went to jail the next day. And that's how my juvenile-hall life started, and just kept on going. . . . It started with a suspension, and then I ended up getting out of juvenile hall. . . . And then me just looking like a suspicious person, and then somebody book me again, just for being out there.

V.R.: So tell me that story. So you had gone to juvy, you got on probation, and then you got out, and someone thought you looked suspicious. Tell me that story.

DARIUS: Actually, I was on my way to school last year, around September, and . . . this dude, right here on my alley, was looking for somebody who looked like the person who robbed him the other day, broke his glasses, and took his phone, his backpack, and his school supplies. I was on my way to school on e-one-four [East 14th Avenue], and a dude try to hit me with his car. I started running 'cause I was scared. He was [a police] undercover. He thought I was guilty 'cause I was running, but I was running 'cause I was scared. I kept moving. This nigga comes hella fast, like he was trying to hit me. Next thing I know, he gets out of his car and arrests me for robbing this kid, even though I wasn't even there.

Darius played out deviant politics by performing the role that he believed teachers expected of a young Black man, defiance and ignorance. However, when it was time to turn in his work or to answer a sophisticated question, Darius was prepared, shocking the teacher and throwing her off. This also played out on the streets. In two encounters with police that I observed, Darius put up a tough front and defied their authority. However, when police officers were ready to handcuff him and throw him in the patrol car, Darius's code switched, he began to be cordial and respectful to the officers, and began to recite his legal rights. This also threw off the officers and led them to release him.

Darius had been arrested twice for violating probation: once for talking back to his probation officer and another time for intimidating a clerk at a Foot Locker shoe store. Darius believed that he was criminalized from a young age. His reaction was to mock the system, to make it seem that he was up to no good, despite his innocence. Doing this, in turn, made him feel empowered. However, Darius did not realize that his performance would lead police to accuse him of a crime he did not commit. Darius had mocked and played the teachers and police to a point that led them to impose a criminal label on him. In the end, as Darius described, "If it walk like a duck, talk like a duck, it must be a duck." In mocking the system, young people gained a sense of empowerment. However, these same strategies added more fuel to the criminalization fire. Many of them realized that they were actively involved in adding fuel to the fire. However, they believed that it was worth the negative consequences. Maintaining a sense of dignity—feeling accepted and feeling that their human rights were respected—was a central struggle. The boys consciously chose to fight for their dignity, even if it meant risking their freedom. Striving for "dignity" is a more accurate way to describe the actions of the boys in this study. "Respect" or "honor," which some ethnographers have used to describe a similar process,[22] may, to a mainstream audience, connote a more antagonistic and fatalistic process, in which young men demand acceptance from the world for any and all of their behavior, often through a rogue approach and a negative attitude. Striving for dignity is a more basic struggle, often overlooked, in which boys are demanding the right to be seen as "normal," to be treated as fellow human beings, to have a sense of positive rites, and not to feel criminalized.

Crimes of Resistance

Many of the young men self-consciously "acted stupid" as a strategy to discredit the significance of a system which had excluded and punished them. These deviant politics garnered attention from the youth control complex, frustrating its agents: the police, school personnel, and others. This frustration led to more punishment, which in turn led to a deeper crisis of control in the community. In the end, it was this crisis of control, when institutions were not able to provide a sufficient amount of social order, which the young men consciously perceived to be a successful result of their defiance. As Flaco put it, "They trying to regulate me, right? So if they can't regulate me, then that means they not doing their job. So my job is to not—what's that word?—confirm [conform]."[23]

One of the classic ethnographies on working-class youth resistance is sociologist Paul Willis's book *Learning to Labour.* Willis argues that working-class youths are reproduced as working-class adults, because of their own resistance to the dominant middle-class culture. For Willis, in practicing an "oppositional working class culture," youth contribute to the "maintenance and reproduction of the social order":

It is their own culture which most effectively prepares some working class lads for the manual giving of their labour power; we may say that there is an element of self-damnation in the taking on of subordinate roles in Western Capitalism. However, the damnation is experienced, paradoxically, as true learning, affirmation, appropriation, and as a form of resistance.[24]

Willis complicates agency by explaining that resistance is often futile and self-damaging but that, paradoxically, this resistance brings about a sense of liberation.[25] Among the boys I observed, even though their resistance to criminalization often led them to become more criminalized, they often developed identities of resistance that allowed them to go beyond self-damnation. Karl Marx's classic statement that people make history but not out of circumstances of their own choosing applies well in this case.[26] As the boys created a dignifying identity, despite punitive consequences, they changed the way in which they perceived themselves, determining modes of interaction and influencing the way in which the system "dealt" with them. Their resistance resulted in harsher punishment, more brutality, and longer incarceration terms, yet they also exposed the massive contradictions and failures of social control dominant in their experience with education, law enforcement, and community institutions.

Infrapolitics

Anthropologist James Scott sees marginalized people's oppositional culture, or "everyday acts of resistance," as a massive and effective, yet scattered and unorganized, social movement.[27] He defines "infrapolitics" as invisible, "tactical" subjectivities among oppressed groups, which seem to follow the status quo but in reality are evading power relations. Although this resistance may seem futile or meaningless, Scott maintains that it has historically made possible huge strides in contesting inequality.[28] Labor historian Robin Kelley applies Scott's theories to today's inner city by applying "infrapolitics" to the cultural practices of the Black working class of the twentieth century.[29] For Kelley, marginalized groups in the United States also practice infrapolitics on an everyday basis. These tactical politics are part of "a dissident political culture that manifests itself in daily conversations, folklore, jokes, songs, and other cultural practices" deployed by oppressed groups, which at first glance seem to maintain an appearance of deviance or absurdity.[30] According to Kelley, even though this infrapolitical mask worn by the Black working class has, on the surface, affirmed the dominant group's myth that the Black working class is passive-aggressive, lazy, criminal, or conniving, at a deeper level, this strategy has managed to transform power relations by providing agency, empowerment, and a voice to those with few resources. It is a strategy that exists outside of "established organizations or organized social movements." Yet, according to Kelley, it is the foundation for what forms social movements of the masses. Kelley provides Malcolm X as an example; Malcolm X's contribution to the civil rights movement could not have been possible without his participation in infrapolitics as a youth. Even though Malcolm X himself, in his autobiography, dismisses his own youthful experience of performing the zoot-suit as a useless negative past of wearing "ghetto adornments," his "participation in the underground subculture of Black working-class youth during the war was not a detour on the road to political consciousness, but rather an essential element of his radicalization."[31] Malcolm X's "ghetto adornments" and culture were an essential building block for his development as a political activist. In the same vein, the "irrational" acts of defiance that the boys in this study deployed may have, at the very least, provided them a sense of dignity and empowerment, and, at best, these acts could become seeds that sprouted into a more critical political and intellectual analysis of the system that criminalized them.

Making the System Believe Its Own Hype

The boys consistently chose to act "bad" in circumstances in which adults expected them to act "good." Almost all the acts that led to an arrest for violating probation were committed as conscious acts of resistance; in the boys' account, they knew they were facing very severe consequences but decided to break the rules in order to make a point. This may have been their way of resisting what they perceived to be unfair treatment and punishment. These transgressions served as a resource for feeling empowered and for gaining redress for the humiliation, stigma, and punishment that they encountered. Because they reported that they committed their transgressions as a way of "getting back at the system," as Ronny explained, I am calling these acts *deviant politics,* by which I mean the political actions—the resistance—that youth labeled by society as deviant use to respond to punishment that they ubiquitously encounter.

At a cultural level, these deviant politics played out through music, dance, and dress. A youth cultural formation, the "Hyphy Movement," became prevalent among the boys. The Hyphy Movement was a subcultural, hip-hop movement started by youth in the San Francisco Bay Area around the year 2000. Underground artists from the Bay Area had rapped about "being hyphy" for years. Eventually, a few of their songs became popular in the national hip-hop scene. Beyond being a discourse used in rap music to indicate a new kind of "cool," hyphy also became a youth cultural practice. *Hyphy* was defined by young people in many ways, and the youths provided the following definitions: acting out, defying authority, breaking rules, being antagonistic, and embracing disreputable behavior as everyday practice. For young people, this was a style that gave meaning to their experiences of marginalization, of being seen by society as "dumb," "stupid," and "hyphy" (hyperactive, crazy, out of control). Some of these practices included dancing in the most ridiculous manner possible, standing on top of a car as the car drove off with no driver to control it, known as "ghost riding," and acting "retarded" in class or on the street in the presence of authority figures who expected otherwise. In a sense, these young people had consciously internalized this disrepute and had made it pleasurable, aesthetic, meaningful, and a form of resilience. As Darius explained, "If you gonna pretend I am dumb, then I'ma pretend I'm dumb. Then you gonna get tricked. Then you gonna— you feel me?—get confused. Then I'ma pull a hustle on you, and you not gonna know what hit you." Darius's understanding of himself as being "dummy smart" came from his subcultural style: hyphy. He was attempting to negotiate the negative aspects of hyphy and give them a positive twist: that you can "act dumb" and still "be smart."

Hyphy was also a hip-hop dance style that involved spontaneous, sporadic, and "dumb" dance moves. Young people danced as if they had no inhibitions; moves were meant to appear ridiculous. Youths used the following language to describe it: "get dumb," "go stupid," "ride the yellow bus." "Riding the yellow bus" referred to the students who were in special education and were picked up from home on a yellow bus. One famous Oakland rapper, Mistah F.A.B, wore a helmet and drove around in a yellow bus so as to appear what he called "retarded." The boys would spontaneously "act retarded" in various contexts, including in the classroom, in stores, and on the street. This would throw off authority figures and make them believe that the youths were ready to commit a crime or destroy property. When police were called in, the boys toned it down and acted "normal." This process of acting up and "going dumb" was a way for young people to resist punitive social control and to play on the fears and expectations that authority figures had. Doing this, in turn, developed a sense of agency, empowerment, and accomplishment in the boys.

This subculture was also deeply embedded in school practices. Some of the boys would spontaneously "act ridiculous" or "go dumb" in the middle of class or in the middle of the school yard. Students would "go dumb" in front of teachers or administrators who had treated them as such. In other words, they played a game and flipped on its head the very stigma which had been imposed on them from a very young age. Eight of the boys in this study reported having been placed in special education classes from a young age. All of them believed that they were not special education students and that the system was using special education classes as a form of control, to discipline them for acting up in the "regular" classroom. This subculture may have been born from the frustration with society's demand for young Black and Latino males to succeed in the mainstream, despite the many structural and punitive barriers that prohibit them from doing so. It may very well be that the Hyphy Movement began as a cultural response to systematic structural processes of neglect, pathologization, and criminalization of an entire community of poor young people in the Bay Area. The Hyphy Movement, and many of the "crimes of resistance" that accompanied it, can be understood as a form of resistance that consciously made the system believe its own hype, when young people acted "dumb" and "criminal" as a means to an end, to feel a sense of freedom and dignity. This process is similar to postcolonial theorist and psychoanalyst Frantz Fanon's explanation of the social-psychological condition which colonized subjects found themselves to be in: "I had rationalized the world and the world had rejected me on the basis of color prejudice. Since no agreement was possible on the level of reason, I threw myself back toward unreason."[32] Moreover, the boys developed a dissident culture that provided self-generated escapes from punishment. Education scholar Jannelle Dance argues in her book *Tough Fronts*, "The mainstream bias of schooling can change temporary, survivalistic attitudes into firm political convictions."[33] She shows that African American male youths develop "tough fronts," performances of being mean and man enough, not because they are pathological or because they resist receiving an education but rather because they have tried and tried to succeed in the system but have been systematically excluded. Some of the boys in this study also described the streets and the subcultures developed on the streets as self-empowering. For some of the boys, these practices became political convictions.

Youth Mobilization against Punitive Social Control

As the youths in this study experienced firsthand the punitive grip of the state, they fought back with the few tools they could find in their social settings, often with only "weapons of the weak," like crimes of resistance, at their disposal. Instead of remaining passive and allowing the system to shame, criminalize, and exclude them, the boys continued to produce scattered acts of resistance. From stealing at the store to cussing out police officers who had once brutalized them, the boys engaged themselves in deviant politics.

While these political convictions can be read as a potential solution for the dire conditions of criminalization that many marginalized people face, we should not romanticize the petty crimes or rebellious acts committed by the boys in this study. Boys who resisted often suffered real and drastic consequences. Sometimes, they did not even realize that they were resisting. Often, they were simply, as they called it, "getting stupid," meaning that they acted "bad" for the sake of being "bad." Moreover, deviant politics were often messy—one example is the perpetuation of misogyny discussed in the following chapter. These kinds of practices had few long-term positive outcomes for any of the boys in the study.

However, these deviant politics may have been a means to an end, the development of oppositional consciousness and political activism, which, in turn, empowered some boys to become agents who fought to dismantle punitive social control and transform other forms of oppression.[34] This is what happened to nine of the boys in this study, who became involved in an organization that protested police brutality and what they called, using feminist scholar Angela Davis's term, "the prison industrial complex," a system of private and government agencies that economically benefit from the incarceration of marginalized populations. These boys had joined grassroots organizations in Oakland after meeting community organizers who had recruited them because of their status as what the community organizers called "survivors of the juvenile justice system." The boys related to and recognized this analysis of the system, which compelled them to join the community organizers in meetings and marches that protested police brutality and the building of incarceration facilities.

During a revisit in 2009, I found that all nine of these young men, four Black and five Latino, continued to participate in formal dissent. They took part in marches, vigils, and meetings that demanded justice for the killing of Oscar Grant by a police officer. Grant was unarmed and handcuffed when the officer shot him in the back. The incident was caught on video and became national headline news. Although none of the boys knew Oscar Grant, all nine boys described Oscar Grant as "one of us." Kobe described a rally that he attended after the killing:

> The march for *my boy* Oscar Grant, man, was downtown on Wednesday, that Wednesday when we was riding it [marching] or whatever, and we gave up. We was in, like, a little part of, like, an alley street, so the crew I was with, we gave in. We was gonna lay down, and they [police] came up to us and was hitting us in the head with the guns and pinned their knees to our backs and twisted my arm. I thought he was gonna break it.

The fact that Kobe continued to be brutalized by police, now as a protestor, bolstered his worldview that all police are part of a system of criminalization and brutality. Prior to Grant's killing, many of these boys had been brutalized or had witnessed friends or family brutalized or killed by police. Eleven of the boys claimed to know a friend or family member who had been severely injured or killed by police. Smoky Man reflected on why he became politically active:

I fight 'cause all the stuff they been doing. They [the police] took [killed] two of my cousins in 2004, for no reason. They came out of a store, and they thought they had some drugs or some guns on them, and they shot both of them. One of them died at the scene. One of them dies like a week later in the hospital. They had no right to do that, so this is payback, man. Anything I saw and been through with the cops, you can't tell me it's a good cop.

Fourteen of the Latino and nine of the Black boys in the study commented on the racial implications of criminalization. They all believed that, despite having differences on the streets with the other racial group, there existed a social order in which interracial conflict was rare, but so too was racial solidarity. The majority of the time the boys in this study found ways to avoid negative interactions with the other racial group, by following certain rules of avoidance and respect. Despite their close living and recreational proximity to one another, Black and Latino boys operated under a "give and take" social order and rarely had conflict with one another.[35]

Whenever the boys in this study talked about racial solidarity, it was often linked to the struggle against criminalization and police brutality. Jordan's perspective is representative of the perspective held by the nine boys who became politically active: "I'm speaking towards the Black perspective, but I understand they treat the Mexicans the same way! They treat the Mexicans the same way, the same way: they all affiliated with gangs. They feel any Mexicans are in gangs—you know what I'm saying? They mess with Mexicans all the same ways they discriminate Black people." Although each racial group may have experienced criminalization in unique ways, what I found with the boys in this study is that they believed that their experiences were very similar. This belief, in turn, generated a racial solidarity among boys who had been criminalized. They held a worldview that informed them that "Mexicans and Blacks are treated in the same way." This feeling of collective racialization facilitated the process by which nine out of the forty boys in this study participated in formal political action against police brutality.[36] Meetings and marches that the boys participated in were multiracial, including Blacks, Latinos, and Whites.

The process of being criminalized developed oppositional identities in all the boys in this study. Some enacted this opposition by committing "irrational" transgressions, such as "going dumb" or disobeying their probation officers. A few boys developed a deeper sense of dissent by participating in marches, protests, and meetings aimed at ending police brutality. While criminalization had many detrimental consequences for the boys, for many it also sparked a deep desire to know why they were targeted, and some developed a keen sense of dissent, often informal and occasionally more formal.

Prominent social-movements scholar Pamela Oliver reminds us that, in the context of mass incarceration generated by the repression of the social movements of the mid-twentieth century, we have to pay attention to the new and unique forms of resistance and mobilization taking place among marginalized populations. She argues that among these populations dissent may also be expressed in crime:

> There is individual dissent and collective crime, and both are common. The more repressive a system, the more dissent takes the form of individual, often anonymous, acts of resistance. . . . We need to ask how oppressed people can gain redress under conditions of extreme repression, and to understand the forms that resistance can take when the possibility of direct resistance is blocked.[37]

In an environment where there were few formal avenues for expressing dissent toward a system, which the boys believed to be extremely repressive, they developed forms of resistance that they believed could change, even if only temporarily, the outcome of their treatment. The boys believed they had gained redress for the punitive social control they had encountered by adopting a subculture of resistance based on fooling the system and by committing crimes of resistance, which made no sense to the system but were fully recognizable to those who had been misrecognized and criminalized. The paradox of punitive social control is that it socially incapacitates too many marginalized populations; at the same time, this system of repression may just be the catalyst for the next wave of massive social movements from below.

6

Proving Manhood

Masculinity as a Rehabilitative Tool

> Willis too easily converts the culture of these young men into a seamless form of resistance, ignoring or textually diminishing internal contradictions such as the male chauvinism and sexism on which the culture of "resistance" is founded.
> —José Limón, *Dancing with the Devil*, 1994

> I'm sicker than SARS, I'm higher than Mars, and I treat my bitch like an ATM card.
> —Mac Dre, "Feelin' Myself," 2004[1]

One late afternoon, Spider, Big Rob, and Bullet passed the time behind a warehouse that bordered the neighborhood park. Bullet made fun of Spider's haircut. Spider had shaved off all his hair except for the back end of his head, where he left a long ponytail. The boys referred to this hairstyle as a "mongolian." The style had been adopted by one of the two largest Mexican American gangs in California, the Norteños, or Northerners. Spider had to be brave to wear this hairstyle, because it immediately marked him as a gang member to rivals and police. However, despite his willingness to show his bravado and manhood to his friends, they found ways to challenge his masculinity. "You look like my sister's Barbie doll, the one that got chewed up by a dog!" Bullet exclaimed, as he covered his mouth. Spider grabbed his pony tail, pumped out his chest, balled his right fist up, and said, "Bullet, why you covering yo' mouth? That's 'cause you got some crack-head teeth." Big Rob intervened: "Remember what the cop said about your hair the other day? He said you look like that bitch that walks around here looking for dope!" The boys' social relations with one another and with community members were saturated with expressions and discourses of manhood.

Criminal justice and disciplinary officials at school often participated in challenging the boys' understanding of masculinity. In this chapter, I argue that beyond the morals and values of manhood which the boys learned from being on the streets, criminalization, specifically encounters with police, juvenile hall, and probation officers, also offered them masculinity-making resources that they used to develop a sense of manhood. One consequence of criminalization and punitive social control for the boys was the development of a specific set of gendered practices. Another outcome of this pervasive criminal justice contact was the production of a hypermasculinity, which obstructed desistance, social relations, and social mobility.

As the boys moved on to another conversation, my mind wandered off, distracted by my thoughts about their future prospects. Perhaps if they were offered another alternative for proving their manhood, this would be sufficient to change their life courses, I thought. My absent-minded moment was quickly interrupted by Big Rob's thick adolescent voice, which occasionally broke into a high pitch: "Here comes those fucking pigs again." I looked toward the park entrance, where a late-model, black and white patrol car rolled into the park toward us. All of us, except Spider, pulled our hands out of our pockets and stood in a position of submission, with our hands open to show that we didn't have a weapon on us, with our eyes looking at the ground to exhibit a nonthreatening stance, and with our bodies slouched over to show that we were not in a position to run away. Spider postured differently. He raised his chest, stared at the officers, murmured curse words at them, and kept his hands in his pockets. He did this to prove himself to his peers and, as I suggested about Jose in chapter 3, in part to intimidate the police officers to avoid future conflicts with them.[2]

This time, Spider's strategy did not work. The officers, one White and one Latino, got out of the patrol car and walked toward us. They said, "Face the wall." The White officer stood by a tree about ten feet away from us, with his hand on his pistol. The Latino officer walked up to each of us and proceeded to search us. He found a knife in Spider's pocket. The officer took him to the patrol car and threw him in the back seat. I intervened, asking the officer why they had stopped us in the first place. After a few seconds of silence, I turned around to face the officer, looking him in the eyes; he reacted by yelling, "Get the fuck back on the wall!" Once I turned around, he handcuffed me and threw me in the car with Spider. Although police officers had the right to conduct pat-downs for weapons if they deemed the boys "reasonably suspicious," they often broke the law by pulling down the boys' pants and emptying their pockets, looking for drugs but under the pretense that they were looking for weapons. They hit boys who disrespected their authority. In my observations, officers constantly violated many of the boys' civil rights. Although I informed the boys that they had the right to report police abuse, many were pessimistic. I learned why, when one day I reported a police officer who had searched my car, ripped part of my door's interior while searching for illegal substances, and then thrown me against his patrol car. When I went to discuss the matter with the officer's superior, he told me, "He has the officers' bill of rights protecting him. I can't tell you what we did with your case." I was never given any further information on the case. The boys often attempted to get legal help for their experiences with the police. However, when they discussed the matter with attorneys, the attorneys would always ask, "Do you have proof?" Besides black eyes and bruises, which were not considered enough evidence, it was the boys' word against the word of the police.

Once in the patrol car, I asked Spider why he was carrying a knife. He told me that Luis, one of the boys in the neighborhood, had disrespected him. Luis had crossed out Spider's name on a wall Spider had tagged up a few days before and then written "*puto*" (fag) over Spider's name.[3] Spider was determined to regain Luis's respect by confronting him. I asked Spider if he intended to stab Luis. He told me that he wanted to "*dale en la madre*" (kick his ass), but his intention was not to stab him. A few days later, I witnessed Spider encounter Luis. Spider went up to Luis and told him off. Luis told Spider that he was not the person who had called him a *puto*. Spider told him, "The next time I see that shit, I'ma slap the shit out of you." Luis continued walking.

During the three years I spent in the field, I regularly encountered knives and guns, often hidden in paper bags and thrown on the curb five feet away from where the boys hung out. Over the years, I asked youth that I studied and encountered, "If I wanted to purchase a gun right now, how much money would it cost me and how long would it take?" All of them responded similarly. They laughed or looked at me funny, as if I was kidding, because in their minds, I should have known how cheap and easy it was to get a gun. They told me that it would cost $150 to $300, depending on the caliber, and that I could get a gun within a few hours. Although many of the boys had easy access to weapons, they rarely used them. The boys understood the potential repercussions of holding a gun. As Slick described, "If you got a thang [gun] on you, you better be ready to use it, and use it all the way." The boys' clear understanding of the danger of killing, being killed, or ending up in prison for life, along with a strong regard for the life of others, deterred the majority from using the guns that were easily accessible to them. Three of the boys were eventually arrested for gun possession or assault with a deadly weapon, and four self-reported using a gun or knife on someone. Although it was difficult to find out whether a youngster had assaulted anyone with a knife or gun unless he was convicted, after a few months of interviews and observations, I was given signals in conversations about who was "putting in work"—committing violence against rivals. I also found out through community members when youths from rival areas had been assaulted. Overall, relative to the high concentration of guns and knives in the lives of these boys, I found that the youths did not typically take up arms and assault others. In most cases, conflicts usually found resolution—or at least a stalemate—in harsh conversations. Even in Oakland, a city that in 2007 was ranked the fourth-most-violent city in the nation, street-oriented young men often found nonviolent ways to deal with conflict.[4]

Conversations often involved references to guns as analogies for resolving conflict and demonstrating manhood. Some examples: "I'ma pistol whip that mothafucka"; "I'll bust a cap in his ass"; "My gat will do the talking." Although the boys most often avoided guns and only discussed guns as metaphors, schools and police often suspected that they were carrying guns or that they were ready to use a gun and treated them as if they had guns in their possession. Misrecognition of subcultural style, talk, and gendered practices also often led to criminalization.

As Spider continued his story about wanting to scare Luis, the White police officer sat inside the patrol car to check our records. As we waited for the officer to gather information on Spider and me, he asked Spider, "What the fuck are you doing carrying a knife? Don't you know I can take you to jail for this?" Rehearsed by the reasoning he had given me earlier, Spider told the officer that he had been disrespected by Luis and that he wanted to fight him but was scared he would get jumped by Luis's older brother. The officer turned to Spider and said, "You want to be a man and get some respect? Get a fucking job! You think this stupid shit is gonna make you a man? It's gonna get you locked up." The officer found no warrants for our arrest. He looked at me and said, "I don't know what the fuck you do, but you need to teach these kids how to be men." The officers drove off. We wiped our hands, shook off our clothes, and talked about what had just happened.

This vignette gives a glimpse of the heavily gendered landscape that the boys in this study navigated. Such scenes show how interactions with peers, police officers, and other social-control agents are often about constructing and contesting masculinity. Whether it was Spider's proving his manhood by premeditating a fight to regain respect or his standing up to police or his peers' questioning his manhood because he looked like a doll, or the officers' urging Spider to prove his manhood by getting a job and asking me to teach him how to do so, or my challenging the officer to treat the boys with respect, we all participated in the making of manhood for Spider.

Criminologist and masculinity scholar James Messerschmidt argues that men are constantly faced with "masculinity challenges" and that this process is what leads to crime:

> Such masculinity challenges are contextual interactions that result in masculine degradation. Masculinity challenges arise from interactional threats and insults from peers, teachers, parents, and from situationally defined masculine expectations that are not achievable. Both, in various ways, proclaim a man or boy subordinate in contextually defined mascu-

line terms. . . . Masculinity challenges may motivate social action towards masculine resources (e.g., bullying, fighting) that correct the subordinating social situation, and various forms of crime can be the result.[5]

Crime is one of the avenues that men turn to in developing, demonstrating, and communicating their manhood. Indeed, criminal activity constitutes a gendered practice that can be used to communicate the parameters of manhood. As such, crime is more likely when men need to prove themselves and when they are held accountable to a strict set of expectations. Furthermore, sociologists West and Fenstermaker contend that this accountability—the gendered actions that people develop in response to what they perceive others will expect of them—is encountered in interactions between individuals and institutions: "While individuals are the ones who do gender, the process of rendering something accountable is both interactional and institutional in character. . . . Gender is . . . a mechanism whereby situated social action contributes to the reproduction of social structure."[6] Conceptualizing gender as structured action, a social process that changes based on interactions with specific types of institutions, in turn, allows us to explore how the criminal justice system shapes the development of specific forms of masculinity.

The young men in this study faced constant interrogation about their manhood on the streets. Questions such as "Is he really a homey?" and "Is he really a man?" if answered in the negative, typically resulted in stigmatization or victimization. At the core of growing up in their community, the boys felt a constant necessity to prove their manhood. Institutions, also, often challenged boys' masculinity in the process of attempting to reform them. Examples included being told that they were not man enough for having committed crime or that being in the criminal justice system meant that they risked being emasculated. The boys, in turn, responded to gendered institutional practices through their own gendered practices. Young men who did not follow this masculinity code ended up putting themselves in a vulnerable position both on the street and in the institutions they navigated.

Many of the collateral consequences of the criminalization and punitive social control of the boys in this study have already been noted in this book: constant surveillance and stigma imposed by schools, community centers, and families; permanent criminal credentials that exclude Black and Latino males from the labor market; and the boys' mistrust and resentment toward police and the rest of the criminal justice system.[7] In this study, I found that an additional consequence of enhanced policing, surveillance, and punitive treatment of marginalized boys was the development of a specific set of gendered practices, which were heavily influenced by interactions with police, detention facilities, and probation officers. Interactions with the youth control complex were heavily gendered: encounters with White female teachers created an "angry male of color" attacking a "White damsel in distress" phenomenon; encounters with police were often a contest between who was a "bigger man"; and probation officers interacted in either a motherly or a heavy-handed way. These patterns of punishment provided the young men with meanings of masculinity that influenced their decisions to commit crime and engage in violence.

Whereas race determined how a young person was treated in the criminal justice pipeline, masculinity played a role in whether they desisted or recidivated as they navigated through the system. One of the outcomes of pervasive criminal justice contact for young Black and Latino men was the production of a hypermasculinity. Angela Harris defines hypermasculinity as an "exaggerated exhibition of physical strength and personal aggression," which is often a response to a gender threat "expressed through physical and sexual domination of others."[8] Drawing on this definition, I contend that the criminal justice system encourages expressions of hypermasculinity by threatening and confusing young men's masculinity. This, in turn, leads them to rely on domination through violence, crime, and a school and criminal justice counterculture. In essence, detrimental forms of masculinity are partly developed through youths' interaction with police, juvenile hall, and probation officers.

Masculinity, Criminalization, and Punitive Social Control

Each of us shapes our behavior according to gendered expectations, and each of us is subject to a system of accountability that is gendered, raced, and classed.[9] The boys in this study were inculcated into a set of hypermasculine expectations which often led them to behaviors that conflicted with the structures of dominant institutions. Many of the boys articulated and performed a "man's expectations," based on the environment they were in.[10] On the street, they would take on a tough persona, posing and acting out hyperaggressive behaviors. In their explanations, these acts were an essential tool for surviving on the street: "You can't act weak, or you'll get taken out," Jose explained. "I can't act like a bitch, . . . 'cause if I do, suckas will try to swoop up on me and take me out. So I gotta handle my business. Even if I am trying to change, I can't look weak," Tyrell explained. In front of probation officers and police, the boys had two choices: play out a masculinity battle or submit to their authority and act passively. This led many of the boys to believe that they lived in a lose-lose predicament. If they acted tough, maybe the officers would hesitate to harass them, but, inevitably, the police might arrest them. However, if the boys acted passively, they would develop resentment and end up taking out their frustration about being humiliated on themselves or others, through drug use or violence. Different environments provided the boys with limited and limiting resources with which to construct their manhood. The boys would often have to default to the manhood that they knew best, those masculine resources that the streets had to offer. These forms of masculinity were often the only concrete bricks the boys had to build their houses of manhood.

To be assigned "real man" status by relevant others and institutions, men must pass multiple litmus tests among peers, family, and these institutions. Masculinity tests, or codes, relevant to delinquent boys, were identified by sociologists as early as the 1920s. In 1924, sociologist Edwin Sutherland discussed how boys were taught to be "rough and tough," rendering them more likely than girls to become delinquent.[11] In 1947, sociologist Talcott Parsons noted that at the very core of American adolescence, an aggressive masculinity was at play: "Western men are peculiarly susceptible to the appeal of an adolescent type of assertively masculine behavior, . . . to revolt against the routine aspects of the primary institutionalized masculine role of sober responsibility, meticulous respect for the rights of others, and tender affection towards women."[12] The boys in this study learned early on to prove their manhood using the few resources made available to them in the social contexts in which they persisted.

Elijah Anderson describes the "young male syndrome" as the perceived, expected, and often necessary pressure to perform a tough, violent, and deviant manhood in order to receive and maintain respect.[13] Psychologist Sandra W. Pyke finds that masculinity is expressed differently by men of varied class positions.[14] While wealthy men can prove their masculinity through the ability to make money and consume products that make them "manly," poor young men use toughness, violence, and survival as a means of proving their masculinity and resilience. Sociologist Nikki Jones has found that young women also use masculinity as a resource for protecting themselves and gaining respect. However, Jones finds that young women are caught in a double bind; they have to act tough on the streets and use masculinity resources, while, at the same time, they have to act "good" in order to meet gendered expectations. They are caught "between good and ghetto."[15] Although these young women are not fighting for "manhood," they are fighting for respect and security, and one of the vehicles to maintain this respect is masculinity. An informal interview with a nineteen-year-old Latina named Kenya, who was previously in a gang but had turned her life around and was now trying to help some of the boys in this study, was representative of the toughness exhibited by the few young women who were visible on the streets where the boys hung out:

> V.R.: You work with these boys; they are disrespectful of women at times. How do you deal with it?
>
> KENYA: I . . . had an understanding of feminism before I had a term for it. . . . You see young women in urban areas fighting for it in different ways, without the terms to define it, but it's still the same thing, fighting. . . . I had to fight dudes. . . . I've fought hella dudes. . . . That's what made hella people scared of me. [She fist fought with males to prove herself.] . . . And, even though he won physically, the story got around that he was a punk for fighting a girl. One time, my friend got raped by this dude. So we beat the shit out of him and took a baseball bat with nails in it to his ass, . . . taking justice into our own hands. I mean, not justice, 'cause beating his ass is not enough. . . . It sent a message out there that . . . that shit, it's just not acceptable.

Observing Kenya and other street-oriented young women interact with the boys made me realize that masculinity does not always correspond to biological sex; instead, it is a resource used by young people in specific settings to accomplish specific goals. Kenya took on the most masculine of boys to gain respect, and she acquired justice by giving a man a taste of his own medicine. In my three years observing the boys, I noticed at least six girls who had taken on these masculinity resources to accomplish their goals. Therefore, although my study was limited in that I did not formally observe young women, I did find that masculinity was indeed used by some young women to survive on the streets and to resist the criminalization that they also encountered.

Toughness, dominance, and the willingness to resort to violence to resolve interpersonal conflicts are central characteristics of masculine identity.[16] Sociologists Kimmel and Mahler argue that most violent youths are not psychopaths but, rather, "overconformists to a particular normative construction of masculinity."[17] I find that by studying these "overconforming" violent and delinquent youths, we uncover clues as to how masculinity is developed in relation to institutional constructions of manhood within the criminal justice system. Mainstream institutions and the criminal justice system expect a masculine conformity that emphasizes hard work, law abidance, and an acceptance of subordinate social conditions. These institutions expect boys to embrace a "positive" working-class masculinity. Many of the boys in this study were familiar with this form of masculinity from growing up with fathers or father figures who worked hard, respected authority, and accepted their subordinate status in society. Some of the young men attempted to embrace this masculinity as a means to reform. However, when they tried to use this form of masculinity in order to transform their lives, they found a dearth of viable jobs in which they could prove they were hard workers. Kimmel explains the context in which proving manhood through work has become jeopardized in times of economic crisis: "Deindustrialization made men's hold on the successful demonstration of masculinity increasingly tenuous; there are fewer and fewer self-made successes and far more self-blaming failures."[18] The boys were consistently told by various adults in the community that a "real man" took responsibility for his own actions. Although this message may have been important for the boys to hear, it seemed that this was one of the only rehabilitative tools that the system used to address the negative behaviors. The boys in turn internalized this logic and often blamed themselves not only for the "bad choices" they made but also for the structural circumstances in which they lived. In other words, the youth control complex was successful at convincing young men that poverty, racism, and neglect were products of their actions. The boys often blamed themselves for "looking and acting" like criminals even when they had not transgressed the law.

The boys also expressed that respecting authority meant accepting their criminalization and, by doing so, giving up their dignity. In addition, they came to realize that embracing this "positive" working-class masculinity did not provide the proper resources to survive on the streets, a place to which they constantly returned. In attempts to manage young men's criminality, institutions developed practices heavily influenced by masculinity. In response, the boys in this study became socialized to specific meanings of manhood that were diametrically opposed to those expected by dominant institutions of control. Thus, gendered interactions with the criminal justice system placed the boys in a double bind. Most bought into the system's ideals of reform by attempting to become "hardworking men." However, frustration with the lack of viable employment and guidance opportunities led them to leap into the seductive arms of hypermasculinity. This double bind was partially generated by the criminal justice system's involvement in the making of hypermasculinity.

Masculinity and Criminalization

Criminalization intensified the boys' conflicts over manhood, and they ran a collision course with the criminal justice system's demands of passivity, compliance, and conformity to a subjugated, racialized social status. Expectations of passivity and compliance, unaccompanied by a change in social conditions, engendered hopelessness in the boys and an inability to function both in mainstream institutions and on the streets, where survival skills were intricately connected to hypermasculinity. Criminalization, policing, and the criminal justice system's pressures on the young men forced them to make a choice: comply or become "hard." The boys, who embraced the system's gendered expectations of them, often experienced a negative change in their social relations with peers. When they complied with authority figures, they felt impotent on the streets, where they became vulnerable to ridicule or victimization. This vulnerability was created not because the other boys rejected a "hard-working" identity but because these boys observed their peers fail in obtaining employment or becoming a better man. The system had dichotomized manhood. It forced the boys to choose between "good" working-class manhood or hypermasculinity and did not allow them room to shift between the two. The reality was that in order to persist on the streets and to successfully desist, they had to learn to employ both forms of manhood.

Although some boys chose the "right path," they were unable to obtain employment or eliminate the criminal stigma marked onto them by the system. When they failed to comply, they were harassed or arrested. When they complied, they were seen as "snitches" by their friends, because police and probation officers often forced these boys to interact with them in public, as a means of demonstrating innocence and reform. The young men further encountered criminalization through gendered interactions as they were pipelined into the system. The first point of contact with hypermasculinity through criminal justice was with the police.

Police

Police officers are themselves embedded in a logic that embraces masculinity. For example, criminologists Prokos and Padavic have found that police academies train officers to practice a rogue and hostile masculinity. Male officers "equate men and masculinity with guns, crime-fighting, a combative personality, . . . and a desire to work in high crime areas."[19] This positioning reverberates in the inner city. Legal scholar Angela Harris explains, "Police officers in poor minority neighborhoods may come to see themselves as law enforcers in a community of savages, as outposts of the law in a jungle."[20] In this context, punitive police treatment of men of color is not only racial violence; it is also gender violence. Harris continues, "Violent acts committed by men, whether these acts break the law or are designed to uphold it, are often a way of demonstrating the perpetrator's manhood. I call this kind of violence 'gender violence' and assert that men as well as women may be its victims."[21] Young people in Oakland encountered this "gender violence" regularly from police on the street, at school, at community centers, and in front of their apartment complexes. The boys often became victims of police officers who were attempting to uphold the law. Officers wanted to teach the young men lessons, by effeminizing them: they manhandled them, constantly called them "little bitches," humiliated them in front of female peers, challenged them to fights, and otherwise brutalized them:

CASTRO: Dude [the officer] was pointing his gun. "I give up, I give up." He hit him [Castro's friend] with a stick and broke his arm, and this other fool had his knee on my neck. All 'cause we were smoking some weed. . . . They beat us down and call us "little bitches."

RAFA: They kick your ass, pistol whip you, even try to kill you. . . . Them bustas [cowards] just trying to prove themselves, you feel me? They trying to prove they are more manly than us, but if they didn't have guns or jails, they would end up being the bitches.

Gendered police interactions and gendered violence began at an early age.[22] The boys consistently reported that they had been taught by disciplinary authorities at school and by police, over the years, that to be a man meant to stand up for themselves without relying on the police; to be a man was to learn to take a beating from police whenever they talked back to them or were caught committing a crime; to be a man was to desist from committing crime by being a responsible man and resisting the seductions of street life.

Eighteen-year-old Franky, a young man who was born in San Francisco, who was on the cusp of graduating from an alternative high school, and whose parents were from El Salvador, pinpointed the very moment when he had to demonstrate his manhood to authority figures. He was driving his mother and two sisters from Little Caesars Pizza restaurant. They were celebrating his five-year-old sister's birthday. Franky had played a father figure in the family since he was a little boy; his father had abandoned them when he was five. Since he was nine, Franky remembered dropping off and picking up his two sisters at daycare and school. He cooked for them and protected them when bullies picked on them at school. His mother worked in San Ramon, an affluent city fifteen miles away, over the hills from Oakland. Franky's mother did not drive. Her daily public-transportation journey took two hours and fifteen minutes, each way. She left home at six in the morning and returned at ten o'clock at night, six days a week. She worked as a house cleaner. The woman for whom she worked paid her sporadically and constantly docked her pay. Franky estimated that, in a good week, his mother made about ten dollars an hour. He decided to work to help his mother with the bills. One summer, he helped an uncle who was a carpenter. At seventeen, he accomplished a lifetime dream: to help his mother with her commute. With the cash he had saved, he purchased a 1988 Nissan Maxima for fifteen hundred dollars. Within a few months, this young man who had been responsible—attending school, caring for his sisters, saving money to buy a car for the family—saw the bounty of his hard work disappear.

> We were coming home from pizza. I parked the car. I turned off the car. I got out of the car, and dude [a police office] turned on his lights. He came up to me, and he pulled out a gun on me. I got out the car and was like, "What the hell?" And then I got back in the car. And he said, "You don't have your lights on." And I said, "Of course I don't have my lights on. I parked the car and turned them off and was about to get out." . . . He's like, "Step out the car." So we did. And my mom stepped out the car. And dude pointed the gun at her. And I was like, "What the hell?" And then I got out the car hella fast to help my mom. I thought she was gonna get shot. And then he tried to grab his gun, but then he grabbed his thing [baton], and he was gonna run up. And I got the adrenaline and pushed him away. He knocked me down hella fast, and he had the stick right here in my neck hella hard. And he arrested me and took me to jail. I had a bruise right here and went to court and told them he hit me, but he told them I pushed him. . . . When I went to the hospital, dude fractured something right here [points to collar bone]. . . . I was in jail for four months, and they took the car away [to impound] for thirty days. I had to leave it there because it cost more to take it out then what I paid—the only car my family had.

Franky's attempt to protect his mother backfired, leading him deep into the criminal justice system. Franky believed that the police officer was wrong in pointing a gun at his mother. Therefore, he was willing to take a bullet or go to jail in an attempt to protect her. In this case, Franky's attempt to contest the officer's rogue behavior led him to become constructed as an aggressor. The officer's gender violence prevailed.

In my observations, I learned that at the epicenter of police-youth interactions, hypermasculinity prevailed: it was taught and learned; it was challenged and embraced; it was fruitful and poisonous. In attempting to teach the young men lessons on being law-abiding gentlemen, officers used a brutal masculinity that inculcated a toughness, manliness, and hypermasculinity in the boys. This hypermasculinity often influenced the young men to perpetrate defiance, crime, and violence, sanctioning police to brutalize or arrest them. Once these young men were in confinement, they adapted a masculinity that made them feel protected not only from the streets and police but also from violence in confinement.

Incarceration

While the young men were incarcerated, they reported being forced to overemphasize their masculinity. Big Rob illustrated this point. He had been arrested for driving a stolen car. Rob's specialty was stealing cars and selling them to chop shops, garages that dismantled the cars and sold them for parts. Rob was driving a 1987 Buick Grand National when he was arrested. Upon arrival at the county's juvenile-justice facility, Rob was stripped and cavity searched. His possessions were confiscated, and he was provided with a dark-blue jumpsuit with the words "Property of Alameda County" printed on it. "The guard told me, 'Take a shower and make sure you don't drop the soap, boy!' I didn't know what he was talking about. It wasn't until I asked some dude that I figured out what he meant." ("Don't drop the soap" was a reference to rape by other inmates in detention showers.) Rob was placed in a cafeteria where about twenty or so boys were congregated; they stared Rob down, giving him dirty looks. A few boys walked up to him and asked, "Where you from?" Rob told them, "Dirty thirties." They responded with the names of their "turfs." "I had to act hard. I balled up my fist and was ready to knock a nigga out." Rob eventually got into a fight while protecting himself from an attack. He was sent to solitary confinement, allowed outside his tiny cell with a cement bed only to take a shower and call home. The officer who supervised his cell commented, "You gonna learn how to be a man the hard way." Once released, Rob brought this repertoire back to the streets, as do other young men like him. "Man! They think I got better. Mothafuckas just taught me how to be more violent, steal tighter rides [nicer cars]. . . . I even ended up with more bitch-ass enemies."

Probation

Probation practices subjected the boys' ideas of manhood to strict evaluation. As agents of reform, probation officers attempted to teach the young men how to be "real men," by demanding that they work toward signs of a proper masculinity: to acquire an education, to attain a job, and to support a family. The boys were told to get a job, do well in school, and stay out of trouble. The likelihood of failure was high, since most avenues of legitimate success were out of reach.

When they failed, the boys abandoned attempts to achieve a "proper" masculinity—the decent, hard-working manhood that authority figures expected of them. Instead, they became significantly more connected to hypermasculinity. Whenever the young men got into trouble, their probation officers threatened them with incarceration to teach them how to be real men. The young men often felt strain from not being able to become the men that the institution expected them to become, because they could not find work—the central vehicle for demonstrating manhood. When the Black and Latino males abandoned these false expectations of obtaining a job, instead of becoming hopeless, they adopted a hypermasculine ideal of survival. In a social context in which jobs were scarce, traditional working-class notions of manhood were nearly impossible to accomplish; in lieu of this gender accomplishment, the boys adopted hypermasculinity to prove themselves.

The boys held a contradictory understanding of the masculinity that they confronted. Jose's statement is representative of many of the boys' perspectives:

They [probation officers] tell us to be "real men," to show respect, but they don't see that if we show respect, we'll get treated like punks. . . . Being a man out here is different. It means smashing on a scrub [beating up an enemy] if he breaks your respect. . . . It means handling your business in order to get paid, . . . not being a bitch and shit. It means going to jail if you have to.

From Jose's perspective, and that of many of the other youths whom I studied, it was extremely self-defeating for probation officers trying to reform them to attempt to do so by teaching them how a "real" man should act. These messages did not provide the boys with tools to navigate the streets, to do well at home and in school, or to succeed at a job and make an income. Instead, the youths saw two extreme worlds of manhood, where only one was accessible: hypermasculinity. At this point, the boys made their decisions to affirm, develop, and demonstrate a manhood that appeared to offer respect, economic gain, and social status, instead of hopelessness.

The ideal of manhood that probation officers tried to inculcate was also one of responsibility. For these officials, the responsibility of a young man was to follow his "program" and not to violate probation. The message became, "A real man does not belong in jail." Once a male enters jail or prison, he is at risk of becoming emasculated. According to Jose, his probation officer, Mr. Bryan, explained the emasculation process of men in confinement: "You want to go to prison, where everybody is gonna pimp you? The guards are gonna run you like a little bitch. The murderers and rapists are gonna make you bend over; they gonna treat you like somebody's wife." In trying to teach a "proper" masculinity, as a set of ideals, probation officers unintentionally pushed young men of color further into hypermasculinity.

T, a sixteen-year-old African American boy from Oakland—after being arrested and placed on probation, unable to continue selling drugs or stealing cars for income and unable to secure a job because of his record—resorted to using women as a central source of income. When T was asked, "Where do you get money from?" he replied, "Pimp a bitch, you know, let that bitch come out her pocket, . . . act like I like her so she'll give me money and shit. . . . Most bitches will give me whatever I need: . . . shoes, shirts, food, bus pass, whatever. . . . Or make her sell shit for me." T made the decision to no longer commit crime. However, his solution was to fully embrace hypermasculinity and dominate women to accomplish what the criminal justice system expected of him—to desist from committing crime. In the process of attempting to reform and resist his criminalization, T adopted a chauvinistic masculinity that called on him to abuse young women, to use them as objects and as a source of income.

Hypermasculinity influenced the criminalized boys to embrace gendered practices that further limited their futures and harmed those around them. The boys reported trying to be "good men," following the criminal justice system's ideals of manhood by being passive, trying to do well in school, or looking for work. However, these strategies often placed them in a double bind such that they were not able to succeed at work or in the streets. When these strategies failed, a seductive alternative surfaced in times of crisis: hypermasculinity.

As adolescent boys practiced masculinity on the street, the institutions of control that managed the boys also generated meanings of manhood, which correlated with the damaging identities these youth formed on the street. In this case, the criminalization of Black and Latino males and the criminal justice system's expectations of masculinity provided the young men with gender resources which often limited their mobility, interrupted their social relations, and pipelined them deeper into the criminal justice system. The gender ideals purveyed by police, probation officers, and others did not translate adequately into the realities of the boys' lives. In this context, hypermasculinity served both as resistance and as a resource for self-affirmation. The criminal justice pipeline imposed gender practices fraught with failure and insolvable contradictions. While hypermasculinity may have been in disrepute, it made its practitioners feel self-fulfilled. This survival strategy, in turn, impeded the youths' desistance and social mobility and entitled the system to further criminalize and punish them. In sum, then, gender is one of the processes in which the criminal justice system and the youth control complex are involved in the reproduction of criminalization, social exclusion, and racial inequality.

7

Guilty by Association

Acting White or Acting Lawful?

Children can't achieve unless we raise their expectations and turn off the television sets and eradicate the slander that says a black youth with a book is acting white.

—Barack Obama, DNC Speech, 2004

The problem is that parents, shopping-mall security, police officers, grocery-store clerks, and even other youth have a hard time distinguishing the delinquents from the wannabes. . . . The many lawful youth take on the stylistic affections of true "wild children" even though they infrequently, if ever, cross the line in their behavior.

—Mary Patillo-McCoy, *Black Picket Fences*, 1999

J.T., an African American sixteen-year-old, was a good student: "I get like A's and B's and sometimes C's, but I try to stay on top," he explained. I saw two of his report cards to verify this. His mother worked for the City of Oakland as a clerk. He described what she does: "The kind of person that checks yo' papers to see if you legit. Like, she'll put the rubber stamp on your paperwork if you paid your taxes, yadadamean [you understand]?" J.T.'s father had moved to Chicago when J.T. was eight years old, and his mother kept him disciplined: "She'll make sure I am doing good, and if I ain't, she'll pull out the whip. . . . One time, when I was little, I stole some shit from the store. My mom found out, and she made me take it back. And she ask the man [store clerk] if I could work to pay him back. He said no. My moms made him give me a job! He made me scrub the piss outside the store. . . . I never stole again." His mother, Angela, worked until 5 p.m., arriving home by 6 p.m. J.T. got out of school at 2:45 p.m.; he had three hours to kill. These three hours, between 3 p.m. and 6 p.m., were often the most dangerous hours for young people in Oakland. This is when most youth crime, violence, and victimization took place. To prevent J.T. from getting into trouble, his mother ordered him to attend one of the few afterschool programs in the community, at the East Side Youth Center (ESYC).

J.T. had never committed a crime or been arrested, despite growing up in a neighborhood where crime was rampant and having an older brother who had been arrested several times. J.T.'s brother, cousins, and childhood friends were involved in gangs and drug dealing. Despite actively avoiding delinquency and never being arrested or suspended, J.T. believed that sometimes he was treated worse than his delinquent peers. He told me that even though he tried to stay away from trouble, authority figures often implicated him in the deviance and crime that his friends committed. "I just always knew it was stupid to do crazy shit, so I just stayed away from stupid niggas. . . . The only thing I did was not go to school. I was just taking care of my lil' sister and trying to make some money cleaning people's yards." Although J.T. claimed that he stayed away from the guys who committed crime, six out of eight of the people he hung out with on a regular basis had previously been arrested. I believe that what J.T. meant when he said he stayed away from guys who committed crime was that he had the unique skills to navigate between what authority figures expected of him and what the streets expected of him. J.T.'s story is representative of the nine other non-delinquent boys in this study. They all reported being and were observed to be treated similarly to the delinquent boys.

Out of the forty youths I studied, ten had never been arrested but came from the same neighborhood, schools, family background, and subculture as those who had been. Four of the youths I studied were siblings of delinquent boys I had observed and interviewed. The other six were close friends with some of the boys who had been arrested. These non-delinquent youths also felt deeply impacted by punitive social control and the youth control complex. An example was Jaime, a sixteen-year-old Latino who received A's and B's at school and who had one brother incarcerated for attempted murder and another brother in a gang. He explained, "School has been very hard. It's like the teachers don't care if we make it or not, and the police is off the hook at the school. They treat us like if we were animals or criminals." At the same time, the boys who had previously been arrested resented the boys who had not been arrested, not for doing well in school but for becoming inculcated in the discourses and practices that criminalization agents—school personnel, police, and other punitive social-control practitioners—had imposed on them. In other words, non-delinquent youths had to prove their innocence by embracing the logic and practice of the youth control complex.

In a study of Black and Latino students, sociologist Prudence Carter found a group of "cultural straddlers," young people who had developed the skills to straddle two worlds, meeting the "expectations of the school's cultural codes" and "co-creating meaning with their peers." These cultural straddlers, Carter argues, "hold on to their native cultural style but also embrace dominant cultural codes and resources."[1] Similar to Carter's cultural straddlers, all of the non-delinquent boys in this study knew how to navigate multiple worlds. Although these boys were not honor students, they received decent grades, stayed away from drugs and crime, and found strategies to avoid police contact, while at the same time knowing how to "keep it real" and use the skills required to persist on the streets, among their primarily delinquent peers.

The non-delinquent boys engaged creative responses to punishment in a different manner than the delinquent boys. The delinquent boys consistently worked at fighting for their dignity, while the non-delinquent boys consistently worked at fighting for their freedom. Fighting for dignity, as discussed in previous chapters, entails being willing to take the risk of harsh discipline or arrest, in order to expose the contradictions of the system and achieve acknowledgment and a feeling of dignity. Dignity work involved acts of resistance that often placed the boys at risk of punishment. The delinquent boys calculated that it was worth taking the risk of losing their freedom in order to gain some dignity from the system.

The non-delinquent boys worked at fighting for their freedom by evading situations in which they might encounter school discipline, police contact, or targeting for criminalization. These boys found creative ways to avoid criminalization. However, despite their hard work, many of the boys encountered contradictions with school officials and police officers: they believed that if they followed the rules, they would not be targeted or harassed; however, despite knowing how to straddle, these boys found themselves treated similarly to their peers.

I found that despite having the skills to navigate between two worlds, the non-delinquent boys often found themselves in a Catch-22: even when they followed the rules, authority figures still criminalized the boys because they lived among the delinquent boys. Like the delinquent boys' parents discussed in chapter 4, the non-delinquent boys who lived in high-crime areas were also granted courtesy stigmas. Even if the boys attempted to adapt to school or police norms and codes, they were still treated with the suspicion that they might commit crime like their peers. The non-delinquent boys held the conviction that they had been criminalized in the same systematic way as their delinquent peers. On the other hand, their peers sometimes accosted them for appearing to have become part of the system that was criminalizing them. The delinquent boys perceived the non-delinquent boys as part of the system that governed them through crime, as snitches who would tell on them not for committing violent crime but for not complying with authority, as individuals who also participated in the stripping of their peers' dignity. The delinquent boys were not disappointed with the non-delinquents for wanting to do well in school or for dreaming of being successful one day; they felt tension with these boys because school officials and police had pitted them against each other. The non-delinquent boys had been told to stay away, avoid, and reject the delinquent boys, who were considered risky and dangerous. Schools and police had imposed a dichotomous identity on the non-delinquent boys. In order to be perceived as "good kids," these boys were expected to relinquish hanging out with neighbors and family members, to embrace a style of dress and talk that was foreign to them, and to keep officials informed of the whereabouts and activity of their "criminal" peers.[2] The message was, as J.T. reported a police officer telling him, "Either you stay away from those punks, or you're going to get picked up just like them." This "either you're with us or against us" mentality placed many of the non-delinquent boys in a precarious situation: they could easily be identified as snitches or cowards on the streets and become vulnerable to victimization. While having the skills to straddle two worlds sometimes paid off for the boys, it also took a toll on them. Many felt that they were betwixt and between, accepted neither here nor there.

The non-delinquent boys, who consciously chose to do well but who had a network of friendship and family with the delinquent boys and, likewise, encountered punitive social control, also had to deal with the wrath of their peers, who saw them as outsiders. In the end, J.T. and the nine other non-delinquent boys attempted to become "code switchers," kids who could navigate both the streets and mainstream institutions.[3] However, they had to constantly perform as if they were not connected to the delinquent boys, which placed a huge stress on the non-delinquents and impacted social relations between delinquent and non-delinquent youths in the same neighborhood. The delinquent boys often chastised the non-delinquents, not because they were "acting white" but because the youth control complex had coerced them into "acting lawful."

Acting Lawful

The non-delinquent boys displayed a strategic approach to avoiding contact with police. For example, when I shadowed J.T., he often abruptly left the park or street corner where he hung out with his delinquent friends and cousin. I asked him, "Why do you leave in the middle of a game or a conversation?" He replied, "You know what time mothafuckas get scraped; you know what time fools get arrested. It all happens at the same times. When I'm feeling it, you know? I start feelin' myself, and I say it's time to run." J.T. seemed to display strong navigational skills necessary to avoid victimization and criminalization. However, despite his attempts at "being legit" and avoiding criminalization, he still encountered stigma, exclusion, and punishment.

The non-delinquent boys felt the weight of punitive social control on their shoulders, and, in response, they developed a navigational skill that

I call *acting lawful*. Acting lawful is the process by which individuals who experience punitive social control attempt to avoid becoming victims of criminalization and punishment. The boys acted lawful by following school rules, complying with police officers, and avoiding situations in which they might be suspected of breaking a rule or violating the law. "Knowing how to talk to police," as J.T. explained, means "saying shit like, 'Yes, sir,' 'No, sir,' 'Please, sir,' and making sure you don't act like you got contraband on you. . . . It means making sure you riding legit, like letting them do their stupid shit and just keeping your mouth shut." In order to avoid further harassment, brutality, or incarceration, J.T. learned not to question police officers when they searched or questioned him, even if he felt that they were violating his rights. When J.T. was stopped and searched by police when he was with his peers, many of them responded negatively to this strategy. They thought that J.T. was being a "coward" for not standing up to the police. This led some of the boys to suspect J.T. was "working for the police" and giving them information about the boys.

Punitive social control impacted social relations between delinquent and non-delinquent youths living in the same neighborhoods in Oakland. While criminal justice officials punished those youngsters who had broken the law, this system and other institutions played a role in making non-delinquent youths feel punished, as well. It was not success in education that led delinquent boys to "hate" on their non-delinquent peers. Instead, the delinquent boys resented their peers for participating in the perpetuation of their criminalization, for becoming inculcated in a system that saw much of marginalized youth culture and action as crime. In addition, the non-delinquent boys had to demonstrate their distance from deviant youths, and deviant youth culture, in order to prove themselves not guilty. In order to gain legitimacy from the youth control complex, from school authorities, police, and other authority figures who constantly scrutinized them, non-delinquent boys had to overcompensate in their behavior. They had to relentlessly prove to authority figures that they were not criminal, that they were acting lawfully. This, in turn, created resentment in the delinquent boys, who then took out their frustrations with the youth control complex on their peers and their relatives who attempted to comply.

The Criminalization of the Non-delinquent Boys

One of the ironies of the conversations and observations I held with those boys who had not been arrested was that they expressed the same feelings and experiences as the boys who had been stigmatized, disciplined, and arrested. Paul, an eighteen-year-old Latino from Oakland, attended City College of San Francisco and had recently moved to San Francisco's Mission District. He described his experiences as a youth who was never involved in criminal or deviant activity: "Even though I have never got wrapped up [arrested], I still get treated like I am about to commit a crime every day. Everywhere I go, from the store to school, I got people sweatin' me 'cause they think I'm gonna steal something or whoop somebody's ass. I mean, I will if I have to, but most of the time I am a cool cat."

Despite never having been arrested, Paul has faced many encounters with police officers that have led to negative consequences. At one point, an officer physically brutalized him:

> The cop, Officer Gonzalez, that was watching me whenever I left the house, grabbed me one day and asked me if I knew which gang member in the neighborhood had shot someone else. I gave him attitude and told him, "How the fuck I'm s'posed to know? I'm not in the gang. Go ask the gang. Oh, I forgot: you're scared of them." He grabbed me and started to choke the shit out of me.

According to Paul, this interaction led him to move to San Francisco, where he thought that maybe he could start over and find a space where police would not harass him. He also reported that he no longer talked back to the police, and this helped him negotiate police officers' orders. Remaining passive when encountering police aided Paul in avoiding an escalation. Paul seemed to embrace the idea that he was working to remain free, even if it meant giving up some of his dignity. "Even in the Mission, I still get hit up by cops. I just stay quiet and let them do their thing. . . . It's just life, man. You got to deal with it. Part of growing up is knowing when to choose your battles."[4] I observed Paul in his new neighborhood in the Mission District of San Francisco and witnessed him encounter police two times there. Both times, he was told he "fit a description." Both times, Paul shrugged his shoulders, remained passive, and allowed the police to run a check on his record. I believe that the police were thrown off by Paul's presence in the neighborhood and had decided to check him out and keep track of him as a new, young, baggy-clothes-wearing community member.

Despite acting lawful, the non-delinquent boys experienced guilt by association. For example, police harassed J.T. for interacting with his childhood friends. One day, J.T. was walking home from school with one of his best friends, Larry. Larry had dropped out of school and been arrested for drug possession a few times. As Larry and J.T. parted ways, J.T. continued walking toward his house. A police officer stopped him. J.T. described the encounter: "He searches me, makes me feel like shit in front of my little cousins. He says, 'Oh, you one of them dope-dealing gang bangers.' He did it to scare my little cousins."

In the three years that I observed and interviewed J.T., he constantly displayed an interest in demonstrating his innocence, in acting lawful. A myriad of opportunities to steal, sell drugs, beat up other teenagers, and be confrontational with adults presented themselves to him. But J.T. lost his cool only one time, when he talked back to a police officer, and the officer responded by gripping his hands on his neck as if prepared to choke him. Although he did not commit crimes, he believed that he was still treated as a potential threat, or a criminal, by police and school officials. J.T., like many of the non-delinquent boys who were imposed with courtesy stigmas, was on his own, with no supportive peer networks he could rely on and with adults who imposed punitive social control on him, despite his innocence and his persistence to do well in school.

Rejecting Criminalized Peers

One day, as I shadowed J.T., we ended up at his afterschool program at the local community center. We were standing outside watching a group of seven Black teenage males play a game of basketball about thirty feet away. One of them was J.T.'s cousin, Ronny, one of the delinquent boys. The boys called each other names and joked about each other's mothers as they took shots. A heavy-set kid, wearing a XXL-sized Ecko sweater with a picture of a rhino on it, ran, dribbled, stopped, and held the ball. He eyed the basket and called out, "If I make this shot, Dante's mother sucked my dick last night." He missed the shot. Dante ran for the ball, cleared the three-point line, and took a shot. He made it. "Nigga, yo mama sucked my dick for a rock last night," Dante proclaimed. A few minutes later, the game ended and the group dispersed. They walked toward us. One of them yelled, "There goes that bitch-ass nigga J.T. Wassup, gay-ass nigga?" His cousin Ronny, walking behind them, began to laugh. Before J.T. could respond, one of them ran up to him with his arm out parallel to the ground. He caught J.T. in a "clothesline," forcing his extended arm into J.T.'s neck. J.T. fell, hitting the back of his head on the concrete. I got in between J.T. and the rest of the group, who ran up to J.T. to kick him. I crouched over him and then tried to help him up. "Come on, fellas, cut this shit out!" I yelled at them. They marched into the community center, laughing and joking about J.T.'s fall. "They mad at me 'cause I don't want to act stupid like them," J.T. exclaimed with frustration, and a few tears on his face. "Mothafuckas think I'm a bitch 'cause I don't want to be stupid."

J.T. believed that part of the reason that his close childhood friends and cousin bullied him was because he had recently joined the program about drug awareness and anger management sponsored by the Alameda County Probation Department. Even though J.T. was not on probation, he had gotten involved in this program because it had been recommended by a community-center worker. It was one of the only programs available for older teenage boys; the center had run out of funds for their D.J. program that J.T. had been in the previous year. The D.J. program taught young people about mixing, writing, and producing hip-hop music. Although he had never demonstrated any anger issues, J.T. decided to participate; his only other alternative was to hang out with the boys who were getting into trouble.

After joining the program, J.T. became stigmatized by his peers; they rendered him a "snitch" who would tell probation officers everything they did. On one occasion, the probation officer who taught the program, Mr. Taylor, encountered J.T., his friends, and I standing outside the community center, and he told J.T. that manhood was about being responsible and denouncing "gangster" practices such as "wearing your pants like you want some guy to come and hump you . . . or acting like an animal when you think someone disrespected you." Pointing to the other boys, Mr. Taylor said, "You gotta stay away from these knuckleheads, man! You want to go to prison?" The other boys looked down. When the probation officer went back into the building, Ronny looked at his cousin with disgust and walked away. The rest of the boys followed.

The threat of going to prison was a recurring strategy used by teachers, probation officers, parents, and police to discipline the boys, and the non-delinquents were constantly told that if they associated with the delinquents, they would likewise go to prison. The boys grew frustrated hearing this discourse repeated across a spectrum of institutions. While they all agreed that this "boogey man" threat did not deter them from hanging out with individuals who were actively engaged in crime, it did create a clear division between them. The non-delinquent boys wanted to do well in school and avoid police harassment, so, in public, they were forced to avoid and reject their friends and family members who were marked as criminals or gang members. The boys had to overcompensate in order to demonstrate to authority figures that they were not criminals. For example, at school they would have to pretend in front of teachers and administrators that they did not hang out with the delinquent boys. This created a strain in social relations between delinquent and non-delinquent youths from the same neighborhood and often resulted in "bullying" and the victimization of the non-delinquent boys. This finding may help us shed light on bullying and analyze it as a response to the resentment that develops from strict rules and punishment. In other words, schools and specific neighborhood effects may very well be responsible for some of the conditions that lead some young people to bully others.

The non-delinquent boys also had to constantly prove they were not criminals. In the store, for example, J.T. stayed away from the candy section until he was ready to purchase a piece of candy. When he walked to the candy aisle, he made sure to reach for the candy he wanted with his arm extended and to keep his body away. "This way," he told me, "the fool doesn't think I'm trying to steal his shit." In the previous chapter, I showed how the delinquent boys interacted at a store, how they sometimes played games with the clerk to send a signal that they were aware that the store clerk believed they were going to steal candy. The non-delinquent boys, on the other hand, kept their distance from the candy, yet, in my fourteen observations with non-delinquent boys at stores, all of them were closely scrutinized by store clerks, regardless of the distance they kept from the candy. The non-delinquent boys grew up forced to overcompensate and to constantly prove to others that they were law-abiding citizens. Their actions and demeanor was adjusted accordingly, to satisfy the system. However, despite acting lawfully, the boys still faced criminalization.

J.T. was trapped in a double bind: if he followed in his cousin's footsteps, he would end up getting "wrapped up" in the system; if he attended the probation program, his peers saw him as a "snitch." While the streets and his peers were a powerful force, J.T. opted to "go legit" and follow what sociologist Martín Sánchez-Jankowski calls a "security-maximizing value system."[5] Sánchez-Jankowski argues that some individuals living in poor neighborhoods choose to "deprive themselves today to avoid future suffering."[6] In other words, J.T. understood that the delinquent boys, as a group, were setting themselves up for failure. Their defiance of criminalization allowed the system to impose the harshest sanctions on them. Although J.T. might suffer stigma at the moment, he believed that he might have a better future if he proved his lawfulness over time.

Acting White or Acting Lawful?

In popular discourse about "minority failure" in the education system, low-achieving students are often blamed not only for their own failures but for developing a culture of opposition that rejects learning and achievement. These students are also held responsible for putting pressure on their high-achieving peers by accusing them of "acting White." Contrary to this widespread belief, all the boys in this study placed a high value on education. They all had dreams of one day having a college degree and acquiring viable, professional employment. However, many had not yet developed the specific skills needed to attain passing grades, graduate from high school, or attend college. Low-achieving students did not "hate on" their high-achieving peers for doing well in school; as a matter of fact, many of the delinquent boys gave their peers "love" for making it in school, getting good grades, and graduating. The delinquent boys were much more interested in "hating on" peers who they perceived had become part of the system that criminalized them; the boys who cooperated with police or school administrators, who rejected their delinquent peers, or who attempted to follow unrealistic advice given to them by police officers were often the targets of chastisement and violence. Much has been written about the "acting White" stigma.[7] However, in this study, I found that when delinquent Black and Latino boys chastised peers who had gone "legit," it was because of the belief that they had become part of the system of punitive social control. They had participated in stigmatizing and excluding their delinquent peers, and this, in turn, earned them "snitch" status, one of the worst labels given by the delinquent boys.

Education scholars Fordham and Ogbu coined the term "acting White" and argued that African American students did not succeed to the best of their potential for fear of being accused of "acting White" by their peers. They argued that cultural attitudes hindered Black students in academic achievement:

> Learning school curriculum and learning to follow the standard academic practices of the school are often equated by the minorities with learning to "act white" or as actually "acting white" while simultaneously giving up acting like a minority person. School learning is therefore consciously or unconsciously perceived *as a subtractive process*: a minority person who learns successfully in school or who follows the standard practices of the school is perceived as becoming acculturated into the white American frame of reference."[8]

Ogbu and Fordham further suggested that it was racist society that led young people to chastise their peers for acting White. Because of racism in White America, Fordham and Ogbu argued, "Black Americans subsequently began to doubt their own intellectual ability, began to define academic success as white people's prerogative, and began to discourage their peers, perhaps unconsciously, from emulating white people."[9] Conservative scholars took this idea and argued that it was this "victimization" ideology that led minority students to act this way toward one another. Linguist John McWhorter argued that some immigrant groups managed to survive because they did not blame the system for their failure, and, as long as Blacks saw themselves as victims of oppression, they would continue to feel the wrath of acting White.[10] By 2004, senator and later presidential candidate Barak Obama jumped on the bandwagon: "Children can't achieve unless we raise their expectations and turn off the television sets and eradicate the slander that says a black youth with a book is acting white."[11]

In 2006, economist Roland Fryer attempted to demonstrate that "acting White" was still prevalent among Black and Latino students. He found that as White students' grades went up, their popularity in school also increased. This was not the case for Black and Latino students; their popularity diminished as their grades went up. Fryer suggested that peers began to dislike "good" students in their racial group because they demonstrated "White" characteristics. Fryer determined popularity by counting the amount of friends students had. If a student was listed by other students as their friend, this student rose up in the "social hierarchy." Black and Latino high achievers were less likely to be chosen as friends by other Black and Latino students. From this data, Fryer concluded that "acting White" was alive and well, since the "smart" kids were disliked by the low achievers.[12]

Other scholars have argued that it is not "White" characteristics that students of color reject but, rather, middle-class standards and culture.[13] Prudence Carter has argued that Black and Latino students do not reject academic achievement and that they do not develop an oppositional culture to it. Instead, she argues that these young people struggle to embrace multiple forms of capital, some of which are used in the social order of their communities.[14] In this study, I found that the delinquent boys did not reject middle class standards; nevertheless, they rejected those practices, discourses, and individuals that treated them as failures, risks, or criminals. Students rendered as "failures" and therefore deviant at school may reject their high-achieving peers not for acting White but for appearing to have turned against their own communities and embraced punitive social control.

Institutional Aggression

I found that the boys who chastised their high-achieving peers did so because they believed that those peers had accepted the criminal label that the system had given them; the delinquent boys felt that the non-delinquent boys had become part of this system. These findings indicate that institutions such as schools are implicated in the process of creating tension between young people. I found the delinquent boys' primary reasons for humiliating their non-delinquent peers was the latter's decision to participate in their stigmatization. Being from a community where most of the residents were imposed with punitive stigmas (e.g., welfare queen, absent father, criminal youth, etc.), the non-delinquent boys felt the weight of this punitive social control pressing down on them. Some took on an identity that attempted to prove to the system that they were "diamonds in the rough." The young people in this category believed that if they could prove to police, teachers, and the community that they were not criminals, then they could enjoy the spoils of being a good citizen. However, three of the ten non-delinquent boys, despite acting lawfully, graduating from high school and attending community college, were eventually arrested. James was one example.

James was a young African American man whose story was very similar to that of many young Black men in poor urban areas of the United States. He grew up in poverty, was criminalized at school and on the streets, and, despite receiving a high school diploma, had no job opportunities. By the end of the three-year study, James was arrested. He had stayed away from trouble and negative peers, had received good grades, and aspired to attend a four-year college. According to James, while growing up, he first experienced police harassment beginning in grade school, when, at the age of ten, his teacher called in the police because James had called her a "bitch." The police officer showed up in his class, pulled James out, handcuffed him, and gave him a scare: "He told me, 'I'm gonna take you to jail, boy. You better respect that teacher.'" For years, as James walked home from school, this same police officer stopped him and searched him for drugs. Eventually, James became accustomed to routine police stops, and he normalized police harassment and brutality, despite the fact that he had never committed a crime. "Police are always gonna be here to make sure you don't get out of place. That's just life. Even if you don't got nothin' on you, you still gotta deal with it." The same officer who had handcuffed James at age ten, and who had systematically harassed him for seven years, arrested him when he was seventeen, a few months prior to graduation. James was walking home from school when the officer stopped him, searched him, and found a rolled-up marijuana cigar in his pocket. James was booked, released, and placed on probation.

Eventually, the probation process facilitated further arrests that led James to felony convictions. From that point on, James was granted a negative credential by the state and civil society. This mark of a criminal record became a central obstacle in James's ability to acquire a job, even though he had a high school diploma. Because he had received an adult drug conviction, he was not eligible to apply for financial aid, which ultimately discouraged him from applying to college. James continued to look for work, but his criminal record limited his ability to obtain one of the few low-wage, low-skill jobs for which many working-class people competed.

To argue that socially marginalized youth do not succeed because their culture teaches them that education is a "subtractive process" is the equivalent of saying that tomato seeds do not sprout in the winter because the soil they are planted in is too acidic. The reality is that cold weather and little sun keeps the tomato from growing in the winter, not just acidic soil. In order for the tomato to thrive in a cold climate, we have to provide it with surrogate conditions such as a greenhouse. Similar to a permanent winter, criminalization and punitive social control provided the youths in this study with perpetually infertile conditions, robbing them of the opportunity to sprout, let alone flourish. Even when non-delinquent young people developed skills to learn how to grow, even when they learned how to "straddle," criminalization became a central obstacle, which still rendered them as threats and as unworthy of positive credentials.

CONCLUSION

Creating a Youth Support Complex

It would seem that sanctions imposed by relatives, friends or a personally relevant collectivity have more effect on criminal behavior than sanctions imposed by a remote legal authority.... Repute in the eyes of close acquaintances matters more to people than the opinions or actions of criminal justice officials.

—John Braithwaite, *Crime, Shame and Reintegration*, 1989

All students cringe under the scrutiny, but those most harshly affected, least successful in the competition, possess some of our greatest unperceived riches.

—Mike Rose, *Lives on the Boundary*, 1989

Social Incapacitation

On a hot summer day in the Bay Area in 2006, I found myself at San Quentin State Penitentiary, infamous for hosting California's only execution chamber. I stood between two rusty iron gates, anxious and claustrophobic, as the bars appeared to inch closer toward me. The guards sat comfortably on the other side of the gate, at the control station, shooting the breeze about football, their kids, and the inmates. Finally, one of the gates opened up, only to dump me deeper into this final frontier of punishment. As I continued walking, I felt the debilitating weight of the prison's iron cages. Now I could begin to imagine the pain that Jose, who had been here for three months, must have been feeling.

Jose was sentenced to five years after being charged with assault with a deadly weapon and a gang enhancement. A gang enhancement is an added sentence to felony cases when the court finds a defendant guilty of committing a crime for the benefit of the gang.[1] A person can receive an additional two to fifteen years' sentence for having participated in a crime to benefit the gang. Jose was arrested because he was present when one of his friends shot a gun at gang rivals. According to Jose, and other young men I interviewed who witnessed the event, he had not instigated the event, nor was he involved in the acquisition or handling of the gun. When prosecutors threatened him with a fifteen-year sentence, Jose accepted a five-year sentence, in a heartbeat, because, he said, "I did not want to spend the rest of my life in jail."

I finally made it to the booth where I was to meet Jose, and, finally, he arrived. But he did not look like the Jose I knew; he looked very different. He was as skinny as a sick pit bull, his eyes full of gloom, and his skin chalky pale. Staring at Jose through a glass window in that cold cell filled me with sorrow and anxiety. I had followed some of the boys through a major part of their journey through the school-to-prison pipeline, and now, as I stared straight into the final destination, I became filled with pessimism. I thought, at this moment, that for a young man like Jose, his destiny had already been chosen for him, that the youth control complex had set him up for failure and incarceration from a young age.

Being criminalized from a young age had devastating consequences for the boys in this study. As I observed and interviewed them, I uncovered a youth control complex made up of punitive interactions between young people and authority figures, where punishment threaded itself into the fabric of everyday social life in an array of institutions; marginalized young men's behaviors and styles were criminalized and subjected them to shame, exclusion, punishment, and incarceration. This hypercriminalization of young people was composed of exclusion, punishment, racialization, gendered violence, harassment, surveillance, and detention by police, probation officers, teachers, community program workers, and even parents. This system shaped the ways in which young men developed worldviews about themselves and their social ecology. Despair and politicized identities became fused together as two dominant responses to the punitive social control that the boys encountered. At the moment, Jose remained in a state of despair.

The thick plexiglass that separated Jose and me was sticky with greasy residue from the many stressed foreheads that had rested there. "How are you, Jose?" I asked. Then I thought to myself, "How stupid of me to ask; of course he's not doing well caged up in here." But he responded, "I'm a'right. Shit's fucked up here, but I'm doing okay." He gave me that same charismatic childish smile, showing his entire set of shiny teeth and a big dimple on his left cheek—the same smile that he'd given when I first met him, back when he was a budding adolescent. "Where do you think you'll go from here?" I asked. He replied, "Man, I gotta live it one minute at a time. I'll get out of here and do good." He dropped his head and stared at the ground as he said this; he didn't seem to believe what he was saying. I asked him what he thought he might do when he got out. He replied, "I don't know, but I think I know I'll be here forever." Even though "forever" referred to his five-year sentence, Jose seemed to believe that he had become a perpetual part of the system. He also talked about the pressure of proving himself inside, of participating in the code of the prison, of having to constantly protect himself, of having to "handle business"—attack other inmates—in order to survive.

Jose's journey through the school-to-prison pipeline had ended. Criminalization and punishment had accomplished themselves: stigmatizing Jose at a young age, excluding him from productive activities as he matured, brewing a resentment and resistance in him that would lead him deeper into criminalization, marking him with negative credentials, preparing him for prison, and ultimately ingesting him into its punitive carceral abyss. Jose and six of the other young men in this study, all ultimately ending up in prison, experienced what sociologist Orlando Patterson calls "social death."[2] "Social death" is the systematic process by which individuals are denied their humanity. Despite being biologically alive, they are socially isolated, violated, and prevented from engaging in social relations that affirm their humanity. Ethnic studies scholar Dylan Rodriguez argues that incarceration is a form of social death. This social death, he argues, is "the political and organizational logic of the prison."[3] But beyond finding that incarceration produced a certain kind of social death, I also found that social death began at a very young age in the form of punishment and criminalization. Growing up, the boys were injected with consistent microdoses of social death. This microaggressive form of social death I refer to as *social incapacitation*. Social incapacitation is the process by which punitive social control becomes an instrument which prevents marginalized populations from functioning, thriving, and feeling a sense of dignity and humanity in their daily interactions with institutional forces. Culture scholar George Lipsitz reminds us of Malcolm X's brilliant analysis of racism: "Racism is like a Cadillac, they bring out a new model every year."[4] Malcolm X might agree that if race and class stratification form the highway by which marginalized populations are excluded from important material and symbolic resources in American society, then punitive social control is the Cadillac that cruises them deeper into social exclusion, marginalization, and ultimately social or physical death (as was the case with young Oscar Grant, shot in the back by a police officer, while handcuffed, in Oakland).

As the boys came of age, and were almost always treated like criminals, they believed, and were often correct, that they were being systematically punished for being poor, young, Black or Latino, and male. In the era of mass incarceration, when punitive social control has become a dominant form of governance, some young people are systematically targeted as criminal risks. "Under this insufferable climate of increased repression and unabated exploitation," Henry Giroux argues, "young people and communities of color become the new casualties in an ongoing war against justice, freedom, social citizenship, and democracy. Given the switch in public policy from social investment to containment, it is clear that young people for whom race and class loom large have become disposable."[5] This process has created a generation of marginalized young people, who, by way of social incapacitation, are prevented from engaging in a full affirmation of their humanity, let alone from gaining entry into roles that might give them social mobility. The logic and practice of punitive social control has prevented many marginalized young people from gaining acceptance, affirmation, and achievement in school, landing a job, or catching a break or learning a reintegrative lesson for minor transgressions from police and probation officers.

The youth control complex is not a new phenomenon. Poor and racialized populations have been criminalized and violently punished in the United States since its inception.[6] The black body has been a target on which criminalization, punishment, social incapacitation, and social death have been executed and perfected. The transatlantic slave trade, savage whippings by slave owners, lynchings, and police brutality have been a few of the many historical forms, often state sanctioned if not state imposed, of violent punishments executed on the black population. Punishment of the brown body has been executed through the genocide of indigenous populations; violent appropriation of Mexican territory by the United States; and vigilante and police brutality against "bandidos," "illegal immigrants," zoot-suiters, and gang youths.[7] In an era of mass incarceration, developed over the past thirty years, punitive social control has fed an out-of-control minotaur, allowing it to expand its labyrinth by embedding itself into traditionally nurturing institutions, punishing young people at younger ages, and marking many for life.

Criminalization is well disguised as a protective mechanism: zero-tolerance policies at schools are declared to provide the students who want to learn protection from bullies and disruptions; increased punitive policing is sold as protecting good citizens from violent gang members; longer incarceration sentences and adult sentencing appear to keep the bad guys from victimizing others and send a clear message to potential criminals; and so on. In order to transform punitive social control and to help young people like Jose live more productive lives, we have to unveil the reality of mass incarceration: it is expensive, financially and socially, for all of society, and it specifically denies many innocent, marginalized young people their humanity. While this study might lead us to believe that marginalized young men are perpetually trapped in a system that slowly shapes them into incarcerable subjects and that they are therefore doomed, victims to the historical tsunami of mass incarceration, there is a beacon of hope, a light that shines, capable of creating a more just way of nurturing marginalized young people—the youth themselves.

Building a Youth Support Complex

Although punitive social control had a debilitating impact on many of the boys in this study, there is a way to short-circuit this system. My personal story of growing up in poverty, being in a gang, going to juvenile hall, and then turning my life around, acquiring a higher education, and becoming a college professor may seem like an anomaly—I was at the right place at the right time and stumbled on resources, such as people who believed in me, academic and cultural programs, affirmative-action programs, and many mentors along the way. But this does not mean that other marginalized young people cannot do the same. My time in the field taught me that if we provide them the right resources to catapult themselves out of marginalization, young people will deliver. Politicians, schools, criminal justice institutions, and community members must create a youth support complex, a ubiquitous system of support that nurtures and reintegrates young people placed at risk. This system must find creative ways to teach young people when they have made mistakes. Healthy adolescent development requires that young people make mistakes and that they learn from their mistakes. Middle- and upper-class children are given ample opportunity to learn from their mistakes. In a survey I conducted with 550 of my "Introduction to Sociology" students, I found that those young people who came from families who made above seventy thousand dollars a year and reported that at one point during their adolescence they were caught getting drunk, smoking a joint, or committing statutory offenses overwhelmingly reported feeling that they had been given an opportunity to learn from their mistakes. The boys in my study never had a chance to learn from their mistakes.

In this study, only three of the forty boys found long-term, meaningful connections with non-criminal-justice programs or mentors who attempted to support them. An intriguing finding was that all three boys reported feeling that these programs and mentors had made a significant difference in their ability to transform. These programs provided these three boys with genuine caring relationships with adults who advocated for them and helped them develop their everyday resistance and resilience into navigational skills, to transform organic capital into social capital, which allowed them to desist, complete high school, and attend college. These three boys found one thing in common—access to resources that allowed them to move from negative credential status to positive credential status. These resources included college-prep programs, youth leadership organizations, mentors, and teachers and law enforcement officers who acknowledged them as young people capable of reaching the peak of human possibility.

As the system punished and entrapped these young people, and developed a reproductive resistance that pipelined many deeper into the system, it also developed within them an oppositional consciousness, as they became well aware of the process by which they were punished.[8] These boys all demonstrated a clear understanding of the process of punishment described in this book. In addition, their deviant and delinquent actions, except when they were drunk or high, served as an attempt to act in their own rational interests. While some of what the boys told me was one-sided, full of half truths, and with a clear bias and misrecognition of their social conditions and the intentions of most social-control institutions to genuinely help them, these young people could clearly articulate the mechanisms by which they ended up marked and tracked into the criminal justice system. Many of their actions, subcultures, and worldviews were developed in direct opposition to punitive social control. This resistance carried the seeds of redemption, self-determination, resilience, and desistance. Embracing the positive aspects of this resistance, teaching young people how to use it to navigate in mainstream institutions, and granting more productive consequences for young people who break the law are all endeavors we must undertake if we are to dismantle punitive social control and help young people who society has rendered as risks, threats, and criminals become productive citizens.

Facilitating Dignity and Freedom for All Young People

Eight of the young men in this study, who desisted from criminal activity for one year or longer, reported that their freedom depended on their ability to recognize that the system was against them, and, therefore, they needed to be strategic in their actions. The actions of those youths who desisted were premised around the notion that by remaining free, they were resisting the system. They analyzed the system's punitive treatment against them and responded by deploying everyday actions aimed at maintaining their freedom.

In the context of an era of mass incarceration, the boys in this study demonstrated the possibilities of political mobilization among marginalized populations. Their preoccupation, their movement, was centered around unshackling handcuffs, prying open prison bars, and shaking iron cages off their backs. I believe that the social movements of the new millennium among the most marginalized classes will be centered on dismantling punitive social control. The ideology of this control is constantly contested and challenged by marginalized young people. Because ideology is always political, ideological change occurs in the everyday interactions that youth have with dominant forces.⁹ If policymakers, scholars, program workers, or activists are to find viable ways of working with those populations most affected by punitive social control, they will have to be willing to hand over some bolt cutters: they will have to be willing to take the "risk" of proposing and implementing policies and programs that provide more reintegration and less disintegration, they will have to be willing to join the movement to dismantle punitive social control and the criminalization that keeps it company.

Urban ethnographer Nikki Jones demonstrates that formerly incarcerated young people have to constantly "work" at maintaining their "freedom." "The intersecting structural, cultural, and personal challenges facing young people who are released from detention facilities, jails, or prisons complicate pathways to freedom in ways that are not reflected in traditional desistance models. . . . 'Freedom' [is] not a static outcome but rather, a dynamic, on-going accomplishment that occurs within a particular structural, cultural, and historical context. . . . Freedom is work."¹⁰ The young people in my study also worked hard at maintaining their freedom. Some of this "hustle" to stay free consisted of young people's maintaining resilience and self-determination by analyzing their condition as a struggle against a system that ubiquitously attempted to incarcerate them and socially incapacitate them. A youth support complex that facilitates marginalized young people's social mobility will have to embrace and legitimize the hard work that young people engage in as they survive the streets, work for their freedom, and strive for their dignity.

One Youngster at a Time

One of the ways in which policymakers, schools, criminal justice institutions, and social programs can help young people desist from crime and become engaged in their education is by finding ways to respect and embrace the work that young people do for dignity and freedom. This entails decriminalizing young people's style and noncriminal actions, listening to young people's analysis of the system, and asking them how to develop programs and policies that can best help them. Asking their perspectives about the system and how the system can be changed to address their needs, and the needs of those in similar conditions, can become a way to empower these young people. In addition, their recommendations, if taken seriously, can lead the system to become more efficient, effective, and egalitarian when it comes to addressing school detachment, juvenile deviance, delinquency, and crime.

When a young man becomes self-empowered and believes he can change his marginal conditions and his environment, his ability to engage in his education and civic participation increases, leading to personal and social transformation. Young G, one of the young men in this study, who by the time this book is published will have already received his Bachelor of Arts degree, serves as a prime example. Young G is one of the forty youths in this study who, thus far, has attended a four-year university; he attends a small liberal arts college. He has been in college for three years, has a 3.0 grade point average, and aspires to attend medical school. When asked, "What were the conditions that helped you turn your life around, from being a gang member whose house got shot at and who witnessed a few murders, and from being someone who participated in crimes that may have led to decades in prison?" Young G replied, "As I was getting close to being eighteen, I started to recognize I could get more heavy into it, or this is my last opportunity. I met this math teacher who really turned backwards and forwards for me. He knew I had potential. He would visit my house. He wrote me letters of recommendation. Even when I cussed him out and threw a desk on the floor in his class, he gave me another chance." Young G found a teacher who broke away from the mainstream of punitive social control at his school. This support, combined with Young G's awareness that he had to work hard to avoid being punished, to break away from, and dismantle, punitive social control, led him into higher education and activism on campus.

Later on, I established a sixty-member student organization. We had our first protest against the messed-up graduation rates at the college. Forty percent of us [that dropped out] were Black, fifty percent Latino. By age thirteen, I learned that the system did not want me to spend my eighteenth birthday free. The system was trying to teach us to be docile, versus rich people taught to be creative. When I was little, before I even joined a gang, I had heavy surveillance of gangs, gang task force on me all the time. Even in middle school, police would search us for marijuana, cocaine, stuff I didn't even know existed. . . . And my teachers were telling me that I wasn't gonna make it. So I always had a political consciousness, because I saw I was oppressed. Being in the gang has to be political. The gang is about principle, loyalty, commitment; we fit in because it serves a purpose. Society don't give us a purpose, so we create a purpose for ourselves. Now I want to be able to have my actions speak louder than words.

Although Young G is the only one of the forty boys in this study who made it to a four-year university, all the other boys shared similar beliefs. The difference is that Young G had been given a formal stage with a supportive audience on which he could perform dignity, freedom, and reform. The other boys were stuck performing for a punitive audience who threw tomatoes at their every attempt to reform or resist. The key is to provide all marginalized youths a stage with good props, good lighting, and a supportive audience. In this way, acts of resistance, resilience, and reform, which go hand in hand, can become the basis for helping young people transform their lives. Policymakers, researchers, and program workers must recognize these seeds of transformation in young people and work with them to pry open the punitive bars that have socially incapacitated so many for so long.

We must eliminate the zero-tolerance policies that are rampant in schools, policing, and community centers. School-based police officers must be given limitations: schools don't allow music teachers to teach math, so why allow police officers to stand in for counselors, administrators, parents, or teachers? Police are trained to find and eliminate criminality; they are not trained to teach or to nurture. Therefore, neither police nor criminal justice practices should monopolize social control. The right arm of the state, the punishing arm, must be restrained and uncoupled from the left arm, the nurturing arm. We must find ways to eliminate the use of criminal justice metaphors and practices as a means of solving everyday social problems. Redistributing resources from criminal justice institutions back into nurturing institutions must become a priority.

I hope this book has demonstrated that the current system of punitive social control, filled with criminalization, zero-tolerance policies, and extreme sentencing, is not working to deter young people from committing crime. Instead, it has the unintended consequence of incapacitating young people, developing resistance in them which is often perceived as criminality, and further pipelines many into the criminal justice system. As I complete this manuscript, Oakland, California, and other cities have implemented gang injunctions, the laws that provide extreme surveillance and punishment for young people who are accused of being in the gang. These policies will only make matters worse. We must take a leap of faith, place trust in these young people, and believe that if we provide them with the right opportunities, they will respond and become productive citizens. We have to be brave. We must believe that one day, that boy who the youth control complex has labeled a "gang banger," "street thug," "dropout," "juvenile delinquent," and "predator" will come back to us and say, "Because of the second chance that you gave me, because of the support you provided, because you invested in me, I am now a productive member of society." He may even write a book that exposes the trials and tribulations that marginalized young people face.

APPENDIX

Beyond Jungle-Book Tropes

Knowledge is from the very beginning a co-operative process of group life.
　　　　　　　　—Karl Mannheim, *Ideology and Utopia*, 1936

We need to understand how structures become sources of meaning and determinants on behaviour in the culture milieu *at its own level*.
　　　　　　　　—Paul Willis, *Learning to Labour*, 1977

Reflexivity

Although I would like to pretend that this study was objective, from an outsider's perspective that could bring to light the issues that young people face in a fair and balanced way, I acknowledge that this study is affected by my own experience. Nevertheless, as a social scientist, I committed myself to generating an empirical and systematic study. This included making sure that I reflected on my own experience so that I could distinguish between my personal "truths" and the "truths" of others. My goal has been to utilize my experience in the production of knowledge but also to generate a study that could be replicated by anyone who is interested in doing so. While I remained reflexive, I also did not want to produce a "poor me" narrative in which I risked creating a study centered around my own subjective experiences and not the concrete array of experiences facing the boys in the field.

The boys in this study unearthed my own past, which I had dug six feet under on the day I buried my best friend, who I mentioned in the Preface to this book. The more I studied them, the more I reflected on my own days growing up in Oakland. During the course of this study some of the ghosts of the past came back to haunt me. Instead of ignoring them, I took sociologist Avery Gordon's advice, "If you let them the ghosts will lead you to what has been missing, which is sometimes everything."[1] This idea emerged in my field notes and reflections during the course of this study. I analyzed my own past and subjectivity and how it pertained to the lives of the boys I was studying.

I began this study because I was trying to make sense of the detrimental lived experiences of my friends and family. However, in my journey to understand the world of punitive social control, I found that many more, if not all, marginalized youths, in one way or another, experienced these systems of punitive control as social fabric stitched into their daily routines. As a native, I had insight into the processes that generated social misery in the inner city. As an intellectual, I maintained a reflexivity and rigor that allowed me to analyze agency and structure through a systematic lens. Sociologist Kathy Charmaz reminds us that "grounded theorists need to remain reflexive during all phases of their research and writing. In this way they may learn how their grounded theory discoveries are constructed."[2] I constantly reflected on how I collected data and what consequences, positive or negative, this may have had on my subjects. Reflexivity is the process by which a researcher understands how personal experience shapes his or her ideas and the way he or she attributes meaning, interprets action, and conducts dialogues with informants.[3]

I wanted to know how Black and Latino boys responded to negative interactions with authority figures and what they thought of their own actions and interactions with others. To find viable solutions to the negative predicaments that young people encountered, I analyzed both attitudes and specific cultural, political, and economic processes that produced the ecologies that youth navigated. Furthermore, I evaded the mistake that recent influential urban ethnographies have been accused of committing: telling "neoromantic tales" in order to appeal to the "moral schemata" of mainstream readers.[4] Instead, I sought to "dissect the social mechanisms and meanings that governed their practices, grounded their morality (if such be the question), and explained their strategies and trajectories."[5]

One of the promises I made to the boys in the study was that I was not there to study their criminality. I told them that I was not interested in hearing about the kinds of crimes they were committing. This could put them in danger if the records would ever end up with police. Inevitably I would witness and hear a plethora of stories about crime. Later I would find myself reminding the young men not to provide me with details about the crimes that they had committed. If I were to expose the names of the youths in this study, reputations and street credibility may be affected and resentment from authority figures may develop. Many of them told me that they did not care if I mentioned their true names. However, I believe that it is my ethical duty to prevent any information that may put them in any kind of harm from being released, even if some of my participants have determined that they are no longer at risk.

Life Stories and Interviews

By understanding both the biographical world and the structural world of youth, I began to further understand the current historical moment: the era of punitive social control. In addition to systematic observation, participants' life stories were elicited in order to gain a sense of when, how, and why the youths were criminalized. More important, their life stories brought light to the hidden structure of juvenile criminalization and punishment that they experienced every day. These life stories put at the forefront testimonies that many studies had failed to acknowledge and had often made invisible.

Five different in-depth sets of questions were asked. After each set of questions was completed—usually taking about two interviews each— each interview was analyzed, and from participant responses I developed more thematic questions that addressed specific themes brought up in the interview. The five sets of questions addressed a specific theme: Set 1 was open ended and centered around the life story and growing-up experience of the youth; Set 2 was semistructured and asked about the youth's interactions with institutions of social control, including school, family, community centers, and the criminal justice system; Set 3 was semistructured and inquired about the youth's experience with being criminalized; Set 4 was semistructured and examined the youth's attitudes toward crime and deviance; Set 5 was semistructured and asked the youth about his socioeconomic status and aspirations.

Bridging Agency and Structure

Social scientists cannot thoroughly understand larger political processes taking shape without also having a sense of how the local "on the ground" context shapes and is shaped by these macro processes. We also cannot understand the local context without a global perspective. We must have a clear sense of the macro processes of power and domination that shape the everyday lives of social subjects. I made sense of the lived experience of youth in this study and the structures that shaped their actions.[6] Structures contribute to our experience, which in turn contributes to the making of social systems: in effect, experience is the essence of who we are and how we shape our society. But analytically this experience must be understood both in terms of the lived experience of the social actors in their world(s) and at the structural level through an analytical and theoretical approach to the observed phenomena (from the perspective of actors) in multiple micro settings. In short, the relationship between human action and social structure is a crucial process to examine if we are to understand any social phenomenon.[7]

While my study was empirically focused on the lives of forty boys, I kept in mind the macro processes of power and domination that shaped the everyday lives of the social subjects I studied.[8] Everyday people serve as prisms through which we can grasp the reality of structural processes. The observer must connect the *habitus* of his or her participants to larger social forces shaping social action. Habitus is the process by which individuals internalize and embody the structures they encounter.[9] In order to avoid the victim premise that would render participants as passive agents at the mercy to the social structures that surrounded them, I also examined the "creative responses" that young people enacted.[10] Simplistic models of victimization or cultural explanations which largely blame victims for their situations and circumstances do not suffice to explain the lives of these youths.

Urban Ethnography in the Twenty-First Century

In the 1980s and 1990s, challenged by feminist and postcolonial scholars, cultural anthropology went into a crisis. A major part of this crisis came about when critical, feminist, postcolonial, and postmodernist scholars analyzed the various ways in which ethnography had been implicated in colonization, racialization, "othering," and placing non-Western populations, who lived in the present, in the past.[11] Anthropologist Johannes Fabian epitomized this critique of anthropology by asking, "What would happen to the West (and to anthropology) if its temporal fortress were suddenly invaded by the Time of the Other?"[12] This line questioning traditional scientific anthropology revived ethnography and brought about a diversification in the anthropological method. Indigenous peoples and formal colonial subjects had asserted a new methodology that addressed knowledge from below. Critical ethnography, reflexivity, feminist ethnography, and indigenous methodologies were introduced, reinventing what had become a stale, colonial enterprise trapped in the nineteenth century.

What would happen to urban ethnography if its subjects, those marginalized populations it has sought to understand and explain to the world, invaded its academic fortress? I believe that urban ethnography may face a "crisis" as well—a crisis in which the stories, worldviews, epistemologies, and systematic empirical studies by individuals who have embodied the experiences that urban ethnographers write about might change the composition of urban ethnography and the ways in which it conceptualizes marginalized populations. Urban ethnography would benefit from embracing solid studies conducted by individuals who have embodied the experiences that they write about. One recent critique by Douglass Hartmann of Scott Brooks's 2009 book on young basketball players is that Brooks, a sociologist with insider status with the people he studied, "exhibits very little distance" from his subjects.[13] Although Hartmann is not an urban ethnographer, in my experience, he personifies the critiques that I have witnessed over the years of urban ethnographers who are of the same race, class, gender, or sexuality as the people whom they have studied or as those who grew up in the communities that they study. It is time to embrace these kinds of perspectives as another form of knowledge that enlightens urban ethnography; otherwise, we will continue to legitimate the jungle-book trope: "I got lost in the wild, the wild people took me in and helped me, made me their king, and I lived to tell civilization about it!" The twenty-first century is experiencing a critical mass of ethnographers who are moving beyond telling journalistic, apologetic, "rogue" stories about marginalized peoples. This generation of scholars promises to change the way we understand marginalized populations and to dislodge those gatekeepers who claim to speak for the masses.

NOTES

Notes to the Preface

1. In this case "homies" are fellow gang members.

2. Out of respect for where I am from, and for safety concerns, I do not mention what gang I claimed.

3. Mills (1959:3).

4. Elijah Anderson (1999) argues that the "code of the street"—violent actions, symbolic or material, people participate in to gain respect—is "the fabric of everyday life" in the inner city. In the same vein, I argue that the culture of punishment, or what I later define as the youth control complex, is another organizing principle in the lives of marginalized youths.

5. Sociologist Paul Hirschfield (2008a) defines *criminalization* in a similar vein: "as the shift toward a crime control paradigm in the definition and management of the problem of student deviance. Criminalization encompasses the manner in which policy makers and school actors think and communicate about the problem of student rule-violation as well as myriad dimensions of school *praxis* including architecture, penal procedure, and security technologies and tactics." Legal scholar Jonathan Simon (2007) argues that everyday social problems, such as student truancy, workplace conflict, and parenting, are symbolically criminalized through the use of criminal justice metaphors and through the use of criminal justice policies and resources.

Notes to Chapter 1

1. Despite my informing Slick's mother and other parents that my study would have little to no benefit to their children, per human-subjects requirements, many of them still saw me as a mentor and role model to their children. In return, I tried to help their children as much as I could by connecting them with programs.

2. Hall et al. (1978).

3. See Wacquant (2009).

4. Stuart Hall and his colleagues (1978) argue that moral panics are created not only as a way of building a Durkheimian solidarity among white middle-class populations but also as a means of managing underemployed populations and racial threats in times when capital is in crisis. Hirschfield (2008b) argues that inner-city black youth are indeed constructed as moral panics and, as a response, are being pipelined by schools into the criminal justice system.

5. Smith (1990:25).

6. Alice Goffman (2009) reminds us that most urban ethnographies have been written prior to the increase in punitive criminal justice policies and mass incarceration.

7. Thomas and Thomas (1928:572).

8. Anderson (1999).

9. The "Superpredator" thesis, created by Princeton professor John DiIulio, catalyzed national media coverage and congressional legislation on youth crime and the need for punitive policy in 1996. DiIulio claimed that "Superpredators"—juvenile criminals with an unprecedented potential for violence—were an emerging risk to society and that serious punitive policies had to be generated to "deter" and "incapacitate" them at as early an age as possible: "Try as we might, there is ultimately very little that we can do to alter the early life-experiences that make some boys criminally 'at risk.' Neither can we do much to rehabilitate them once they have crossed the prison gates. Let us, therefore, do what we can to deter them by means of strict criminal sanctions, and, where deterrence fails, to incapacitate them. Let the government Leviathan lock them up and, when prudence dictates, throw away the key" (DiIulio 1996:3). Pushing the "Superpredator" thesis a step further, in 1996 DiIulio and former U.S. secretary of education William Bennett coauthored *Body Count: Moral Poverty and How to Win America's War against Crime and Drugs*, in which they introduced the idea of "moral poverty." According to Bennett and DiIulio, "moral poverty" stems from the increase in single-parent households and homes where one or more of the parents are "deviant" or "criminal" themselves. Specifically, the authors argue that "in the extreme, it is the poverty of growing up surrounded by deviant, delinquent, and criminal adults in a practically perfect criminogenic environment—that is, an environment that seems almost consciously designed to produce vicious, unrepentant predatory street criminals—that repeats the cycle" (Bennett, DiIulio, and Waters 1996:14).

10. "At-promise" youth are those youth who have traditionally been labeled "at-risk"—youth who lived in marginalized conditions. An issue with labeling young people as "risks" is that this may generate the very stigma that I am analyzing in this study. Therefore, I am calling them what many community workers call them: "at-promise."

11. Weiss (1994).

12. Mario Luis Small (2008) argues that unique cases are a crucial area of study. In the following hypothetical scenario, he explains how unique cases matter: "Suppose that Bill had chosen a neighborhood with a 40 percent poverty rate but little garbage or graffiti and a unique architectural design due to the influence of a mayor interested in promoting architecture in the city. . . . Suppose the mayor in the second case also had instituted a radical and unique policy whereby mothers received significantly higher rent subsidies plus $1000 per child for a college fund if they married before the birth of their second child. This rare case would suddenly present Bill an exceptional opportunity to examine the relationship among high poverty, policy, and out-of-wedlock births in ways that cases that happen to be at the mean might not. In case studies, rare situations are often precisely what the researcher wants" (169).

13. For examples, see Anderson (1999); Bourgois (1995); Duneier (1999); and Venkatesh (2006).

14. For this approach, I used a case-study research approach (Small 2008; Yin 1981, 1984, 1993). Due to the nature of this study, I did not seek a sample of forty youth who would be representative of a specific population. Instead I created a set of forty cases which could provide insight into how young people develop an understanding of punishment (see Small 2008).

15. See Brunson and Miller (2006); Chesney-Lind and Shelden (2004); Diaz-Cotto (2006); N. Jones (2010); and Miller (2008).

16. See Chesney-Lind and Jones (2010).

17. See N. Jones (2009) and Miller (2008) for an understanding of adolescent girls' experiences with violence. At the outset of my study, I believed that I was not prepared to adequately address the power relations that exist between male researchers and female participants. I also sought to avoid what Meda Chesney-Lind calls the "stag effect"—the assumption that theories of male experiences can be universally applied to women (Chesney-Lind and Shelden 2004). I understood that gender shapes the experiences of men and women differently and that each group requires a thorough analysis of this process.

18. Jody Miller (2008) and Nikki Jones (2009) provide groundbreaking analysis of how girls experience gender, violence, racism, and agency in the inner city.

19. Irwin (2003).

20. N. Jones (2009:177–178).

21. I borrow from standpoint theory, as developed by Dorothy Smith (1990) and Patricia Hill Collins (1990), to develop this approach. Standpoint theory, developed by feminist scholars, argues that a person's personal experience is a central pillar for knowledge production. A person who has experienced gender, class, or racial marginalization may have a unique standpoint from which to study the social world: "Collins argues that 'personal and cultural biographies [are] significant sources of knowledge' for 'outsiders within' the academy (Naples 2003:53). She explains that

since working class Black women are 'much more inclined to be struck by the mismatch of [their] own experience and the paradigms of sociology itself' (Naples 2003:50), they are more likely to identify 'anomalies' between their experiences and those represented by normalized, yet distorted, sociological accounts" (Naples 2003:52). For an excellent application of this approach to urban ethnography, see N. Jones (2009).

22. Werner and Schoepfle (1987:16).

23. Denzin (1989) calls this "intersubjectivity."

24. Diego Vigil explains his experience as an insider with gangs: "It is also important to stress that my background as an insider at various times, places, and levels of gang reality enables me to examine and pinpoint the dynamic, multi-dimensionality of gang behavior and plumb the deeper private motives behind the public 'gang' or 'cholo' image. Likewise, I claim no distance here, for a self-reflective examination provides liberties to speak to several levels of the issue" (1988:14).

25. E. Goffman (1989:125).

26. This is not to say that an outsider could not gain trust from youth. In fact, most urban ethnography has been conducted by outsiders, and most have gained the trust of community members and have even been accepted as insiders by the community because of the time they spent researching the community.

27. Becker (1963:141).

28. I used selective coding to "cut across multiple interviews and thus represent recurrent themes" (Charmaz 2002:686).

29. In *Racism without Racists*, sociologist Eduardo Bonilla-Silva (2006) describes how colorism affects the Latino community and how light-skinned Latinos attract more privilege. I would like to note that I am a dark-skinned Chicano. I found that many darker-skinned Latino youths had deeper bonds with Black youths than lighter-skinned Latinos did. I found that light-skinned Latinos used racism against Blacks and colorism against dark-skinned Latinos. In other words, some Latinos were able to escape punishment easier than darker-skinned Latinos and Blacks were; punishment discriminates based on hue.

30. In *Everyday Surveillance*, sociologist William Staples (2000) reminds us that "no matter the stated motivations, the intent of social control is to mold, shape, and modify actions and behaviors" (3).

31. Here I am making the distinction that Alford Young (2004) makes between "beliefs and thoughts" and "values and norms." He argues that beliefs and thoughts have been given too little attention by urban poverty research, which instead has "focused upon the presumed values and norms adopted by these men while reducing investigations of belief that the men think that their path to a better life is obstructed by their entrenchment in the turbulent and pernicious social world of the inner city" (5).

32. Staples (2000) reminds us that "as new forms of social control are localized in everyday life, they are capable of bringing wide-ranging populations, not just the official 'deviant,' under the watchful gaze" (6).

33. See Devine (1996); Ferguson (2000); Giroux (2003, 2009); Hagedorn (2008); Hirschfield (2008a, 2008b); Kupchik (2006); Parenti (2000); Simon (2007); and Vigil (2002).

34. Witt (2007).

35. Whitlock (2007).

36. Witt (2007).

37. See Giroux (2009) for an explanation of the criminalization of youth at a global level. For an analysis of the criminalization of youth as a neoliberal system of controlling surplus populations in a transnational context, see Rios and Rodriguez (2011). While this book does not have the capacity to analyze transnational punitive social control, my observations and analysis may be applied to other communities throughout the globe, keeping in mind the local histories of race, class, gender, and nation.

38. I borrow from Mary Patillo-McCoy's (1999) and Clifford Shaw's (1966) approach of adding character to theory by providing an in-depth account of the life stories of youths.

Notes to Chapter 2

1. Later in the book I argue that punitive social control in Oakland has led many young people to become politically active, to use crime as a form of protest, or to formally protest against debilitating criminalization.

2. H. Harris (2010).

3. Oakland has a crisis when it comes to teen prostitution. Dozens of female teens prostitute at various intersections in Oakland on any given day.

4. See U.S. Census Bureau (2000).

5. Aihwa Ong (2003) has written an excellent book that focuses on this population in the San Francisco Bay Area. She discusses the predicaments of Southeast Asian youth caught in the midst of poverty, drugs, and incarceration.

6. I define *social control* as the mechanisms in place that socialize individuals to follow rules and laws.

7. Rhomberg (2007:18–19).

8. U.S. Census Bureau (2009).

9. U.S. Census Bureau, U.S. Census 2006.

10. U.S. Census Bureau, U.S. Census 2000.

11. U.S. Census Bureau, U.S. Census 2000.

12. U.S. Census Bureau, U.S. Census 2000.

13. Bagwell (1982).

14. Oakland Community and Economic Development Agency (2010).
15. Robinson (2004:73).
16. Willis (1977).
17. Hirschfield (2008a).
18. See Rios and Rodriguez (2010).
19. Self (2003).
20. Murch (2007:334).
21. Ward (2009).
22. Ward (2009); also see Wacquant (2009) for an analysis of the prison as a race-making system.
23. Murch (2007:337).
24. Davis (1999); Garland (2001a); Gilmore (2007); Parenti (2000); Wacquant (2002a); J. Young (1999).
25. Davis (1999); Gilmore (2007); Mauer (1999); Parenti (2000).
26. Parenti (2000).
27. Lynch (1998); Martinson (1974); Mauer (1999).
28. Alexander (2009); Gilmore (2007); Mauer (1999); Parenti (2000).
29. Beckett (1997).
30. Semple (1968).
31. Parenti (2000).
32. Rosenfeld (2002).
33. See Coleman (1986).
34. Murch (2007).
35. Churchill and Vander Wall (2002); Parenti (2000).
36. It is important to note that there is currently an active youth movement in Oakland (Martinez 1998; Rios 2006). As recently as October 2008, high school students had shut down the city's commuter rail system during rush hour to protest Immigration and Customs Enforcement (ICE) raids and anti-immigrant legislation (Jones et al. 2008).
37. See Harcourt (2001). One of the most influential articles of the time was Martinson's "What Works? Questions and Answers about Prison Reform" (1974). It should be noted that Martinson concluded that rehabilitation programs did not work but recanted his broad conclusions in a later article that received much less attention (Mauer 1999). The theory of "broken windows" later contributed to the argument that zero-tolerance policing must exist in order to maintain order (Lynch 1998).
38. Mauer (1999); Parenti (2000).
39. Between 1980 and 1993, federal spending on employment and training programs was cut nearly in half, while corrections spending increased by 521 percent (Mauer 1999).
40. California Penal Code § 186.21.
41. California Penal Code § 186.21.
42. See Rios and Navarro (2010).

43. Rios and Navarro (2010) have shown how young people are erroneously defined as gang members by gang experts in the courtroom.

44. U.S. Department of Justice (2006).

45. City Councilwoman Pat Kernighan was quoted stating this to Police Chief Wayne Tucker by the *San Francisco Chronicle* (C. Jones 2008).

46. Warren (2008).

47. Sabol and Couture (2008).

48. NCCD (2009). Scholar and activist Angela Davis has called the structure responsible for this mass incarceration, specifically of people of color, the "prison industrial complex": "All this work, which used to be the primary province of government, is now also performed by private corporations, whose links to government in the field of what is euphemistically called 'corrections' resonate dangerously with the military industrial complex. . . . Taking into account the structural similarities and profitability of business-government linkages in the realms of military production and public punishment, the expanding penal system can now be characterized as a 'prison industrial complex'" (Davis and Gordon 1998:146).

49. Wacquant (2002a).

50. Garland (2001a).

51. Davis (1999); Gilmore (2007); Western (2006); J. Young (1999).

52. Parenti (2000).

53. Wacquant (2009) and Rusche and Kirscheimer (1939) argue that incarceration is a system by which precarious labor is imposed on poor populations.

54. This component of Wacquant's argument is reminiscent of Durkheim's functionalist understanding of crime: "But so that the originality of the idealist who dreams of transcending his era may display itself, that of the criminal, which falls short of the age, must also be possible. One does not go without the other" (Durkheim 1982:85). Crime is a communicative apparatus by which morals and values are proscribed.

55. Wacquant (2009).

56. For exceptions see Pager (2007) and Western (2007).

57. David Garland (2001b) coined the term "mass imprisonment," referring to the historically exponential and peculiar incarceration rate in the United States. I refer to it as "mass incarceration" to account for juvenile and county jail populations as well (see Wacquant 2002a; Western and Wildeman 2009).

58. This was also true for thirty-two of the seventy-eight youth in the additional interview sample.

59. Martín Sánchez-Jankowski (2008) has found that gang neighborhoods are negatively affected by incarceration: as older gang members who in the past have maintained a less violent social order are incarcerated, younger gang members looking to prove themselves emerge, often leading to an increase in crime and violence by the gang. I found this to be true in this study.

60. Mauer and Chesney-Lind (2002:4).

61. This demonstrates Wacquant's (2002b) notion of the "hyperghetto," in which the culture of the prison and that of the ghetto are indistinguishable. However, to the youths in this study, it was the culture of the prison and the cultures of school and police institutions that were perceived as indistinguishable. Although none of them had been to prison at the time that I met them, they had an imagined understanding of prison and prison culture.

62. Mauer and Chesney-Lind (2002) have argued that the disproportionate incarceration of people of color has had unintended consequences in poor communities. They contend that such punishment not only adversely affects confined individuals but also creates negative effects for families and communities, as well as for the future livelihoods of those who come into contact with the criminal justice system.

63. Mauer and Cheney-Lind (2002:12).

64. Mauer and Chesney-Lind (2002) have produced an excellent book that speaks to these "collateral consequences of mass imprisonment." Also see Bruce Western (2006) for an exceptional study of how families and women suffer when their loved ones come home after being incarcerated and lose the ability to generate social bonds in the community.

65. Western (2006).

66. For exceptions, see Brunson and Miller (2006); Ferguson (2000); A. Goffman (2009); Hagan (1991); Kelley (1997); Kozol (1991); Kupchik (2006); Nightingale (1993); and Simon (2007). Here I am using Yasser Payne's notion of "street life–oriented" youths (2006). He uses this term to avoid perpetuating stereotypes of Black boys and to develop a more accurate understanding of the population under study. In my case, the boys in this study are street oriented in that the street is a space in which the boys choose to, or are forced to, inhabit, claim, and make their own.

67. A. Goffman (2009:2).

68. Philippe Bourgois reported that while police brutality was a reality, "it was not one of our primary daily concerns. . . . We were considerably less worried about being brutalized by the police if they raided the crackhouse compared to what we risked at the hands of our fellow inmates" (1995:37). Martín Sánchez-Jankowski (1991) found that police bond with and become a structural support for gangs. MacLeod found that police brutality is a "graphic and straightforward" form of racial domination (1995:244). Duneier (1992) found that police are a friendly force for Black men in specific contexts. He later found that zero-tolerance policing gripped the lives of poor Black men (1999). See A. Goffman (2009) for a discussion of the new police presence in the inner city.

69. Anderson (1990:185).

70. Jonathan Simon makes this point in his book *Governing through Crime* (2007).

71. Simon (2007); also see Kupchik (2010).

72. "When we govern through crime, we make crime and the forms of knowledge historically associated with it—criminal law, popular crime narrative, and criminology—available outside their limited original subject domains as powerful tools with which to interpret and frame all forms of social action as a problem for governance" (Simon 2007:17).

73. Simon (2007:4).

74. Simon (2007:4).

75. Pager (2007:4).

76. Pager (2007:4).

77. See Anderson's discussion of the "campaign for social regard" (1990:194).

78. Lind and Tyler (1988:237).

79. Chester Pierce (1970) coined the term "microaggression." He argues that racialized individuals are impacted every day by subtle but cumulatively devastating forms of racism. Critical race theorists build on his concept: "Like water dripping on sandstone, they can be thought of as small acts of racism" (Delgado and Stefancic 2001). Tara Yosso (2006) uses the term to describe how Chicana/o students experience the U.S. education system.

80. Ferguson (2000).

81. For a critique of the social disorganization literature, see Sánchez-Jankowski (2008).

82. Blomberg and Cohen (2003:6).

Notes to Chapter 3

1. See Ageton and Delbert (1974); Becker (1963); and Hepburn (1977).

2. See Dodge (1983) and Lebel (2008).

3. Matsueda (1992).

4. Hirschfield (2008a).

5. See Anderson (1990); Bourgois (1995); Horowitz (1983); Sánchez-Jankowski (1991); Venkatesh (2006); Vigil (1988).

6. Kelley (1997).

7. In March 2009, a twenty-six-year-old Black male killed four police officers, just a few miles from this neighborhood. The day before, two blocks from where the murders happened, I had been interviewing Black and Latino boys about their experiences with the police. The day after, I returned to ask them about their perspectives on the killings. In a nutshell, the youths believed that their lives were not valued as much as police lives. A few weeks prior to the police murders, an unarmed fifteen-year-old boy had been killed by police in the same area. Police had earned themselves a reputation as a violent occupying army among the boys, and some of the boys therefore perceived their deaths as justice.

8. Herbert Gans (1962) and Claude Fischer (1976) have found that despite ecological change, social organization remains the same in urban settings.

9. Matsueda (1992).

10. Payne (2008) has developed a "sites of resiliency" theory, in which he argues that the streets organize meaning for street-oriented youths around feeling safe, secure, and fulfilled. Young people engage in behaviors which will make them feel this way. These behaviors are often seen as criminal and oppositional. However, Payne argues, street-oriented youths are not oppositional; they are actually attempting to accomplish a mainstream lifestyle with marginal resources.

MacLeod (1995) argues that inner-city Black men are neither victims nor victimizers. Instead, they live in a context in which committing crime can be seductive, but at the same time there is very little choice but to commit the act. Young people are both agents and subjects. Covington (1995) has warned researchers about explanations that attempt to explain crime committed by racialized groups. She urges researchers to understand that cultural and structural theories of crime have often assumed that all poor Blacks are at risk of committing crime, when in reality only a small number of poor Blacks commit crime. The problem, she contends, is that Black crime has almost always been measured in relation to White crime. Covington reminds us that poor Black criminals have more in common with poor White criminals than they do with other poor Blacks.

11. A quinceañera is a coming-of-age ceremony for girls turning fifteen, celebrated by many Latino families.

12. Anderson (1999) and Venkatesh (1998) have written about underpolicing and the impetus for residents to take justice into their own hands.

13. Anderson (1999); Pinderhughes (forthcoming).

14. Anderson (1999:10).

15. Anderson (1999:326).

16. Also see Pinderhughes's idea of "violence as a violence prevention strategy" (forthcoming).

17. This phenomenon may become more prevalent as gang injunctions, laws that prevent gang members from hanging out with each other, continue to spread around the country. The gang may become prone to hide away and concentrate in private spheres, where innocent families pay the price.

18. Paul Hirschfield (2008b) argues that criminalization has created a process for marginalized youths by which the criminal justice system becomes an institution that grants young people their "rite of passage" as they become adults.

19. Durkheim (1912); E. Goffman (1967).

20. Braithwaite (1997).

21. Hagan and McCarthy (1997) explain that "the implication is that when . . . unresolved personal shame . . . interacts with the unremitting criminal stigma . . . , a defiant criminal response is likely to follow" (183). Furthermore, Flores-Gonzalez (2002) finds that "most students cope with stigma in one of two ways: living up to the myth, or countering the myth" (51). She also finds that the school amplifies street-oriented youths' desire to become more street oriented.

22. Nilda Flores-Gonzalez (2002) finds that schools play a major role in shaping street identity or school identity in Latino youths: "School produces school kids and street kids by giving or denying them certain conditions needed to become engaged in school" (12).

23. Contrary to popular belief and court testimony from gang police, most crimes committed by gang members in this study were not committed to directly expand the gang enterprise. Instead, each individual picked up a specialization (e.g., drug sales, auto theft, burglaries) in an attempt to make money to help himself, to have fun, or to help his family.

24. Venkatesh (1998).

25. The CalGang database was created in 1998 by a private corporation. The database is used by all major police departments in California. It categorizes and organizes various "gang information," including the nicknames, tattoos, and clothing styles of suspected and known gang members.

26. In order to maintain trust with the boys, I decided to minimize my interactions with police. I did not want to take any risks of the boys finding out that I had discussions with police. Therefore, I decided not to interview police officers. In addition, many officers seemed to have animosity toward me; I was seen by them as an advocate for the boys who did not respect police presence in the community.

27. Sociologists John Hagan and Bill McCarthy (1997) have found that the combination of negative experiences at home and in the community can lead young people to embrace criminality: "Family-based experiences of shame and rejection can interact with state-imposed criminal stigma to provoke what . . . labeling theory referred to as secondary deviance—that is, criminal behavior that follows sanctioning" (183).

28. For studies on poor women on welfare and their everyday struggles with welfare-to-work policies and programs, see Hays (2004) and Collins and Mayer (2010).

29. Liebow (1967).

30. A. Goffman (2009:15).

31. Stewart, Schreck, and Simons (2006) find that young Black men who use the code of the street are more vulnerable to victimization.

32. A. Young (forthcoming).

Notes to Chapter 4

1. Garland (1993:276).
2. Garland (1993:282).
3. Kelley (1994:5).
4. Urbina (2010).
5. The school name is a pseudonym.
6. For an understanding on how the family is penetrated by the state's project to regulate its population, see Donzelot (1979).
7. E. Goffman (1967).
8. Alice Goffman (2009) finds that family members of Black male felons in Philadelphia use the criminal justice system in an attempt to regulate their behavior.
9. During my time in the field, and according to community members, for many years past, as public and private funding for community programs diminished, community organizations applied for grants and partnerships with law-enforcement agencies, whose budgets continued to increase.
10. Historian Carl Nightingale (1993) argues that the harsh and corporal punishment of children is a central theme in American culture. "For both parents and children, the tradition itself, the respectability of its Christian and mainstream origins, and the official sanction it received from the law-and-order policies of America's police, courts, and prisons, all help to make the forceful child-rearing approach an important source of legitimacy for values of violence in the inner city" (81). The youth control complex has very deep historical roots in a three-hundred-year-old legacy of racialized social control and an equally old American idea of harsh discipline for children. Also see Greven (1992).
11. Foucault (1977).
12. The decline of the welfare state and deindustrialization taking place from the 1960s to the 1990s (see Parenti 2000 and Wilson 1987) broke down the "old school" forms of social control that often worked in marginalized communities. The "old school" form of social control included when grandmothers, neighbors, caring business people, and other community members took on an "it takes a village to raise a child" approach and took discipline into their own hands to teach young people a lesson that in the end helped them become productive citizens. At a larger scale, social control has shifted from informal social control and collective efficacy in poor communities to social control through state violence and mass incarceration. This state violence influences other institutions to become equally punitive at the material and symbolic level as well.
13. Hagan and McCarthy (1997:181).
14. Anderson (1999:36).

Notes to Chapter 5

1. As a commitment to helping the youths in this study, I had given them my phone number and told them to call me if they ever needed help with school- or employment-related matters.

2. Gramsci (1996).

3. Yosso (2006).

4. Sánchez-Jankowski (2008).

5. Payne (2006).

6. Devah Pager (2007) has found that young Black men without a criminal record have less of a chance of obtaining a job than White men with a criminal record.

7. See Takaki (1993) and Apel (2004) for a detailed discussion of this history.

8. This racialized sexual control is reinforced by close scrutinization of Black and Latino boys when they interact with White female teachers, students, or community members. Although it may be important to discuss the differences between African American and Latino youth, I have decided to focus here on commonalities. Lamont and Small (2008) have argued that "the idea that races have a culture—for example that there is an Anglo-American culture that differs from Asian culture or Afro-American culture—is unhelpful to the study of racial differences in poverty" (78). This conception has failed in the study of urban poverty because often it has created fixed understandings of specific populations. Lamont and Small argue that "instead of imputing a shared culture to groups, we [should] study empirically how people make sense of their lives" (78). The approach, then, is to make sense of the resources available to urban young for them to engage in social action and the meanings they make as they deploy these resources. Punishment, at least in the lives of the youths in Oakland, had what I call a *collective racialization* effect. In other words, poor Black and Latino youths experienced similar forms of punishment when it came to crime control and made sense of their experience with punishment in similar ways. It is time for scholars to move beyond the "four food groups of racialization" and examine how some social phenomena, such as punishment, might be experienced collectively.

9. Bourgois (1995).

10. Bourgois (1995).

11. Castells (1997:9).

12. Swidler (1986).

13. It is important to point out that this resistance contradicts the idea that young Black and Latino men reject mainstream values and prefer to embrace the streets (Anderson 1999).

14. Quinney (1977).

15. Hagedorn (2008:xxv).

16. Padilla (1992).

17. Quoted in Padilla (1992:5).

18. Becker (1963).

19. Swidler (1986:276). Lamont and Small (2008) argue that this method of observing culture as repertoire allows for the study of culture and poverty without blaming the victim.

20. Scheff (2006).

21. Scheff (2006).

22. See Anderson (1999), Bourgois (1995), and Horowitz (1983).

23. See Rios (2005).

24. Willis (1977:3).

25. Urban ethnographers such as Elijah Anderson (1999), Mercer Sullivan (1990), and Sudhir Venkatesh (2006) have found a similar paradox among marginalized urban Black youths.

26. "Men make their own history, but they do not make it as they please; they do not make it under circumstances of their own choosing, but under circumstances existing already, given and transmitted from the past." Marx (1963:15).

27. Scott (1985).

28. Scott contends that the "imperial inspirations of many a monarch [were] ... undone by the social avalanche of petty acts of insubordination carried out by an unlikely coalition ... with no name, no organization, no leadership, and certainly no Leninist conspiracy behind it" (quoted in Duncombe 2002:90).

29. Kelley (1994).

30. Kelley (1994:8).

31. Kelley (1994:13).

32. Fanon (2008:102).

33. Dance (2005:7). Payne (2008) discusses how these kinds of acts are forms of resilience in a context where there are no other opportunities.

34. Kelley reminds us that the forces of punishment also become a basis for controlling resistance: daily acts of resistance have had consequences for existing power relations, and the powerful have deployed immense resources in order to avoid those consequences or to punish transgressors. Knowing how those in power interpret, redefine, and respond to the thoughts and actions of the oppressed is just as important as identifying and analyzing resistance (1994:9).

35. For a more in-depth discussion, see Martinez and Rios (forthcoming).

36. This is a different process from that described by Padilla (1992), who finds that Puerto Rican gang members gripped onto their ethnic culture as a form of resistance. While the boys in my study were proud of being Black or Latino, their analysis and resistance to criminalization was not based on "cultural superiority" but on a consciousness of "collective racialization," as a sense of solidarity and formal and informal resistance.

37. Oliver (2008:19).

Notes to Chapter 6

1. From the album *Ronald Dregan: Dreganomics* (2004). Mac Dre is considered the "godfather" of the hyphy subculture that many of the youths in this study ascribed to.

2. Martín Sánchez-Jankowski (2008) describes a similar process, whereby some of the urban poor will sometimes make a sacrifice in the present in order to avoid future suffering. I believe that some of these young men understood that their preemptive verbal attacks on police and other authority figures served as a way of attempting to structure the relationship, to tell the officer, "Don't mess with me because I will give you a hard time," in order to prevent future harassment and brutality. Sometimes this strategy worked, but often it backfired. The boys were aware of the high failure rate of this strategy. However, many of them believed that it was worth the gamble.

3. Homophobic language was a common bonding and exclusionary practice for these boys. Chauvinism and homophobia went hand in hand and served as a basis for the development of masculinity. It is important to note that homophobia and chauvinism were not only a street creation but were also created and perpetuated in other institutions, by authority figures.

4. Morgan and Morgan (2007).

5. Messerschmidt (2000:13).

6. West and Fenstermaker (1995:21).

7. For policing and gender, see Brunson and Miller (2006); for mistrust, see Fine and Weiss (1998); for negative credentials, see Pager (2007).

8. A. Harris (2000:785).

9. West and Fenstermaker (1995).

10. Ferguson (2000) has demonstrated that schools participate in the making of Black masculinity in children as young as ten years old.

11. Sutherland and Cressey (1955).

12. Quoted in Kimmel (2006:82).

13. Anderson (1999); see also Dance (2005) and Duneier (1999).

14. Pyke (1996).

15. N. Jones (2009).

16. Anderson (1999); Messerschmidt (1993).

17. Kimmel and Mahler (2003).

18. Kimmel (2006:216).

19. Prokos and Padavic (2002:442).

20. A. Harris (2000:22).

21. A. Harris (2000:6).

22. See Brunson and Miller (2006); and Ferguson (2000).

Notes to Chapter 7

1. Carter (2005:12–13).

2. As this book goes to press, Oakland, and other cities in California, have imposed gang injunctions in specific neighborhoods where marginalized youths live. These injunctions require individuals to relinquish any contact with others named in a lawsuit, including family members and neighbors. Injunctions may accentuate this process of straining social relations and hypercriminalization and may place many youths at risk of being victimized for being seen as snitches by peers.

3. Here I am referring to Elijah Anderson's (1999) notion of "code-switching," when individuals who live in a violent environment learn to shift their behaviors within the different institutions they navigate.

4. Hagan, Shedd, and Payne (2005) found that Black youths in Chicago understand regular negative police interactions as a normal part of life. I found this to be true also with Black and Latino youths in Oakland.

5. Sánchez-Jankowski (2008).

6. Sánchez-Jankowski (2008:22).

7. See Fordham and Ogbu (1986).

8. Fordham and Ogbu (1986:6).

9. Fordham and Ogbu (1986:6).

10. McWhorter (2000).

11. Obama (2004).

12. Fryer (2006).

13. Ainsworth-Darnell and Downey (1998) have found that levels of disdain for academic achievement are very similar across racial lines, including among Whites.

14. Carter (2003).

Notes to the Conclusion

1. See Rios and Navarro (2010).

2. Patterson (1982).

3. Rodriguez (2006:5).

4. Lipsitz (2006:183).

5. Giroux (2009:2).

6. Feld (1993); Krisberg (2004); Takaki (1993); Ward (2009).

7. See Mirande (1987).

8. For more on reproductive resistance, see Rios and Rodriguez (forthcoming).

9. See Gramsci (1996); Hall (1985).

10. N. Jones (2010).

Notes to the Appendix

1. Gordon (1998:54).
2. Charmaz (2002:692).
3. Meyerhoff and Ruby (1982).
4. Wacquant (2002b).
5. Wacquant (2002b:3).
6. Simmel (1950).
7. Simmel (1950); Berger and Luckmann (1966); Bourdieu (1972).
8. Burawoy et al. (1991).
9. Bourdieu (1972).
10. "Creative responses" refers to the agency that young people enact. Ferguson (2000), Kelley (1997), and MacLeod (1995) have argued that inner-city youth constantly resist inequality. Their resistance is an important social force that has the potential to generate change (Kelley 1997) but often also leads to further criminalization and detriment (MacLeod 1995). When institutions embrace this resistance and allow young people to express themselves, children and youth become empowered to succeed (Ferguson 2000).
11. See Asad (1973) on colonization and decolonization; Fabian (1983) on temporality; Geertz (1988) on the crisis in anthropology; Said (1978) on "Othering"; and Behar (1996) on feminism.
12. Fabian (1983:35).
13. Hartmann (2010:146). See Alford Young's (2008) critique of white ethnographers, their journalistic accounts, and his experience as an African American male of being "too close" to his subjects.

REFERENCES

Ageton, Suzanne, and Elliot Delbert. 1974. "The Effect of Legal Processing on Delinquent Orientation." *Social Problems* 22:87–100.

Ainsworth-Darnell, James W., and Douglas B. Downey. 1998. "Assessing the Oppositional Culture Explanation for Racial/Ethnic Differences in School Performance." *American Sociological Review* 63:536–553.

Alexander, Michelle. 2009. *The New Jim Crow: Mass Incarceration in the Age of Colorblindness.* New York: New Press.

Anderson, Elijah. 1990. *Streetwise: Race, Class, Change in an Urban Community.* Chicago: University of Chicago Press.

———. 1999. *Code of the Street: Decency, Violence, and Moral Life of the Inner City.* New York: Norton.

Apel, Dora. 2004. *Imagery of Lynching: Black Men, White Women, and the Mob.* New Brunswick, NJ: Rutgers University Press.

Asad, Talal, ed. 1973. *Anthropology and the Colonial Encounter.* London: Ithaca.

Bagwell, Beth. 1982. *Oakland: The Story of a City.* Novato, CA: Presidio.

Becker, Howard. 1963. *Outsiders: Studies in the Sociology of Deviance.* New York: Free Press.

Beckett, Katherine. 1997. *Making Crime Pay: Law and Order in Contemporary American Politics.* New York: Oxford University Press.

Behar, Ruth. 1996. *The Vulnerable Observer: Anthropology That Breaks Your Heart,* Boston: Beacon.

Bennett, William J., John J. DiIulio, Jr., and John P. Walters. 1996. *Body Count: Moral Poverty and How to Win America's War against Crime and Drugs.* New York: Simon and Schuster.

Berger, Peter L., and Thomas Luckmann. 1966. *The Social Construction of Reality.* New York: Doubleday.

Blomberg, Thomas G., and Stanley Cohen. 2003. Introduction to *Punishment and Social Control.* Hawthorne, NY: Walter de Gruyter.

Bonilla-Silva, Eduardo. 2006. *Racism without Racists: Color-Blind Racism and Racial Inequality in Contemporary America.* Lanham, MD: Rowman and Littlefield.

References

Bourdieu, Pierre. 1972. *Outline of a Theory of Practice*. Cambridge: Cambridge University Press.

Bourgois, Philippe. 1995. *In Search of Respect: Selling Crack in El Barrio*. New York: Cambridge University Press.

Braithwaite, John. 1989. *Crime, Shame and Reintegration*. New York: Cambridge University Press.

———. 1997. "On Speaking Softly and Carrying Sticks: Neglected Dimensions of Republican Separation of Powers." *University of Toronto Law Journal* 47:1–57.

Brunson, R. K., and J. Miller. 2006. "Young Black Men and Urban Policing in the United States." *British Journal of Criminology* 46:613–640.

Burawoy, Michael, Alice Burton, Ann Arnett Ferguson, and Kathryn J. Fox. 1991. *Ethnography Unbound: Power and Resistance in the Modern Metropolis*. Berkeley: University of California Press.

Carter, Prudence. 2003. "'Black' Cultural Capital, Status Positioning, and Schooling Conflicts for Low-Income African American Youth." *Social Problems* 50 (1): 136–155.

———. 2005. *Keepin' It Real: School Success beyond Black and White*. New York: Oxford University Press.

Castells, Manuel. 1997. *The Power of Identity*. Oxford, UK: Blackwell.

Charmaz, Kathy. 2002. "Qualitative Interviewing and Grounded Theory Analysis." In *Handbook of Interview Research: Context and Method*, ed. J. Gubrium and J. A. Holstein, 675–693. Thousand Oaks, CA: Sage.

Chesney-Lind, Meda, and Nikki Jones, eds. 2010. *Fighting for Girls: Critical Perspectives on Gender and Violence*. Albany: SUNY Press.

Chesney-Lind, Meda, and Randall G. Shelden. 2004. *Girls, Delinquency, and Juvenile Justice*. 3rd ed. Belmont, CA: Wadsworth/Thomson Learning. First edition published in 1992.

Churchill, Ward, and Jim Vander Wall. 2002. *Agents of Repression: The FBI's Secret Wars against the Black Panther Party and the American Indian Movement*. Cambridge, MA: South End.

Coleman. Kate. 1986. "The Roots of Ed Meese: Reagan's Polemical Attorney General Has Prompted a Major Constitutional Debate, Surprising Those Who Knew Him in His Pragmatic Early Days, in the Quiet Hills of Oakland and during the Turbulent 60's." *Los Angeles Times Magazine*, May 4.

Collins, Jane L., and Victoria Mayer. 2010. *Both Hands Tied: Welfare Reform and the Race to the Bottom of the Low-Wage Labor Market*. Chicago: University of Chicago Press.

Collins, Patricia Hill. 1990. *Black Feminist Thought: Knowledge, Consciousness, and the Politics of Empowerment*. Boston: Unwin Hyman.

Covington, Jeannette. 1995. "Racial Classification in Criminology: The Reproduction of Racialized Crime." *Sociological Forum* 10:547–568.

Dance, Jannelle. 2005. *Tough Fronts: The Impact of Street Culture on Schooling.* New York: Routledge.

Davis, Angela, and Avery Gordon. 1998. "Globalism and the Prison Industrial Complex: An Interview with Angela Davis." *Race and Class* 40 (2–3): 145–158.

Davis, Nanette J. 1999. *Youth Crisis: Growing Up in the High-Risk Society.* Westport, CT: Praeger.

Delgado, Richard, and Jean Stefancic. 2001. *Critical Race Theory: An Introduction.* New York: NYU Press.

Denzin, Norman K. 1989. *Interpretive Biography.* Thousand Oaks, CA: Sage.

Devine, John F. 1996. *Maximum Security: The Culture of Violence in Inner-City Schools.* Chicago: University of Chicago Press.

Diaz-Cotto, Juanita. 2006. *Chicana Lives and Criminal Justice: Voices from El Barrio.* Austin: University of Texas Press.

DiIulio, John J., Jr. 1996. "The Cycle of Poverty Produces 'Super-Predators.'" *Star-Ledger,* June 23, 1.

Dodge, Kenneth. 1983. "Behavioral Antecedents of Peer Social Status." *Child Development* 54:1386–1399.

Donzelot, Jacques. 1979. *The Policing of Families.* Trans. Robert Hurley. New York: Pantheon.

Duncombe, Stephen. 2002. *The Cultural Resistance Reader.* New York: Verso.

Duneier, Mitchell. 1992. *Slim's Table: Race, Respectability, and Masculinity.* Chicago: University of Chicago Press.

———. 1999. *Sidewalk.* New York: Farrar, Straus and Giroux.

Durkheim, Emile. 1912. *The Elementary Forms of Religious Life.* Trans. Karen E. Fields. New York: Free Press.

———. 1982. *The Rules of the Sociological Method.* Ed. Steven Lukes. Trans. W. D. Halls. New York: Macmillan.

Fabian, Johannes. 1983. *Time and the Other: How Anthropology Makes Its Objects.* New York: Columbia University Press.

Fanon, Frantz. 2008. *Black Skin, White Masks.* New York: Grove.

Feld, Barry C. 1993. *Justice for Children: The Right to Counsel and the Juvenile Court.* Boston: Northeastern University Press.

Ferguson, Ann Arnett. 2000. *Bad Boys: Public Schools in the Making of Black Masculinity.* Ann Arbor: University of Michigan Press.

Fine, Michelle, and Lois Weiss. 1998. *The Unknown City: Lives of Poor and Working-Class Young Adults.* Boston: Beacon.

Fischer, Claude S. 1976. *The Urban Experience.* San Diego, CA: Harcourt Brace Jovanovich.

Flores-Gonzalez, Nilda. 2002. *School Kids/Street Kids: Identity Development in Latino Students.* New York: Teacher's College Press.

Fordham, Signithia, and John Ogbu. 1986. "Black Students' School Success: Coping with the 'Burden of "Acting White."'" *Urban Review* 18:176–206.

Foucault, Michel. 1977. *Discipline and Punish: The Birth of the Prison*. Trans. Alan Sheridan. New York: Pantheon.

Fryer, Roland. 2006. "'Acting White': The Social Price Paid by the Best and Brightest Minority Students." *Education Next*, Winter.

Gans, Herbert J. 1962. *The Urban Villagers: Group and Class in the Life of Italian-Americans*. New York: Free Press.

Garland, David. 1993. *Punishment and Modern Society: A Study in Social Theory*. Chicago: University of Chicago Press.

———. 2001a. *The Culture of Control: Crime and Social Order in Contemporary Society*. Chicago: University of Chicago Press.

———. 2001b. "The Meaning of Mass Imprisonment." *Punishment and Society* 3 (1): 5–7.

Geertz, Clifford. 1988. *Works and Lives: The Anthropologist as Author*. Stanford, CA: Stanford University Press.

Gilmore, Ruth Wilson. *Golden Gulag: Prisons, Surplus, Crisis, and Opposition in Globalizing California*. Berkeley: University of California Press.

Giroux, Henry A. 2003. *Democracy beyond the Culture of Fear*. New York: Palgrave Macmillan.

———. 2009. *Youth in a Suspect Society: Democracy or Disposability?* New York: Palgrave Macmillan.

Goffman, Alice. 2009. "On the Run: Wanted Men in a Philadelphia Ghetto." *American Sociological Review* 74 (2): 339–357.

Goffman, Erving. 1967. *Interaction Ritual*. New York: Pantheon.

———. 1989. "On Fieldwork." *Journal of Contemporary Ethnography* 18 (2): 123–132.

Gordon, Avery. 1998. *Ghostly Matters*. Minneapolis: University of Minnesota Press.

Gramsci, Antonio. 1996. *Prison Notebooks*. New York: Columbia University Press.

Greven, Philip. 1992. *Spare the Child: The Religious Roots of Punishment and the Psychological Impact of Physical Abuse*. New York: Vintage.

Hagan, John. 1991. "Destiny and Drift: Subcultural Preferences, Status Attainments and the Risks and Rewards of Youth." *American Sociological Review* 56:567–582.

Hagan, John, and Bill McCarthy. 1997. *Mean Streets: Youth Crime and Homeless*. New York: Cambridge University Press.

Hagan, John, Carla Shedd, and Monique Payne. 2005. "Race, Ethnicity and Youth Perception of Criminal Injustice." *American Sociological Review* 70:381–407.

Hagedorn, John. 2008. *A World of Gangs: Armed Young Men and Gangsta Culture*. Minneapolis: University of Minnesota Press.

Hall, Stuart. 1985. "Signification, Representation, and Ideology: Althusser and the Post-structuralist Debates." *Critical Studies in Mass Communication* 2 (2): 91–114.

Hall, Stuart, Chas Critcher, Tony Jefferson, and John N. Clarke. 1978. *Policing the Crisis: Mugging, the State, and Law and Order*. New York: Holmes and Meier.

Harcourt, Bernard E. 2001. *Illusion of Order: The False Promise of Broken Windows Policing*. Cambridge, MA: Harvard University Press.

Harris, Angela P. 2000. "Gender, Violence, Race, and Criminal Justice." *Stanford Law Review* 52 (4): 777–807.

Harris, Harry. 2010. "Official from Governor's Office Called Gang Problem in Oakland 'Dire.'" *Oakland Tribune*, August 24.

Hartmann, Douglass. 2010. Review of *Black Men Can't Shoot*, by Scott Brooks. *Contemporary Sociology: A Journal of Reviews* 39 (2): 145–146.

Hays, Sharon. 2004. *Flat Broke with Children: Women in the Age of Welfare Reform*. New York: Oxford University Press.

Hepburn, J. R. 1977. "The Impact of Police Intervention upon Juvenile Delinquents." *Criminology* 15:235–262.

Hirschfield, Paul. 2008a. "The Declining Significance of Delinquent Labels in Disadvantaged Urban Communities." *Sociological Forum* 23 (3).

———. 2008b. "Preparing for Prison? The Criminalization of School Discipline in the USA." *Theoretical Criminology* 12:79–101.

Horowitz, Ruth. 1983. *Honor and the American Dream: Culture and Identity in a Chicano Community*. New Brunswick, NJ: Rutgers University Press.

Hughes, Langston. 1995. "Montage of a Dream Deferred" (1951). In *The Collected Poems of Langston Hughes*, ed. Arnold Rampersad. New York: Random House.

Irwin, John. 2003. Preface to *Convict Criminology*, ed. Jeffrey Ian Ross and Stephen C. Richards. Belmont, CA: Wadsworth.

Jones, Carolyn. 2008. "Oakland Police Brass Say Arrests Not Answer." *San Francisco Chronicle*, April 23.

Jones, Carolyn, Matthew B. Stannard, Jill Tucker, and Rachel Gordon. 2008. "Protesting Teens Shut 3 BART Stations." *San Francisco Chronicle*, November 1.

Jones, Nikki. 2009. *Between Good and Ghetto: African American Girls and Inner-City Violence*. New Brunswick, NJ: Rutgers University Press.

———. Forthcoming. *Beyond Desistance, Toward Freedom: Notes from the Field*. New Brunswick, NJ: Rutgers University Press.

Kelley, Robin D. G. 1994. *Race Rebels: Culture, Politics and the Black Working Class*. New York: Simon and Schuster.

———. 1997. *Yo' Mama's Disfunktional! Fighting the Culture Wars in Urban America*. Boston: Beacon.

Kimmel, Michael S. 2006. *Manhood in America: A Cultural History*. New York: Oxford University Press.

Kimmel, Michael S., and Matthew Mahler. 2003. "Adolescent Masculinity, Homophobia, and Violence." *American Behavioral Scientist* 46 (10): 1439–1458.

Kozol, Jonathan. 1991. *Savage Inequalities: Children in America's Schools*. New York: Crown.

Krisberg, Barry. 2004. *Juvenile Justice: Redeeming Our Children*. Thousand Oaks, CA: Sage.

Kupchik, Aaron. 2006. *Judging Juveniles: Prosecuting Adolescents in Adult and Juvenile Court*. New York: NYU Press.

———. 2010. *Homeroom Security: School Discipline in an Age of Fear*. New York: NYU Press.

Lamont, Michelle, and Mario Small. 2008. "How Culture Matters for the Understanding of Poverty: Enriching our Understanding." In *The Colors of Poverty*, ed. Ann Chih Lin and David R. Harris. New York: Russell Sage Foundation.

Lebel, Thomas P. 2008. "Perceptions of and Responses to Stigma." *Sociology Compass* 2 (2): 409–432.

Liebow, Elliot. 1967. *Tally's Corner: A Study of Negro Streetcorner Men*. Lanham, MD: Rowman and Littlefield.

Limón, José E. 1994. *Dancing with the Devil: Society and Cultural Poetics in Mexican-American South Texas*. Madison: University of Wisconsin Press.

Lind, Edgar Allan, and Tom R. Tyler. 1988. *The Social Psychology of Procedural Justice*. New York: Plenum.

Lipsitz, George. 2006. *The Possessive Investment in Whiteness: How White People Profit from Identity Politics*. Philadelphia: Temple University Press.

London, Jack. 1907. *The Iron Heel*. New York: Regent.

Lynch, Mona. 1998. "Waste Managers? The New Penology, Crime Fighting, and Parole Agent Identity." *Law and Society Review* 32:839.

MacLeod, Jay. 1995. *Ain't No Makin' It: Aspirations and Attainment in a Low-Income Neighborhood*. Boulder, CO: Westview.

Mannheim, Karl. 1936. *Ideology and Utopia: An Introduction to the Sociology of Knowledge*. New York: Harcourt Brace Jovanovich.

Martinez, Elizabeth Sutherland. 1998. *De Colores Means All of Us: Latina Views for a Multi-Colored Century*. Cambridge, MA: South End.

Martinez, C., and Victor Rios. In press. "Examining the Relationship between African American and Latino Street Gangs: Conflict, Cooperation and Avoidance in Two Multi-racial Urban Neighborhoods." In *Black and Latino Relations*, ed. Edward Telles et al. New York: Russell Sage Foundation.

Martinson, Robert. 1974. "What Works? Questions and Answers about Prison Reform." *Public Interest* 35:22–54.

Marx, Karl. 1963. *Eighteenth Brumaire of Louis Bonaparte*. New York: International Publishers. Originally published 1852.

Matsueda, Ross. 1992. "Reflected Appraisal, Parental Labeling, and Delinquency: Specifying a Symbolic Interactionist Theory." *American Journal of Sociology* 97:1577–1611.

Mauer, Marc. 1999. *Race to Incarcerate*. New York: New Press.

Mauer, Marc, and Meda Chesney-Lind. 2002. *Invisible Punishment: The Collateral Consequences of Mass Imprisonment*. New York: New Press.

McWhorter, John. 2000. *Losing the Race: Self-Sabotage in Black America*. New York: HarperPerennial.

Messerschmidt, James. 1993. *Masculinities and Crime: Critique and Reconceptualization of Theory*. Lanham, MD: Rowman and Littlefield.

————. 2000. *Nine Lives: Adolescent Masculinities, the Body, and Violence*. Boulder, CO: Westview.

Meyerhoff, Barbara, and Jay Ruby. 1982. "Introduction: Reflexivity and Its Relatives." In *A Crack in the Mirror: Reflexive Perspectives in Anthropology*, ed. Jay Ruby, 1–38. Philadelphia: University of Pennsylvania Press.

Miller, Jody. 2008. *Getting Played: African American Girls, Urban Inequality and Gendered Violence*. New York: NYU Press.

Mills, Charles Wright. 1959. *The Sociological Imagination*. New York: Oxford University Press.

Mirande, Alfredo. 1987. *Gringo Justice*. Notre Dame, IN: University of Notre Dame Press.

Morgan, Kathleen O'Leary, and Scott Morgan, eds. 2007. *City Crime Rankings: Crime in Metropolitan Areas*. 14th ed. Washington, DC: CQ Press.

Murch, Donna. 2007. "The Campus and the Street: Race, Migration, and the Origins of the Black Panther Party in Oakland, CA." *Souls: A Critical Journal of Black Politics, Culture and Society* 9 (4): 333–345.

Naples, Nancy A. 2003. *Feminism and Method: Ethnography, Discourse Analysis, and Activist Research*. New York: Routledge.

National Council on Crime and Delinquency (NCCD). 2009. *Racial and Ethnic Disparities in the U.S. Criminal Justice System*. Oakland, CA. Retrieved November 7, 2000, from http://nccd-crc.issuelab.org/research/5/program/Reports/filter/date.

Nightingale, Carl Husemoller. 1993. *On the Edge: A History of Poor Black Children and Their American Dreams*. New York: Basic Books.

Oakland Community and Economic Development Agency. 2010. *Market Profile: Labor Force*. Retrieved January 3, 2010, from http://www.business2oakland.com/main/laborforce.htm.

Obama, Barack. 2004. DNC Speech. Transcribed in "Illinois Senate Candidate Barack Obama: FDCH E-Media," *Washington Post*, July 27.

Oliver, Pamela. 2008. "Repression and Crime Control: Why Social Movement Scholars Should Pay Attention to Mass Incarceration as a Form of Repression." *Mobilization* 13 (1): 1–24.

Ong, Aihwa. 2003. *Buddha Is Hiding: Refugees, Citizenship, and the New America*. Berkeley: University of California Press.

Padilla. Felix. 1992. *The Gang as an American Enterprise*. New Brunswick, NJ: Rutgers University Press.

Pager, Devah. 2007. *Marked: Race, Crime, and Finding Work in an Era of Mass Incarceration*. Chicago: University of Chicago Press.

Parenti, Christian. 2000. *Lockdown America: Police and Prisons in the Age of Crisis*. London: Verso.

Patillo-McCoy, Mary. 1999. *Black Picket Fences: Privilege and Peril among the Black Middle Class*. Chicago: University of Chicago Press.

Patterson, Orlando. 1982. *Slavery and Social Death: A Comparative Study*. Cambridge, MA: Harvard University Press.

Payne, Yasser A. 2006. "A Gangster and a Gentleman: How Street Life–Oriented U.S.-Born African Men Negotiate Issues of Survival in Relation to Their Masculinity." *Men and Masculinity* 8 (3): 288–297.

———. 2008. "'Street Life' as a Site of Resiliency: How Street Life–Oriented Black Men Frame Opportunity in the United States." *Journal of Black Psychology* 34 (1): 3–31.

Pierce, Chester M. 1970. "Offensive Mechanisms: The Vehicle for Microaggressions." In *The Black 70s*, ed. F. B. Barbour, 265–282. Boston: Porter Sargent.

Pinderhughes, Howard. Forthcoming. *Dealing with Danger: How Inner-City Youth Deal with the Violence That Surrounds Them*. Philadelphia: Temple University Press.

Prokos, Anastasia, and Irene Padavic. 2002. "'There Oughtta Be a Law against Bitches': Masculinity Lessons in Police Academy Training." *Gender, Work and Organization* 9 (4): 439–459.

Pyke, Karen D. 1996. "Class-Based Masculinities: The Interdependence of Gender, Class, and Interpersonal Power." *Gender and Society* 10 (5): 527–549.

Quinney, Richard. 1977. *Class, State and Crime*. New York: Longman.

Rhomberg, Chris. 2007. *No There There: Race, Class, and Political Community in Oakland*. Berkeley: University of California Press.

Rios, Victor M. 2005. "From Knucklehead to Revolutionary: Urban Youth Culture and Social Transformation." *Journal of Urban Youth Culture* 3 (1).

———. 2006. "The Hyper-criminalization of Black and Latino Youth in the Era of Mass Incarceration." *Souls: A Critical Journal of Black Politics, Culture and Society* 8 (2).

Rios, Victor M., and K. Navarro. 2010. "Gang Enhancements and Gang Experts: The Case for Non-police Gang Experts in the Courtroom." *Critical Criminology: An International Journal* 18 (1).

Rios, Victor M., and Cesar Rodriguez. 2011. "Incarcerable Subjects: Working-Class Black and Latino Male Youth in Two California Cities." In *The Trouble with Young Men: Predicaments in Coming of Age*, ed. Noel Dyck and Vered Amit. Oxford, UK: Berghan.

Robinson, William I. 2004. *A Theory of Global Capitalism: Production, Class, and State in a Transnational World*. Baltimore: Johns Hopkins University Press.

Rodriguez, Dylan. 2006. *Forced Passages: Imprisoned Radical Intellectuals and the U.S. Prison Regime.* Minneapolis: University of Minnesota Press.

Rose, Mike. 1989. *Lives on the Boundary.* New York: Penguin.

Rosenfeld, Seth. 2002. "Reagan, Hoover and the UC Red Scare: The Governor's Race." *San Francisco Chronicle,* June 9. Retrieved January 1, 2009, from http://www.sfgate.com/cgi-bin/article.cgi?f=/c/a/2002/06/09/MNCF3.DTL.

Rusche, George, and Otto Kirscheimer. 1939. *Punishment and Social Structure.* New York: Russell and Russell.

Sabol, William J., and Heather Couture. 2008. "Bureau of Justice Statistics: Prison Inmates at Midyear 2007." Washington, DC: U.S. Department of Justice, NCJ221944.

Said, Edward. 1978. *Orientalism.* New York: Pantheon.

Sánchez-Jankowski, Martín. 1991. *Islands in the Street: Gangs and American Urban Society.* Berkeley: University of California Press.

———. 2008. *Cracks in the Pavement: Social Change and Resilience in Poor Neighborhoods.* Berkeley: University of California Press.

Scheff. Thomas. 2006. "Aggression, Hypermasculine Emotions and Relations: The Silence/Violence Pattern." *Irish Journal of Sociology* 15 (1): 24–37.

Scott, James. 1985. *Weapons of the Weak: Everyday Forms of Peasant Resistance.* New Haven, CT: Yale University Press.

Self, Robert O. 2003. *American Babylon: Race and the Struggle for Postwar Oakland.* Princeton, NJ: Princeton University Press.

Semple, Robert B., Jr. 1968. "Nixon Works on His Strategy and Image." *New York Times,* August 18, E2.

Shaw, Clifford Robe. 1966. *The Jack-Roller: A Delinquent Boy's Own Story.* Chicago: University of Chicago Press.

Silko, Leslie Marmon. 1977. *Ceremony.* New York: Penguin.

Simmel, Georg. 1950. *The Sociology of Georg Simmel.* Comp. and trans. Kurt Wolff. Glencoe, IL: Free Press.

Simon, Jonathan. 2007. *Governing through Crime: How the War on Crime Transformed American Democracy and Created a Culture of Fear.* New York: Oxford University Press.

Small, Mario Luis. 2008. "Lost in Translation: How Not to Make Qualitative Research More Scientific." In *Workshop on Interdisciplinary Standards for Systematic Qualitative Research,* ed. Michéle Lamont and Patricia White, 165–171. Washington, DC: National Science Foundation.

Smith, Dorothy. 1990. *The Conceptual Practices of Power: A Feminist Sociology of Knowledge.* Boston: Northeastern University Press.

Staples, William G. 2000. *Everyday Surveillance: Vigilance and Visibility in Postmodern Life.* Lanham, MD: Rowman and Littlefield.

Stewart, Eric A., Christopher J. Schreck, and Ronald L. Simons. 2006. "'I Ain't Gonna Let No One Disrespect Me': Does the Code of the Street Reduce or Increase Violent Victimization among African American Adolescents?" *Journal of Research in Crime and Delinquency* 43:427–458.

Sullivan, Mercer. 1990. *"Getting Paid": Youth, Crime and Work in the Inner City*. Ithaca, NY: Cornell University Press.

Sutherland, Edwin, and Donald R. Cressey. 1955. *Principles of Criminology*. 5th ed., Philadelphia: Lippincott.

Swidler, Ann. 1986. "Culture in Action: Symbols and Strategies." *American Sociological Review* 51 (2): 273–286.

Takaki, Ronald. 1993. *A Different Mirror: A History of Multicultural America*. Boston: Little, Brown.

Thomas, William I., and Dorothy Swaine Thomas. 1928. *The Child in America: Behavior Problems and Programs*. New York: Knopf.

Urbina, Ian. 2010. "Mobs Are Born as Word Grows by Text Message." *New York Times*, March 24.

U.S. Census Bureau. U.S. Census 2000, 2006. Retrieved June 15, 2006, from www.census.gov.

———. 2000. "Figure 1: Percent below Poverty Line Near East 14th Street, Oakland, California 94606." Retrieved from http://www.census.gov/mso/www/casestudies/resources/oakf1.jpg.

———. 2009. "Population Estimates." Retrieved January 4, 2009, from www.census.gov/popest/metro.html.

U.S. Department of Justice, Office of Justice Programs, Bureau of Justice Statistics. 2006. "Corrections Facts at a Glance." May 31. Retrieved June 15, 2006, from http://www.ojp.usdoj.gov/bjs/gcorpop.htm#JailRace.

Venkatesh, Sudhir Alladi. 1998. "Gender and Outlaw Capitalism: A Historical Account of the Black Sisters United 'Girl Gang.'" *Signs* 23.

———. 2006. *Off the Books: The Underground Economy of the Urban Poor*. Cambridge, MA: Harvard University Press.

———. 2008. *Gang Leader for a Day: A Rogue Sociologist Takes to the Streets*. New York: Penguin.

Vigil, James Diego. 1988. *Barrio Gangs: Street Life and Identity in Southern California*. Austin: University of Texas Press.

———. 2002. *A Rainbow of Gangs*. Austin: University of Texas Press.

Wacquant, Loïc. 2002a. "From Slavery to Mass Incarceration: Rethinking the 'Race Question' in the US." *New Left Review* 13 (January–February): 41–60.

———. 2002b. "Scrutinizing the Street: Poverty, Morality, and the Pitfalls of Urban Ethnography." *American Journal of Sociology* 107 (6): 1468–1532.

———. 2009. *Punishing the Poor: The Neoliberal Government of Social Insecurity.* Durham, NC: Duke University Press.

Ward, Geoff. 2009. "The 'Other' Child-Savers: Racial Politics of the Parental State." In *The Child Savers: The Invention of Delinquency,* ed. Anthony M. Platt. New Brunswick, NJ: Rutgers University Press.

Warren, Jenifer. 2008. *One in 100: Behind Bars in America 2008.* Washington, DC: Pew Center on the States.

Weiss, Robert. 1994. *Learning from Strangers: The Art and Method of Qualitative Interview Studies.* New York: Free Press.

Werner, O., and G. M. Schoepfle. 1987. *Systematic Fieldwork.* Vol. 1. Newbury Park, CA: Sage.

West, Candace, and Sarah Fenstermaker. 1995. "Doing Difference." *Gender and Society* 9 (1): 8–37.

Western, Bruce. 2006. *Punishment and Inequality in America.* New York: Russell Sage Foundation.

———. 2007. "The Prison Boom and the Decline of American Citizenship." *Society* 44:30–37.

Western, Bruce, and Christopher Wildeman. 2009. "Punishment, Inequality, and the Future of Mass Incarceration." *Kansas Law Review* 57:851–877.

Whitlock, Jason. 2007. "Jena 6 Case Caught Up in Whirlwind of Distortion, Opportunism." *Kansas City Star,* September 29.

Willis, Paul E. 1977. *Learning to Labour: How Working Class Kids Get Working Class Jobs.* Farnborough, UK: Saxon House.

Wilson, William Julius. 1987. *The Declining Significance of Race.* Chicago: University of Chicago Press.

Witt, Howard. 2007. "Racial Demons Rear Heads: After Months of Unrest between Blacks and Whites in Louisiana Town, Some See Racism and Uneven Justice." *Chicago Tribune,* May 20. Retrieved August 26, 2007, from www.chicagotribune.com/news/nationworld/chi-elf2u1mmay20,0,5086697.story.

Yin, Robert K. 1981. "The Case Study as a Serious Research Strategy." *Science Communication* 3:97–114.

———. 1984. *Case Study Research: Design and Methods.* Thousand Oaks, CA: Sage.

———. 1993. *Applications of Case Study Research.* Thousand Oaks, CA: Sage.

Yosso, Tara Joy. 2006. *Critical Race Counterstories along the Chicana/Chicano Educational Pipeline.* New York: Routledge.

Young, Alford, Jr. 2004. *The Minds of Marginalized Black Men: Making Sense of Mobility, Opportunity, and Future Life Chances.* Princeton, NJ: Princeton University Press.

———. 2008. "White Ethnographers on the Experience of African American Men." In *White Logic, White Methods,* ed. Tukufu Zuberi and Eduardo Bonilla-Silva. Lanham, MD: Rowman and Littlefield.

———. Forthcoming. "Rethinking the Relationship of African American Men to the Street." In *The Oxford Handbook of Cultural Sociology,* ed. Jeffrey C. Alexander, Ronald Jacobs, and Philip Smith. New York: Oxford University Press.

Young, Jock. 1999. *The Exclusive Society: Social Exclusion, Crime and Difference in Late Modernity.* London: Sage.

ABOUT THE AUTHOR

VICTOR M. RIOS is Assistant Professor in the Department of Sociology at the University of California, Santa Barbara. He is also author of *Street Life: Poverty, Gangs, and a Ph.D.* (2011), an autobiography written for a young adult audience.

Made in the USA
Middletown, DE
24 September 2016